/

Ending the torment: tackling bullying from the schoolyard to cyberspace

Publication produced by the Office of the SRSG on Violence against Children in 2016

Cover photo: © UNICEF/UN013287/LeMoyne
Young Colombian woman.

© 2016 United Nations

All rights reserved worldwide

Requests to reproduce excerpts or to photocopy should be addressed to the Copyright Clearance Center at copyright.com.

All other queries on rights and licenses, including subsidiary rights, should be addressed to:
United Nations Publications,
300 East 42nd Street,
New York, NY 10017,
United States of America.

Email: publications@un.org;
website: un.org/publications

Language: English
Sales no.: E.16.I.14
ISBN: 978-92-1-101344-3
eISBN: 978-92-1-058324-4

Printing: UNON, Publishing Services Section/Nairobi, ISO 14001:2004-Certified

Contents

Preface v
    Protecting Children from Bullying and Cyberbullying
    Marta Santos Pais, Special Representative of the Secretary-General on Violence against Children v

I. Empowering Children and Awareness Raising 1

1. Respecting children's rights and promoting a participatory culture of peace and respect in schools
George Moschos 1

2. U-Report: children and young people are agents of social change
María Luisa Sotomayor 9

3. The role of independent human rights institutions in preventing and responding to bullying
Anne Lindboe and Anders Cameron 17

II. Legislation and Public Policies 25

4. A national multi-facetted approach to prevent and address bullying and cyberbullying
Brian O'Neill 25

5. Combating bullying in schools: changing perceptions to change public policies
Eric Debarbieux 33

6. Poverty and inequity: multi-country evidence on the structural drivers of bullying
Kirrily Pells, María José Ogando Portela and Patricia Espinoza 41

7. Promoting an inclusive and equitable education for all learners in an environment free from discrimination and violence: Ministerial Call for Action
Christophe Cornu and Yongfeng Liu 49

8. The role of pediatricians in bullying prevention and in addressing emergent and increasing forms of violence against children
Bernard Gerbaka, Fares BouMitri and Carla Haber 57

III. School Interventions 67

9. Five key components in a global strategy against bullying
Dan Olweus and Susan Limber 67

10. Making large-scale, sustainable change: experiences with the KiVa anti-bullying programme
Sanna Herkama and Christina Salmivalli 75

11. Bullying from a gender-based violence perspective
Julie Hanson Swanson and Katharina Anton-Erxleben 83

12. Tailoring different bullying prevention approaches to a national context
Ersilia Menesini and Annalaura Nocentini 93

IV. Children's Exposure to Bullying: Data and Regional Trends 101

13. Global data on the bullying of school-aged children
    Dominic Richardson and Chii Fen Hiu 101

14. Cyberbullying: incidence, trends and consequences
    Sonia Livingstone, Mariya Stoilova and Anthony Kelly 115

15. Bullying and Cyberbullying in Southern Africa
    Patrick Burton 123

16. Bullying and educational stress in schools in East Asia
    Michael Dunne, Thu Ba Pham, Ha Hai Thi Le and Jiandong Sun 131

17. Bullying in the Arab region: a journey from research to policy
    Maha Almuneef 139

18. Lithuanian anti-bullying campaign and child helplines
    Robertas Povilaitis and Child Helpline International 147

Notes on the Contributors 157

Preface

"It's like being caught in a net. You can't get out if you don't say anything. If you say something and the net does not go away, it just gets bigger."

Protecting children from bullying is not just an ethical imperative or a laudable aim of public health or social policy: it is a question of human rights.

Indeed, bullying and cyberbullying compromise children's rights to freedom from violence, to protection from discrimination, to an inclusive and relevant education and the highest attainable standard of health, to the right to be heard and have their best interests regarded as a primary consideration in all decisions affecting their lives; and more often than not, child victims feel precluded from accessing counselling, justice and redress, and from benefitting from support for their healing, recovery and reintegration. These are rights enshrined in the United Nations Convention on the Rights of the Child, which is in force in virtually all countries around the world.

Whether physical, verbal or relational, bullying is a hurtful and aggressive pattern of behaviour perpetrated repeatedly against a less powerful victim. It is often part of a continuum, a torment that shapes children's lives at different moments and in different settings: from the school yard to the neighborhood and increasingly into the online world.

The impact of any form of violence on children's development and well-being is pervasive, serious and long-lasting. In the case of bullying and cyberbullying it is also surrounded by a deep sense of fear, loneliness and helplessness.

These devastating impacts are strongly reflected in the many heartfelt personal testimonies that children convey when I meet them during my missions around the world. But they are equally confirmed by sound data and research gathered by leading experts across regions, as well as by the significant measures undertaken as a response by governments, education institutions, local communities and families at large in their efforts to prevent and address this serious phenomenon.

Bullying, including cyberbullying, affects a high percentage of children at different stages of their development, often severely undermining their health, emotional well-being and school performance. Victims may suffer sleep disorders, headaches, stomach pain, poor appetite and fatigue as well as feelings of low-self-esteem, anxiety, depression, shame and at times suicidal thoughts; these are psychological and emotional scars that may persist into adult life. Bullies themselves are equally affected and are also more likely than their peers to be involved with anti-social and risky behaviour later on in life. And much beyond, bullying affects those who may be silent or complicit, frightened or uncertain to act, diminishing the overall climate of the school and the broader community.

Bullying is a key concern for children. It is one of the most frequent reasons why children call a helpline. It gains centre stage in surveys conducted with school children, and generates a special interest when opinion polls are conducted through social media with young people.

The recent U-Report initiative supported by UNICEF with more than 100,000 children and young people around the world illustrates this well: nine in every ten respondents considered that bullying is a major problem; two thirds reported having been victims; and one third believed it was normal and therefore did not tell anybody, while many did not know whom to tell or felt afraid to do so.

Serious concerns were equally expressed by the children who participated in a Latin American Regional Consultation on bullying and cyberbullying, held in Montevideo in May 2016.

Coming from ten different countries across the region, the young participants were united in an unshakable commitment to prevent and eliminate all forms of violence against children. They reflected on their perceptions of bullying as a serious form of violence; shared their often painful experiences, especially at school and in cyberspace; and presented compelling recommendations for action:

"Listen to our voices: bullying as any form of violence hurts and it lasts… it is urgent to stop it; violence does not teach good behaviour, being a good model and promoting non-violence conveys a good example for our lives; use dialogue and mediation before you let incidents happen! Help us learn about prevention and our rights; help those who care for us so that they can help us better; and don't forget: legislation is important and everyone needs to know it and respect it."

Although the effect of bullying in any of its forms may differ from victim to victim, in essence it violates a child's integrity and dignity, and it is commonly associated with anxiety, distress, confusion, anger, insecurity, lowered self-esteem, and a deep sense of exclusion, powerlessness and helplessness.

Bullying has long been part of the social, community and school life of children. With the growing access to information and communication technologies, and the wide use of smartphones by children and young people, online bullying – cyberbullying – has also become a source of concern. Spreading rumours, and posting false information, hurtful messages, embarrassing comments or photos, or being excluding from online networks can affect victims deeply. Anonymity may aggravate cyberbullying by encouraging young people to act in ways they would not in face-to-face interactions. But in addition, cyberbullying can strike its victims at any time, while the harmful messages or materials can spread faster and further to a very wide and an exponentially growing audience, in turn magnifying the risks and its impact.

Social engagement through the digital world is now a fundamental part of children's lives, and they shift easily between what is real and what is virtual, regarding the distinction between online/offline as ever less relevant. At the same time, cyberbullying is often an extension of the in-person bullying that takes place in school classrooms, halls and cafeterias, thus the two easily feed into each other, forming a continuum of damaging behaviour.

Although all children are at risk of being bullied, some are particularly threatened by their situation from stigmatization, discrimination or exclusion. These include children with disabilities; from disadvantaged backgrounds; those who are refugees, displaced or seeking asylum; who are indigenous or belong to ethnic, racial, linguistic, cultural or religious minorities; who are unable to go to school or are excluded from it; who face discrimination because their appearance does not meet cultural preferences; or who have or who are perceived as having a sexual orientation or gender identity different from what is seen as the norm.

For children in these groups who already feel isolated from the mainstream culture of their schools or communities, the danger of being bullied may be even greater. They can be more likely to share sensitive information and engage in riskier behaviours in order to gain acceptance and attention, especially when they are eager to overcome the deep sense of marginalization and exclusion they daily endure. This often results in further bullying and its impact has been called the "double jeopardy effect": wherein children with existing psychological vulnerabilities who are being bullied and are desperately seeking to escape, suffer even greater harm by resorting to behaviours that provoke further bullying, both online and offline.

It is clear from the available evidence that the impact of bullying is brutal and life-long, that it is widespread and that it compromises the rights of the child. Taking action to prevent such harm and to mitigate its damaging effects is therefore imperative on all those whose lives are touched by such violence.

Children's protection from bullying in both the built environment, in particular in and around school, and in cyberspace, is a widely shared accountability. It falls on state institutions, on school authorities, as well as on families and communities. By joining hands and expressing a clear resolve to prevent and address this phenomenon, they can achieve lasting change, including by securing safe and welcoming spaces where adults show leadership in supporting young people and modelling positive behaviour, and leading by example by avoiding aggressive, intimidating and abusive behaviours. Their leadership is crucial in promoting a culture of respect for children's rights – for all children, everywhere and at all times.

By enhancing children's sense of responsibility in preventing discrimination and violence, in promoting solidarity and mutual respect and tolerance, adults can help build an inclusive environment where no child is left behind and where children are supported in gaining life skills, learning to cope with adversity, and strengthening their resilience and self-confidence.

Children need to feel empowered to prevent and address bullying and its associated risks. Both at school and as digital citizens they need guidance in developing their ability to make informed decisions, and in building and strengthening solid values including responsibility for their actions towards others. And they need to feel confident and knowledgeable about how to access counselling, reporting and complaint mechanisms.

Whole-school and whole-community programmes, awareness-raising initiatives and media campaigns contribute to whole-society efforts to combat the danger to children posed by bullying and cyberbullying.

Only then will it be possible to overcome the persistently wide empathy gap surrounding bullying, mobilizing adults who may miss it even when occurring in plain sight, those who fail to sense the torment it causes, or still more those who view it simply as a rite of passage. Only then will children stop fearing to speak out and feeling invaded by a deep sense of hopelessness.

Ten years ago the United Nations General Assembly adopted the UN Study on Violence against Children which for the first time offered a global overview of this phenomenon, alongside an action-oriented policy agenda to prevent and address bullying, and all other forms of violence against children.

As a result, the protection of children from violence has evolved from a largely neglected topic into a global concern; a concern that is now included as a distinct target in the 2030 Sustainable Development Agenda.

The Agenda recognizes the profound impact of violence against children in all aspects of life, and includes concrete commitments to bring this violation of children's rights to an end. But the Agenda also conveys a very special sense of urgency to act and to ensure that no one is left behind. It is incumbent upon all governments and other stakeholders to show leadership, to mobilize and inspire action, championing this noble cause in broad alliances committed to freeing children from all violence, including bullying and cyberbullying.

This is no time for complacency. Bullying leaves a long-lasting blight on children's lives, and often has irreversible consequences on their development and well-being and their opportunities to thrive later in life. As with any other form of violence, it also weakens the very foundation of social progress, generating huge costs for society, slowing economic development and eroding nations' human and social capital.

But this is not a fate! The movement to improve on the realization of children's rights and to overcome passivity or complacency when violence occurs is ongoing and growing. Through enhanced cooperation, and with serious investment in proven strategies for violence prevention, bullying can become part of the distant past.

Agenda 2030 promotes an ambitious vision and it marks the start of the most important countdown: towards a world free from fear and from violence for all children, leaving no one behind. Investing in violence prevention, protecting children's lives and futures and saving nations' resources means time gained in the countdown to a brighter future.

It is imperative to seize this historic opportunity to place the protection of children from violence at the heart of the policy agenda of every nation and make a reality of children's vision of a world where fear and incidents of violence are part of the distant past.

While there are still many gaps in the data collected on children's exposure to bullying and on the effectiveness of programmes designed to address it, there is a considerable wealth of information and research that could be shared more widely with all stakeholders. This publication is a contribution to such knowledge-sharing.

It is designed to reach out to government leaders and decision-makers, as well as researchers, educators, health professionals and child protection actors who can help design sound policies and laws and promote their effective implementation, while supporting families and making a lasting difference in the life of children. The analysis, experiences and advice provided are both well-researched and accessible – the data can further advance knowledge in the field, the evidence of what works provides practical examples, and the voices of children reflected in some of the articles provide essential insights for all who are interested in tackling bullying.

I am confident the publication will contribute to the growing impetus worldwide to prevent and address bullying and cyberbullying and support the international drive to end all forms of violence against children, leaving no child behind.

Marta Santos Pais,
Special Representative of the Secretary-General on Violence against Children

Themes of the Publication

This publication seeks to bring together key elements of the rich global expertise on the issue of bullying in order to share information, ideas and examples of best practice with all those who are interested in tackling such a scourge. It offers a complement to the United Nations Secretary-General's Study on Violence against Children and will hopefully provide further impetus to the drive by countries throughout the world to understand and better prevent the bullying of children and young people in all its ugly manifestations.

As on all issues that affect children, it is essential that their ideas and views are sought and heard. The perceptions, experience and recommendations of children are of fundamental importance in tackling any issue of concern to them and their ideas are an important part of this publication. Their views and perspectives feature particularly in the chapter on UNICEF's U-Report. The U-Report is an electronic platform that reaches two million children, the majority in Africa, seeking their views and offering them an opportunity to widely share their experiences. But we also hear their voices in articles from other authors.

The key themes of this publication focus on the areas that need to be developed and strengthened in order to prevent bullying and to effectively mitigate its harm.

Providing information on, and raising awareness of, the insidious and damaging nature of bullying, as well as providing guidance on coping with its negative impacts are an important part of addressing the issue: so too are efforts to enable children to take action themselves to combat the problem. Their empowerment must be at the heart of any holistic approach to bullying.

Chapter 1 of this publication therefore looks at these issues and draws on expertise from different perspectives and regions. From Greece, George Moschos looks at respecting children's rights and promoting a participatory culture of peace and respect in schools. Maria Luisa Sotomayor brings us the responses from the U-Report and considers new approaches to participation and the use of ICTs. And finally, Anne Lindboe and Anders Cameron, from Norway, consider the role of independent human rights institutions in preventing and responding to violence and in particular bullying.

In Chapter 2, the publication moves into a consideration of legislation and public policies with the first article by Brian O'Neill, from Ireland, examining a national multi-facetted approach to the prevention of bullying and cyberbullying. The second article, by Eric Debarbieux, considers the school climate in Europe, and France in particular, and looks at the ways in which changing perceptions can lead to a change in public policies. Kirrily Pells, Maria Jose, Ogando Portela and Patricia Espinoza draw on evidence from a number of countries to understand the structural drivers of bullying: these include poverty and inequity. Christophe Cornu and Yongfeng Liu look at the importance of an inclusive and equitable education for all learners in an environment free from discrimination and violence based on sexual orientation and gender identity/expression and how this can be supported by governments. And finally, Bernard Gerbaka and Fares BouMitri introduce a new topic with a look at the role of the medical community in addressing bullying.

Chapter 3 looks at the essential field of school interventions. In this section Dan Olweus, a pioneer in the field and creator of the Olweus Bullying Prevention Program, and Susan Limber, consider the building blocks for an effective bullying prevention and response model. Then Sanna Herkama and Christina Salmivalli look at the success of the KiVa anti-bullying programme in Finland, which uses a whole-school approach. Julie Swanson and Katharina Anton-Erxleben, from the USA, give an important and strong gender perspective on bullying and school-related gender-based violence. And finally in this section Ersilia Menesini and Annalaura Nocenti look at tailoring different prevention approaches to the national context in Italy.

Chapter 4 examines the importance of data, without which we cannot understand or assess the extent of the problem. Dominic Richardson and Chii Fen Hiu lead off this section with a review of existing data and a look at what is needed to develop a solid response on prevention. This is followed by an article in which Sonia Livingstone, Mariya Stoilova and Anthony Kelly examine the evidence for the claim that new media bring new problems, arguing in conclusion that bullying and cyberbullying are inextricably linked in complex and challenging ways. Patrick Burton takes a look at data on bullying and cyberbullying in southern Africa, while Michael Dunne, Thu Ba Pham, Ha Hai Thi Le and Jiandong Sun, consider the impact of bullying and severe educational stress and the challenges faced in East Asian schools. Maha Almuneef presents a review of bullying in the Arab region, suggesting future policy development directions, and finally in this section, Robertas Povilaitis analyses experiences of projects in Lithuania while the International Child Helpline presents interesting case studies and data.

The contributors to this publication represent all regions, their expertise ranges across a number of different fields, and their research examines different aspects of bullying and cyberbullying. Further information on the authors is included later in the publication.

This publication has sought to identify issues to which we should be giving greater visibility and prominence, new facets of the problem that should be shared, concerns that should addressed, and examples of good practices that can stimulate and boost action by governments, policy makers, teachers and children themselves in the fight against bullying.

A girl stands to speak, in a crowded Primary School in a rural district, Malawi
© UNICEF/UNI40429/Gubb

Chapter I. Empowering Children and Awareness Raising

1. Respecting children's rights and promoting a participatory culture of peace and respect in schools

George Moschos

Introduction

Is "school violence" a matter of school only? Understanding school violence in the wider social context and the need to build defense mechanisms in schools

School violence has become an issue of major public concern globally in recent years. The general public has become aware of its seriousness in children's lives, following reports based on studies and statistical data illustrating that a considerable number of children are involved in violent incidents or practices, taking place inside and outside school, either as victims or as violators. The media repetitively report serious incidents of conflicts and bullying between children, raising the question of whether schools can really do something to prevent the evolution of such behaviours.

Many scientists have stressed the need to develop new methods and techniques to deal with the phenomenon and to empower students as well as teachers to tackle it effectively. There have been approaches focusing more on the actors – the persons involved in every incident - and others that stress the need to change the whole culture of every school community in order to effectively deal with such incidents. Before referring to what can be done at school though, it is important to understand and analyze the roots of school violence.

Despite the fact that many believe school contributes to the tolerance and even the development of various forms of violence, its real causes lie in the broader social context in which children are brought up: their life is flooded by violent stimuli, insecurity, selfishness and lack of respect for anyone competing for the same goals or representing different values. Many societies –especially in the free market economy context- reward the individuals' survival, competitiveness and differentiation, rather than adopt collective values and co-operation in the common interest. This is something that smaller communities could develop, if they aimed to cultivate a common consciousness and their own strong sense of community, by promoting the values and strengths of peaceful coexistence.

In every society there are members who suffer. There are children living in extreme poverty, who are experiencing domestic violence: children confronted in their everyday life with tensions, conflicts, disabilities, diseases, disorders, separations, migration, crime, drugs, clashing emotions and other difficulties. What is more, children facing such difficulties are usually not included in having a say about what is happening in their lives. And when they do express their thoughts or feelings, they are often treated with contempt or aggression. These children need to be heard and understood, in order to find ways to prevent the escalation of their trauma.

On the other hand, children have a great capacity for joy and pleasure, they can relate well to others if they feel secure. Children easily learn from others' examples, especially from the adults who are responsible for them; they can be inspired by and adapt to the culture of their social frame of reference and can achieve great heights when their social environment allows and favours them to do so.

School, as the first (after family) large powerful socialization mechanism, can and should be the "port" that embraces the diverse range of children's situations and feelings, their difficulties and experiences acquired within their own families and social environments, enabling them to process and to transform these into power. However, this power should not be the power of sovereignty and domination, which would create new tensions. It should be a power leading to free personal expression, creative synthesis and peaceful coexistence with all different members of the community.

In this article I will try to present my opinion that school does not need special advice from experts or highly specialized tools to successfully manage violence and conflict, but rather needs a pedagogy of belonging: belonging to a community with common positive values and practices. It needs a culture of participation and collaboration, in order to be able to develop ideas and peaceful relations. Any particular techniques or practices to achieve the peaceful resolution of conflicts should be part of this culture. What should be required by governments and ministries is not so much to fill up school life with new laws, new responsibilities and new systems of penalties, but rather to improve the system of intercommunication and sharing of responsibilities, with the participation of children themselves, in making school life attractive and the school environment a safe space which children love, respect and defend as their own second "home". In this way, schools can operate as mechanisms protecting and defending children from social malfunctions that affect their personal lives and can provide them with skills for the successful management of those difficulties and conflicts that derive from the wider social system.

What children say…

As Children's Ombudsman in Greece, since 2003, I have been listening to children of all ages for many years and have dealt with all sorts of violations of their rights in many social contexts. I have been talking with children about school violence in schools both in group, as well as with individuals that have been involved in violent incidents as victims or violators. Based on this experience I could summarize some of their strongest sayings in the following (see box):

Children in fact believe in sharing and need to take part in team work in relaxed school environments, inspired by trustworthy teachers who demonstrate genuine interest in their feelings, their efforts, their internal conflicts and their concerns. Children need to know that their point of view is being truly respected and taken into serious consideration by adults.

The school as a learning and caring community: core pedagogical principles and values: learning needs and children's rights

Undoubtedly, school is a socialization mechanism that serves the reproduction of society, and hence of the economic system. Therefore, structurally, school is designed mostly for the accumulation of necessary knowledge, while guaranteeing the conformity and discipline of its students, in order to prepare them for their successful entrance to the labour market.

Twentieth-century pioneer pedagogues, like Freinet, Montessori, Piaget, Neil, Steiner, Freire and others tried to break away from this mould, and focused on the need for a child-centred educational model, that would respect children's needs and developmental phases and would build on experience and participation, rather than on simply transmitting knowledge. Learning through experience and participation has been pointed out as the most crucial element for children; they need to be emotionally involved in the process of learning and to cultivate bonds with their school communities and teacher who has been described

Children's voices

"Adults do not pay serious attention to tensions and conflicts happening in our lives among us. Most parents cannot easily understand our experiences outside home and our feelings. When they learn about an incident of violence that we have been involved in, they are either overprotective, trying to immediately intervene with other people in order to protect us, or they are too distant and indifferent, trying to calm us down without recognizing and understanding our stress or trauma.

On the other hand, teachers usually prefer to ignore what seems to be a "minor incident", such as teasing or quarrelling, which can in fact be very painful, and deal superficially and occasionally clumsily with more challenging conflicts, that may disturb school life and rules or in any way may stimulate the interest of our parents. In such cases teachers tend to impose easily sanctions or give us strict warnings, without really trying to investigate, understand and tackle the reasons of our conflicts. They tend to be too busy with other concerns such as curriculum, order, attainment and school grades.

We need teachers to listen to us more carefully, to offer us time and understanding and to respect our privacy. We need to trust them and not to be afraid to talk to them. When teachers want and try to bring us together, either through group activities or through organized discussions, then we feel that we are a group that can find better solutions to any kind of problem or challenge. The most difficult problems can be solved if we feel that we are a team, with common goals and efforts!"

as the one who "cultivates environments ....for learning".[1] A dilemma that schools are faced with is whether to invest their efforts on individual performance, differentiation and excellence (counted by high grades, disciplined behaviour, good manners, success in exams and competitions, etc) or on collective principles and common operational goals (such as good school climate, positive atmosphere, cooperation, creative and team spirit, etc). Parents usually favour individual goals and cannot always appreciate the importance of a happy atmosphere in schools. However, core pedagogical principles supported by contemporary theories of education insist on the need to build a positive school culture and climate in order to secure the development of the student's full personality and potential, creating young citizens who understand and embrace their responsibilities.

The UN Convention on the Rights of the Child (1989) has highlighted the importance of children's right to freely express their views in all matters affecting them (Article 12), as a right that needs to be combined with all other rights, such as the rights to personal development, education, protection from any form of violence, non discrimination and equal treatment, protection of their private life, access to information, participation in social and cultural life, etc.

As was stated by the Committee on the Rights of the Child:[2]

> The overall objective of education is to maximize the child's ability and opportunity to participate fully and responsibly in a free society. It should be emphasized that the type of teaching that is focused primarily on accumulation of knowledge, prompting competition and leading to an excessive burden of work on children, may seriously hamper the harmonious development of the child to the fullest potential of his or her abilities and talents. Education should be child-friendly, inspiring and motivating the individual child. Schools should foster a humane atmosphere and allow children to develop according to their evolving capacities.

Also, the Committee in its General Comment no. 13, among other proposed educational measures,[3] has referred to the:

> provision of accurate, accessible and age-appropriate information and empowerment on life skills, self-protection and specific risks, including those relating to ICTs and how to develop positive peer relationships and combat bullying; empowerment regarding child rights in general - and in particular on the right to be heard and to have their views taken seriously - through the school curriculum and in other ways.

These attitudes and approaches are also strongly supported in the UN Study on Violence Against Children[4] which clearly states that:

> States should ensure that children rights are disseminated and understood (and that) States (a) should encourage schools to adopt and implement codes of conduct applicable to all staff and students that confront all forms of violence, taking into account gender-based stereotypes and behaviour and other forms of discrimination; (b) Ensure that school principals and teachers use non-violent teaching and learning strategies and adopt classroom management and disciplinary measures that are not based on fear, threats, humiliation or physical force; (c) Prevent and reduce violence in schools through specific programs which address the whole school environment including through encouraging the building of skills such as non-violent approaches to conflict resolution, implementing anti-bullying policies and promoting respect for all members of the school community.

Based on the principles set out in the Convention and the findings of scientific studies and research, the Council of Europe has pointed out the necessity for the promotion of the principles of "learning and living democracy" in schools. Human rights education at all school levels, taking place with the use of participatory and experiential methods has emerged as a very important element of schools. Democratic school governance, in the sense of empowerment and involvement of students, staff and stakeholders in all important decisions within the school, as a way to practically safeguard the respect of children's rights, has been promoted as a crucial element of the operation of schools.[5] The Council of Europe has also published six "Living Democracy" manuals[6] that provide teachers with high-quality lesson materials and enable teachers to introduce citizenship and human rights education into their schools in a fun, interactive and challenging way.

A school that favours participation, group activities and common values is a school that also helps children to learn freely and to resolve their conflicts in the most successful way.

Thus, it has been well-documented that schools should simultaneously seek the acquisition of knowledge through supporting a child-friendly and interactive learning environment in the classroom, and promote the active involvement of all students in the creation of a pleasant, attractive and safe school environment. In order to succeed and secure these, it is crucial to build up relations of trust between teachers, students and their parents, while cultivating systematically relations of understanding and collaboration among students.

Teaching children's rights is crucial!

Teaching children's rights is not a simple process of transferring knowledge of existing rules and laws, but a pedagogical empirical process of helping children to understand the deeper meaning of rights and their function in safeguarding peaceful human relations.

Teaching children's rights should include: a) developing an understanding of everyone's rights and ways to successfully and peacefully defend them from any violation; b) respecting other people's rights, individually or collectively, by becoming able to step into their shoes; and c) showing solidarity when someone else's rights are violated. This teaching should be part of a wider human rights education that should help children, using participatory methods, to develop values and attitudes such as tolerance and understanding, and to encourage sustainable actions, so that they become responsible local and global citizens.

Although teaching children's rights should be adapted to every different social and educational setting, we could summarize the following general principles that are universal for teachers involved in activities aiming at teaching children's rights.

Children should be helped and advised through discussions, games and simulation exercises and roles:

- To **identify children's rights,** as set out in the Convention and in the national legislation and connect them with real life situations

- To understand that all rights are correlated and their implementation always needs a **careful balance** between different rights that may be in conflict with each other

- To understand the **limits** of the exercise of each right and the **boundaries** between the rights of different persons

- To know who is the right person to refer to and to address a **complaint** when their rights are violated. Teachers should be able to act as persons of confidence and mediators to other professionals when this is necessary and to provide any necessary information or advice to the students affected or involved

- To **carefully express their opinion and sentiments** in each case of rights' violation or conflict and look for a peaceful and effective way to stop such violations

- To understand and **respect** other people's rights

- To be able to **listen** to other people's opinions, **share their feelings** and experiences and imagine what it would be like if they were in their position/situation

- To **take action** when someone else's rights are violated and show solidarity, without risk of worsening their situation

- To **act as a team,** with commonly agreed rules and principles

- To always carefully consider how any violation of children's rights can be stopped and any **harm** could be **reversed** in a peaceful way.

One can easily understand that in order to create a safe environment in school where children's rights can be taught, understood and properly defended, it is essential that a good climate is created in the classroom but also in the whole school.

Dealing with incidents of violence in the school environment

Despite the fact that students may be sensitized about the need to respect each other's rights, often violence occurs for reasons that cannot be easily identified or affected by school itself. In order to successfully deal with such incidents it is important that every school develop both preventive and interventive/protective strategies and mechanisms.

Every school should carefully focus on all factors that may contribute to the prevention as well as to the effective intervention to protect victims and to treat violators, in order to avoid the repetition of such violent behaviour.

Regarding the crucial factors connected with the occurrence and handling of violent behaviour, schools should be able to address questions such as these:

School environment: Is it organized and supervised in a way that allows students to freely move and communicate, but also to know that they are not exposed to arbitrary attacks or misbehaviours?

School rules: Are rules clearly communicated to all teachers, students and parents and are they implemented in a fair way, without injustice or discrimination? Are they formulated with the contribution of students, so they are better understood, accepted and followed by them? Are there adequate provisions for a careful handling of all violent incidents occurring inside or outside school among students, with careful consideration of their opinion and of the point of view of all those involved?

School principals and teachers: Are they well-informed and sensitized regarding the suggested ways for handling school violence, following agreed rules and principles? Are they well-trained to intervene effectively when a violent incident occurs and to approach victims and perpetrators in a child-friendly manner and listen to them in a confidential way?

Perpetrators: Are they offered the assurance of a careful consideration of their case and understanding of their point of view? Are they given an opportunity to understand the harm they have caused and to take action for the restoration of their relationships? Are they given alternative and legitimate ways to earn the recognition that they seek for?

Victims: Are they offered the opportunity to talk in confidence with a teacher or another professional and present their case, without fearing that their reactions will worsen their position? Are they supported in understanding the perpetrator's point of view?

Witnesses: Are they sensitized about the important role they could play to stop violent or offensive behaviours? Is their testimony sought in a careful way, so that they are protected from any revenge reactions?

Class and peers: Are class mates and student representatives sensitized about their possible contribution in stopping the occurrence and repetition of violent incidents? Are they helped to consider any relevant incident as an issue concerning and affecting them? Are they advised how to mediate in order to find peaceful ways to handling conflicts?

Parents: Are they informed about the ways schools deal with violent incidents? In case their children are involved, are they helped to react in a way responding to the principles adopted by the school community? When their parental responsibilities are not properly fulfilled, are they advised and assisted by specialized professionals?

Supportive and community services: Are schools well-connected with social workers, psychologists and other community services that could assist them in handling difficult behaviour cases, especially when families' responsibilities arise? Are teachers aware and supported about the ways in which they can refer to local community social services and collaborate with them for the best interest of the children who are involved as victims or perpetrators in violent incidents?

Internet and other factors threatening school life: Are the members of school communities (teachers, students and parents) sensitized and advised how to deal with threats to school life deriving from external factors, such as students' contacts and communications on the internet or in other social contexts, such as those resulting from other peers or people abusing, exploiting or having a dangerous influence on them?

Involvement of police and prosecutors: Are school authorities aware of the duties and ethics of collaboration with police or judicial authorities, so that no excessive use of them is made, while their support can be provided when needed?

Suggestions for the formation of a democratic culture in schools that can help successful handling of violence

To answer questions like the ones raised above, schools are advised to combine efforts in order to develop a democratic culture that can be very helpful in handling violence that occurs in their area of competence. In particular, it is suggested that every school takes all appropriate steps to:

- Organize **teachers' training** through seminars (with participatory methods) on developing democratic school governance and teaching, and on including the respect for children's rights and the promotion of students' participation in school life.

- Build up a **positive school climate,** by consistently trying to communicate in upbeat and child-friendly ways the desirability of looking after the school environment and helping children to feel that school belongs to them.

- Agree at the teachers' level on a **school regulation** that will summarize the major principles to be adopted by school community. Invite students to discuss its content and participate in its final formation. School regulation should summarize the basic rules of school life, in a child-friendly language, and refer to the ways in which students are expected to express their views and to participate in decision-making in all matters affecting them.

- **Eliminate punitive sanctions** that may cause negative reactions without real behaviour adjustment. Agree on common principles of dealing with offending behaviours and implement methods alternative to punishment, when a conflict or a violent behaviour occurs, involving actors in discussions and in undertaking the restoration of damage or harm caused to the victims.

- Promote **human rights' education** and organize **discussions in the classroom** on children's rights, common rules and ways to take decisions on issues of common interest, to reach agreements and to resolve conflicts. Children should learn by experience to listen to each other and to respect each other's rights.

- Promote activities to sensitize students on the use of **new technologies** and the respect of other people rights – learning how to self-protect from cyberbullying and other dangers on the web.

- Develop interesting **group activities** in the fields of culture, arts and crafts, sport, mental health education, environmental protection, media and communication, personal expression, solidarity initiatives, etc. Every group should operate on agreed rules and students should be assisted to assess their progress and levels of cooperation.

- Promote **school democracy,** by regularly holding class and school assemblies, giving attention and offering roles to students' elected representatives, sharing responsibilities regarding school life, consulting with students, respecting and counting on them.

- Appoint **"teachers of trust"** and **teachers - mediators,** offering them also special training, support and supervision. Explain to all students, teachers and parents their role, tasks and functions.

- Agree on a **peer mediation model** to be adopted in school. Choose and train students to act as peer mediators and to deal with conflicts in peaceful ways. Younger students could mediate with class mates, while older students (in high school) could form peer mediation groups, who undertake to seek peaceful resolution of conflicts.

- **Involve parents,** both in problem solving (by supporting their children in more successful handling of conflict situations) as well as in planning prevention activities such as lectures and discussions with parents, excursions and exhibitions with the involvement of children.

- Collaborate with **social services and community agencies,** both in particular cases that need their intervention, as well as at preventive level, in order to offer children and their parents additional support and counselling to overcome their difficulties.

- Organize **monitoring and evaluation** meetings and procedures, regarding any kind of interventions aimed at tackling all kinds of problems in school. Evaluation can help every partner to realize their weaknesses and improve their skills and competencies in relating to each other.

- **Open schools to the community:** Organize outdoor activities with the involvement of school students, visit public spaces and services, observe various aspects of social life and take initiatives for children to take action in the community for issues of public concern such as environmental protection, peaceful use of public spaces, protection of children's rights and promoting artistic expression. Organize activities and workshops inside the school area, during evenings and weekends, for the members of the community, including school students, other young people, parents and neighbours, including the less privileged. Careful designing and monitoring of such activities could help the school have a more social character and stronger connections with neighbourhood life and needs.

Conclusion

In this article I tried to present my opinion that, in order to handle the issue of school violence in the most successful way, we should mostly focus on the implementation of the right of all children to enjoy their participation in school. Governments, parliaments, universities and all field specialists should work together to ensure that children should be offered a safe, democratic and attractive school environment that develops their full potential, favours their free expression, teaches them to respect each other's rights through experience and dialogue, cultivates their responsibilities, gives them the opportunity to work and be creative in groups, facilitates the building of bonds and the peaceful resolution of all conflicts, and practically rejects every form of violence and discrimination.

In order to successfully cope with bullying and cyberbullying, we mostly need legislation and administration to focus on securing positive functions and rights-based activities in schools, strengthening their character as democratic communities and steadily improving their own pedagogic tools and internally- agreed regulations, by appropriately training, guiding and supervising teachers instead of turning to and being dependent on penal mechanisms and external "specialists".

Endnotes

[1] Carver, R (1996). Theory for practice: A framework for thinking about experiential education. *Journal of Experiential Education* 19(1): 8-13

[2] UN Committee on the Rights of the Child (2001) General Comment 1, Article 29 (1): *The Aims of Education.*

[3] UN Committee on the Rights of the Child (2011) General Comment 13, *The right of the child to freedom from all forms of violence.*

[4] United Nations Secretary-General's Study on Violence Against Children (2006). New York: United Nations. http://www.unviolencestudy.org/

[5] Bäckman, E & Trafford, B (2007). *Democratic Governance of Schools,* Council of Europe publishing.

[6] http://www.coe.int/t/dg4/cultureheritage/resources/publiforum/Citoyennete-democratic_en.pdf.

Young Ugandans gather around to use the solar-powered Digital Drum.
© UNICEF/UNI118945/Tylle

2. U-Report: children and young people are agents of social change

María Luisa Sotomayor

Introduction

Over the last few years, Information and Communication Technologies (ICTs) have taken a dominant position in the lives of children and young people, to the extent that they now rely on the Internet for a wide range of basic needs and rights.[7] Globally, it is estimated that one-third of all Internet users are children,[8] that children are spending more and more time online and that they start using the Internet at younger ages than ever before. Although children's access to ICTs is highest in high-income countries, the rapid expansion of affordable, accessible Internet through mobile technologies in low- and middle-income countries means that children are gaining access to the Internet worldwide. Even in countries where the overall Internet penetration is relatively low, usage among young people is sometimes as much as double the national average.[9] This immediate and ongoing access to ICTs has redefined both participation and engagement for young communities. With this newfound access comes great opportunity for change - real change.

Participation, at its core, is linked to one's access to information,[10] and when we examine participation, "it is necessary to consider power differentials in terms of social class, age, gender, race, and ethnicity, because they affect both offline and online worlds and constrain access to opportunities".[11] Young people are doubly affected - in the decision-making process they tend to be under-represented, and they are also not a homogeneous group. According to Andrés Lombana-Bermudez, "Not all youth and children have access to the same social, cultural, human, financial, and technology resources."[12]

Are ICTs, then, a democratic source for ensuring youth participation and engagement? Not necessarily, due to behavioural norms. We know that "civic technologies are gaining increasing interest as a way to engage hard-to-reach populations in community planning and decision making."[13] However, we must ensure that these civic technologies can also adapt to the behaviours and channels the community already uses. Asking a community to adapt their behaviour to fit with specific channels and technologies that are foreign to them would be an additional barrier that would negatively impact an already under-represented group. Therefore, civic technologies must offer varied means of participation, so each audience may choose the technology which best accommodates their context.

Another question raised when we think of ICTs as a fertile land for youth engagement and participation, is "has participation changed with digital technologies?" An immediate response would likely be "yes, it has", but we must examine whether it is participation that has changed, if society has changed, or if participation has actually changed because of societal transitions. An interesting way of looking at this comes from what Heinmans and Timms refer to as "new power". Through this power framework they reveal that "a much more interesting and complex transformation is just beginning, one driven by a growing tension between two distinct forces: old power and new power".[14] The latter is made by many; it is open, participatory and peer-driven. This new framework shares, uploads and distributes, and the goal today is to learn how to channel the different models of new power (such as governance, economy and participation, to name a few). People under the age of 30 are the demographic most heavily engaged with new power,[15] especially in areas where young people have a higher access to ICTs. In these places, "a common assumption is emerging: We all have an inalienable right to participate. For earlier generations, participation might have meant only the right to vote in elections every few years or maybe to join a union or religious community. Today, people increasingly expect to actively shape or create many aspects of their lives."[16]

It might just be the way society is evolving, but "new power" values also meet many of today's social networks and civic technology principles including: informal, opt-in decision making, self-organizing, networked governance, open source collaboration, crowd wisdom, sharing, radical transparency, do–it-ourselves, short-term, and more overall participation. Complete transparency, and the gradual process of getting there, particularly draws attention, as "the shift towards increasing transparency is demanding a response in kind from institutions and leaders, who are challenged to rethink the way they engage with their constituents."[17]

In summary, to properly address under-represented communities who most likely share new power rules and have access to a range of ICT tools and to encourage a positive use of the Internet for improving their lives, we must:

- Utilize civic technologies that foster engagement, and drive participation with the goal of achieving change.

- Consider different means and channels that adapt to different audiences and communities.

- Create civic technologies that represent some of the "new power" characteristics: transparent, open, engaging, easy to access, used by many, adaptable to different audiences and shareable.

- Ensure civic technologies designed for children and young people foster their security and well-being.

In the next two sections of this article we'll look at a few examples of civic technologies used to protect children from violence, exploitation and abuse.

How ICTs are used to protect children from violence, exploitation, and abuse

While it is widely recognized that the rapid expansion of ICTs has revolutionized children's access to information, education health services, entertainment and social networks, ICTs can also reinforce inequities among children and lead to harmful consequences and risks to their safety, personal development and well-being. Although children have long been exposed to violence and exploitation, ICTs have changed the scale, form, impact and opportunity for the abuse of children everywhere. Many children are now experiencing widespread victimization through online bullying, harassment and intimidation: being groomed online for sexual encounters; and even victimized in child sexual abuse materials or through live streaming of their sexual abuse.

At the same time, ICTs help protect children and reduce risks of violence, exploitation and abuse. Mobile and digital technology is being used to gather and transmit data by child protection service providers facilitating for example: birth registration, case management, data collection and mapping of violence. Increasingly the Internet and mobile phones also provide important reporting mechanisms for different forms of violence, exploitation and abuse. Child helplines, for instance, have become key components of an effective response to violence against children. Through helplines, children and families can report violence, receive counselling, and be referred to appropriate support services. Increasingly, child helplines rely on ICTs for service provision, providing web-based services including online chat and reaching children through email services and text messages. The introduction of ICTs into the child helpline services often increases the demand for these services. For example, in Kenya when the helpline introduced text messaging, the demand for helpline services increased 20 times.[18]

Countries are also moving beyond traditional helplines, creating innovative platforms including online platforms, social media and mobile phone applications for the reporting of violence, exploitation and abuse. The use of ICTs in these services often helps children voice their concerns and reach out for help. This, in turn, increases the number of reports of violence and the demand for ICT services as children may feel these services are a more readily accessible, anonymous, confidential and safe means of reaching out for help.

UNICEF is working with governments, civil society and the private sector to set up child friendly reporting mechanisms for reporting violence, such as child helplines, online platforms and mobile applications. This is taking place in a number of countries including Albania, Algeria, Brazil, Hungary, Kenya, Madagascar and Serbia. In Brazil, UNICEF, in collaboration with the Government, CEDECA (a Brazilian NGO) and IlhaSoft, launched the "Proteja Brasil"[19] application in 2014, through which reports of violence and exploitation can be made to authorities. As a result of the launch of "Proteja Brasil", during the 2014 World Cup, operators of the 100-hotline received more than 15,000 calls, representing a 17% increase from the previous year. In 2015, the "Proteja Brasil" app was upgraded to process online child sexual abuse complaints, and it shares the same database as the 100-hotline, resulting in an improved coordination of case data sharing.

In Albania, the "ISIGURT", mobile application was developed with UNICEF's support to enhance the "National Platform for Child Safety Online".[20] To date, "ISIGURT" has successfully served as an information-sharing and reporting channel with 40 cases of online child sexual abuse having been reported.

Hotlines that enable the general public to anonymously report child sexual abuse materials and other content that they suspect is illegal in their country are another key component in an effective response to violence against children. These channels are critical for the effective reporting and removal of child sexual abuse materials. In Serbia, with UNICEF support, the "Net Patrol Hotline"[21] was upgraded through a mobile application[22] to allow reports from mobile phones and other devices. This upgrade resulted in a more than doubling of the number of reports received per month (from an average of 40 to 100) following its launch in February 2016.

Finally, the Internet, social media platforms and mobile networks play an important role in awareness raising campaigns on violence prevention by facilitating messaging to a larger audience. In Madagascar, collaboration with three major telecommunication companies (Airtel, Orange and Telma), and four ISPs (Airtel, Blueline, Orange and Telma), representing over 70% of all mobile subscribers, led to over seven million Internet and mobile phone users being provided with information about online risks for children. Further, UNICEF's first-ever digital youth engagement campaign, #ReplyForAll, which was launched in June 2016 as part of UNICEF's End Violence Online Campaign, successfully leveraged social media channels and platforms to give adolescents relevant information about online risks, prevention, and reporting. This campaign reached approximately 2.6 million viewers.

U-Report: civic technology for youth

ICTs are a powerful tool for engaging as well as protecting children, when being used for that purpose. U-Report shows us how. U-Report is a large scale messaging tool, powered by UNICEF and partners, designed to give young people and communities a chance to voice their opinions on issues that they care about, report on what is happening in their community and receive messages with valuable, sometimes life-saving, information.

To start, young people opt in through the channel that best fits their social context (SMS, Twitter, Facebook Messenger, U-Report App or Telegram). Once they have joined, they then receive weekly polls on various issues on which they can give their opinions. The collective poll results are visualized on a public dashboard. Afterwards, collected data is used to achieve social change by showing decision makers popular opinions and experiences U-Reporters have shared about issues that matter to them. Through U-Report channels, young people and their communities use real time data to become agents of change.

U-Report was born in Uganda in 2011 via SMS, and the original purpose of U-Report as a youth empowerment tool was (and is) to create a global movement of young people whose views and opinions could be gathered at scale and mapped in real time. By using a basic mobile phone to send and receive messages the tool was open to even the most disadvantaged and marginalized people, including women and children. The theory of change was founded on people being able to express themselves in vast numbers creating a virtual voice so loud that leaders would have to listen and make decisions based on their collective views. As change-makers and policy influencers, U-Reporters would become empowered.

With U-Report, a few things are accomplished at once: young people become empowered by gaining access to information and having a say on issues that impact them, and governments are able to make better-informed decisions.

Originally, UNICEF's role in fulfilling this purpose was to provide the technical support required, supporting scale-up and utilizing UNICEF relationships with government to partner and use the information for a valuable social purpose. Early Ugandan partners included the Ministry of Labour, Gender and Social Development, which also included the Commissioner for Youth.

As soon as U-Report began to scale in Uganda other applications for the U-Report data became obvious, and it was evident that while youth empowerment and civic engagement was the original vision, there were applications to many aspects of community development; there was a much wider group of potential beneficiaries than originally envisaged. Over time the applications of U-Report have evolved to address certain issues for a variety of population groups including children, adolescents, youth, adults, mothers, victims of abuse, and women in general, many of whom can be considered under-represented communities. At the same time, the use cases have expanded dramatically. U-Report has been used to encourage sexual reproductive health behaviour change, promote safe elections, coordinate UNICEF field responses, educate farmers and even to connect Members of Parliament to constituents. Actions and engagements have been coordinated across the globe on HIV/AIDS, bullying and women's economic empowerment, none of which was part of the original vision, but all of which have been important contributions to community-led development.[23]

U-Report is a tool whose evolution is driven by demand for data and UNICEF has aimed to ensure U-Report features are developed to meet this demand. As of July 2016, U-Report is live in 24 countries,[24] has more than 2.2 million registered U-Reporters, and has enabled different channels of engagement, so that young people may participate through the means that best fit their contexts: SMS (so that the programmes continue to reach the most vulnerable communities), Twitter, Facebook Messenger, Telegram and the U-Report App available on Android and IOS.

The strength of U-Report is that, along with these evolutionary cycles, the tool changes to support new needs and demands. As the technology improves, the speed of implementation, data analytics and modes of communication with U-Reporters also improve, so it becomes easier, faster and cheaper to set up, and arguably more effective. The one constant is the data type: this comes from communities. Effectiveness thereafter falls on the decisions of the stakeholder(s) to apply or not apply U-Report data in solving dynamic development challenges. To date, U-Report has been used in a variety of ways including to influence government programmes and policies, to influence behaviour change and counselling, to influence international policy and in emergency response.[25]

ICTs are presented today as an opportunity to monitor and report issues and to speak out and share opinions. But how can we assure that data is used in a positive way and to achieve change? Technology does not achieve change, humans achieve change. That's why civic technologies need to be built with clear purposes and goals. The purpose of U-Report is to:

- empower young people to share opinions on issues that matter to them

- provide valuable information to community members and governments

- amplify voices for advocacy at local, national, and global levels

- reduce the distance between governments and constituents

- use citizen data to improve accountability and strengthen programmes

- influence positive behaviour change

To achieve these outcomes, in each one of the countries where U-Report is based the programme has three goals: scale, engage and achieve positive change.

U-Report has to scale in each country, ensure marginalized populations are included, and then generate volumes of important data that can be used at local levels for programme monitoring and for local/national decision-making. In order to acquire useful and current data, U-Reporters must remain engaged. This requires incentives that keep U-Reporters interested, such as knowledge sharing, being involved in movements they feel passionate about, and a belief their voice will lead to the final objective: positive social change. For change to happen, a stakeholder must apply U-Reporter data to change a situation identified either in advance or as a result of U-Report messages. A stakeholder can be the government, UNICEF staff, a UNICEF sister agency, civil society organizations, a community movement, or U-Reporters themselves.

Using U-Report to improve the lives of young people

U-Report has the ability to reach a large number of children and young people - at very low cost and via different channels - and to overcome traditional challenges of distance or remoteness and secure children's participation.[26] Collecting real time data can, in fact, help improve young people's lives when being used in the advocacy process. U-Report does not intend to provide scientific data, or survey samples, as it is not a survey tool. Rather, it is a participation tool which can add value to scientific data. As such, it reaches out to children, young people and their communities, and helps collect information from participation. Through U-Report, UNICEF country offices and partners are asking young people what they know, and their responses can help achieve change if used in advocacy processes by stakeholders. Through civic technologies today, we are seeing how youth participation is shifting from asking people what they think, to also asking people

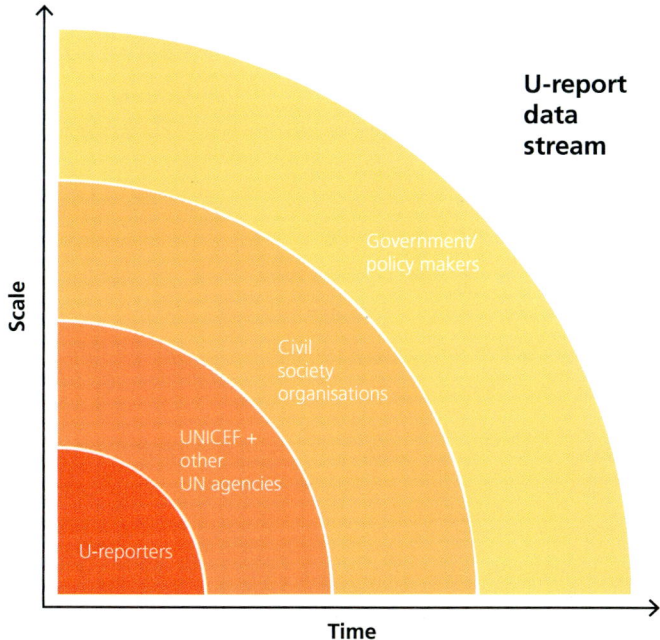

what they know, and considering their answers valuable data that can be utilized to achieve change.

Given that U-Report is a tool by the people and for the people, collected information is first shared with U-Reporters. Throughout time, and in line with advocacy goals and programmes, data is shared inside UNICEF and other agencies, with civil society and other organizations, and ultimately with governments and policy makers for achieving social change. It takes time, scale and data advocacy to achieve expected outcomes.

The same ICT channels, through which children may be victims of violence, can also become tools used to learn about their experiences and protect their rights. In May 2016, U-Report ran a global poll about bullying, engaging more than 100,000 young people in over 20 countries simultaneously. The information was requested by the Office of the Special Representative of the Secretary General on Violence against Children (OSRSG-VAC) to include in the report, Protecting Children Against Violence, requested by the General Assembly to the Secretary General. The same set of questions was sent to all U-Reporters in Senegal[27], Mexico[28], Uganda[29], Sierra Leone[30], Liberia[31], Mozambique[32], Ukraine[33], Chile[34], Malaysia[35], Nigeria[36], Swaziland[37], Pakistan[38], Ireland[39], Burkina Faso[40], Mali[41], Guinea[42], Indonesia[43], Zambia and the U-Report Global[44] platform where anyone from anywhere in the world can join and participate.

Results varied from country to country, but overall, 88.6% of U-Reporters stated that bullying is a problem, and 67% replied "yes" when being asked if they had ever been a victim of bullying. The poll also addressed the reasons for being bullied, why bullying happens in school, and what should governments be doing to stop it. Findings were particularly revealing around who victims talk to when they are bullied: one third of U-Reporters decided not to tell anyone (as they perceived bullying as something normal), one quarter of victims did not know who to tell and almost half of U-Reporters did not tell anyone because they were either afraid or ashamed of doing so.

U-Reporters' views on what the solution to bullying should be directly relates to the programme's participatory nature: over eight in ten children and young people believe they need to be part of the solution by raising awareness and addressing bullying in school. Less than one in ten believe the approach should be just legal prohibition, and even fewer believe that bullying will decrease or disappear by training teachers. This provided valuable insights for the few countries which have since taken their own approach to addressing bullying. In Ukraine, 38% of U-Reporters told no one about being bullied mostly because they were shy (40%).[45] Only 4% told their teachers[46] and 56% of U-Reporters said that teachers should be properly trained to help stop bullying, revealing that teachers should also be considered as a target audience when helping to prevent bullying. These results caused UNICEF's Youth and Education section in their Ukraine office to re-evaluate the way they were addressing bullying. And the Commissioner of the President of Ukraine for Children's Rights published on his Facebook page the results of the poll suggesting the need to "listen to the kids, show interest in their lives and build trusting relationships for tackling child violence". With these U-Report poll results, UNICEF Ukraine started to plan an anti-bullying campaign in Ukrainian schools to reduce violence among children. Results were also presented to the Ombudsman for Child Rights, who was invited to take part in the strategy and campaign. Involving young people in their campaign planning strategy was also an outcome of the U-Report poll, as results showed that young people were willing to be part of the solution by sharing their knowledge and views on such a delicate issue that directly affects them. UNICEF's reaction in Ukraine showed a capacity to embrace real time information, which, as we have seen, provides an excellent opportunity to stop and rethink strategies.

As stated previously, technology doesn't achieve change, humans do. If being used properly, real time information can help determine the direction that programmes to support children and young people should take, and can help shape the way in which authorities address problems.

The actions taken by UNICEF Ukraine provide an excellent example of using real time information to reshape the way of addressing a problem, by transforming young people's knowledge into actionable insights. U-Report receives data from U-Reporters, then uses it to achieve positive social change, and then shares it back with the same young people who initially provided it. By circling back to U-Reporters with results, UNICEF encourages young people to move from participation to engagement. Providing that stakeholders make responsible and prompt use of the U-Report data they receive, U-Report can help motivate young people to continue to engage in issues, to become agents of change and to use ICT's to improve their well-being.

ICTs: empowerment, participation and protection

It is estimated that a third of all internet users are children.[47] With this growing population of children online, we are facing the enormous challenge of understanding when and how ICTs can help protect children and young people from violence, exploitation and abuse. We know that ICTs are excellent participation and engagement tools and that they can also reinforce inequities and present risks that can lead to harmful consequences regarding children's safety, personal development, and wellbeing. Therefore, as children gain access to ICTs, and as civic technologies are designed to encourage children and young people to shape their own lives and adopt positive change, we must acknowledge associated risks, and put the needs and well-being of the community at the core of any system or programme. When designed with children's best interest in mind, ICTs can help foster a child's right to participate in his or her present and future.

We also must continue to ask: "How do ICTs embrace today's "new power" values and assure children's and young people's right to participate through open, transparent and easy-to-access channels?", "How can we make them available to different audiences?" and "How can the Internet help protect children and young people from violence, abuse and exploitation, while providing the mechanisms for empowering them to influence the decision-making process?" These seem to be today's main challenges when shaping civic technologies for children and young audiences.

Through ICTs like U-Report, we have connected communities to their decision makers with more information faster than ever before. However, we must always remember that technology is just a means to an end: the remaining challenges are how the collected information is used to achieve social change and how to ensure children's safety while using ICTs.

Technology by itself does not achieve change; humans achieve change, and ICTs, when used responsibly, can help us get there.

Endnotes

[7] Livingstone, S, Carr, J and Byrne, J (2016). *One inThree: Internet Governance and Children's Rights.* Innocenti Discussion Paper No.2016-01, Florence: UNICEF Office of Research.

[8] https://www.unicef-irc.org/publications/pdf/idp_2016_01.pdf

[9] Measuring the Information Society Report 2013, International Telecommunication Union, 2013. See: http://www.itu.int/en/ITU-D/Statistics/Pages/publications/mis2013.aspx

[10] Lombana-Bermudez, A (2015). Re-thinking Youth Participation and Civic Engagement in the Digital Age. In S Cortesi & U Gasser (Eds), Digitally connected: *Global perspectives on youth and digital media* (p.88). Retrieved from http://papers.ssrn.com/sol3/papers.cfm?abstract_id=2585686

[11] Ibid.

[12] Ibid.

[13] Locantore, J (2014). *Best Practices in the Use of Technology in Engaging Underrepresented Communities in Planning.* Retrieved from https://www.livingcities.org/blog/476-engagement-tech-for-all

[14] Heinmans, J & Timms, H (2014). Understanding "New Power", *Harvard Business Review,* Retrieved from https://hbr.org/2014/12/understanding-new-power

[15] Ibid.

[16] Ibid.

[17] Ibid.

[18] UNICEF WCAR0, (2010). Mobile technologies for Child Protection: *A briefing note,* New York: UNICEF.

[19] Available at: *www.protejabrasil.com.br/br/)*

[20] Available at: www.isigurt.al

[21] The Net Patrol Hotline (2013), along with the Safer Internet Centre, is a mechanism for online reporting of suspected illegal content on the national level. The Net Patrol Hotline handles CSAM reports, cyberbullying and hate speech. Any report received by the Net Patrol Hotline containing suspected illegal material that is not hosted in Serbia is forwarded to the database via an International Association of Internet Hotlines Report Management System electronic mechanism to the member state determined by the Net Patrol's analysis to host the provider of the suspected illegal material. Sign Out patrols are further analyzed by a local mechanism which forwards them to state bodies of the country and/or other adequate bodies in accordance with local laws.

[22] Net Patrol mobile application: http://www.netpatrola.rs/en/mobile-application.1.102.html (last accessed 20 May 2016).

[23] In each country U-Report polls and works around the issues that affect young people and their communities locally. Therefore, each U-Report programme is different, as it looks to adapt to country needs and context.

[24] To date, U-Report is live in Brazil, Burkina Faso, Burundi, Cameroon, Central African Republic, Chile, Guinea, Indonesia, Ireland, Liberia, Mali, Mexico, Mozambique, Nigeria, Pakistan, Senegal, Sierra Leone, Swaziland, Uganda, Ukraine, United Kingdom, Zambia, Zimbabwe. Each country website can be found in ureport.in. Additionally, there are 25 other countries which are in the pipeline of deploying U-Report locally.

[25] U-Report has been applied to a range of use cases, which to date include:
- Increasing risk awareness and knowledge levels among young people.
- Improving communities' disaster preparedness & response: U-Report has mapped results in real-time. This data has complemented nationally available data and has highlighted vulnerable areas, allowing for preparedness efforts to be targeted accordingly.
- Providing support and addressing bottlenecks in service delivery. Information provided by U-Reporters has allowed for quick responses and improvements.
- U-Report poll flows have been used to identify and monitor bottlenecks in policy and programme implementation by collecting relevant data related to the success of each implementation stage.
- Detecting emergencies and outbreaks through keyword detection within U-Reporters' messages, allowing for real-time and rapid response.
- Improving accountability by reducing the distance between governments and their constituencies.
- Understanding gaps and demand for information among young people (experience from U-Report has shown that about 2/3 of all unsolicited messages consist of requests for information).
For more information on U-Report case studies visit ureport.in

[26] While assuring their participation, it also safeguards their anonymity: U-Report is free and anonymous. Phone numbers are hidden in the system. Even those with the highest level of access cannot view a U-Reporter's phone number, Twitter handle, or Facebook profile. U-Reporters are also given the option to have a nickname or remain private. For those who choose a nickname these aren't used outside of the system without a U-Reporter's permission.

[27] Poll results available in http://senegal.ureport.in/poll/556/

[28] Poll results available in http://mexico.ureport.in/poll/570/

[29] Poll results available in https://uganda.ureport.in/polls/

[30] Poll results available in http://sierraleone.ureport.in/polls/

[31] Poll results available in http://liberia.ureport.in/polls/

[32] Poll results available in http://mozambique.ureport.in/polls/

[33] Poll results available in https://ukraine.ureport.in/poll/566/

[34] Poll results available in http://chile.ureport.in/poll/637/

[35] Poll results available in https://malaysia.ureport.in/polls/

[36] Poll results available in http://nigeria.ureport.in/poll/558/

[37] Poll results available in https://swaziland.ureport.in/poll/573/

[38] Poll results available in http://ureport.pk/poll/571/

[39] Poll results available in http://ireland.ureport.in/polls/

[40] Poll results available in https://burkinafaso.ureport.in/poll/578/

[41] Poll results available in http://mali.ureport.in/polls/

[42] Poll results available in https://guinea.ureport.in/poll/606/

[43] Poll results available in http://indonesia.ureport.in/polls/

[44] Poll results available in http://ureport.in/poll/575/

[45] Poll results available in http://ukraine.ureport.in/poll/566/

[46] Which was in line with global poll results where only 8 % told their teachers.

[47] https://www.unicef-irc.org/publications/pdf/idp_2016_01.pdf

A counsellor speaks to children, Occupied Palestinian Territory
© UNICEF/UNI9394/Pirozzi

3. The role of independent human rights institutions in preventing and responding to bullying

Anne Lindboe and Anders Cameron

Introduction

"Getting beat up doesn't hurt, but the psychological stuff really hurts. It ruins your life. Your life is stolen from you. It's loss of freedom, that's what bullying is". This quote from a 19-year-old boy who suffered many years of bullying in school shows how serious bullying or cyberbullying over time can constitute grave human rights offences. Bullying limits children's fundamental right to develop and reach their full potential. There can be no doubt that bullying and cyberbullying should be on the agenda of independent human rights institutions for children, and that such institutions can make a difference for both children that are bullied and the children that bully others.

The UN Convention on the Rights of the Child (CRC) is almost universally ratified, and there is a broad global consensus to protect the rights of children. Still, children as a group are nearly invisible in many countries. Their voices and roles in policy making and budgeting are weak or non-existent. There is an enormous gap between children's rights on paper and the reality in the communities where they live. This is the main reason why independent human rights institutions for children are needed. These should be strong, independent institutions that can voice children's interests in society and ensure that policies to secure children's rights are developed and implemented.

In this article we will give a short outline of what independent human rights institutions for children's rights are, and then we will elaborate on their role in the protection of children against bullying and cyberbullying, using examples from the work of the Ombudsman for Children in Norway.

We will use the term bullying in a wide sense, not distinguishing between bullying and cyberbullying. In our work, we see that most cases involve both bullying and cyberbullying. Cyberbullying has some important distinct features that need to be addressed, but essentially many of the measures that need to be in place to tackle traditional bullying will also have effect on cyberbullying.

What are independent human rights institutions for children?

Independent human rights institutions for children take many forms. Some countries, including the Nordic countries, have separate ombudsman institutions for children. Other countries have chosen different models – for example by including protection and promotion of children's rights in the mandate of a wider, more general national institution for human rights or a human rights commission. Even though there are differences both with regard to structure, mandate and working methods, independent human rights institutions for children should fulfill some minimum standards. The Paris Principles[48] and the General Comment no. 2 by the UN Committee on the Rights of the Child[49] formulate some criteria which include, among others:

- A clear mandate and power
- Independence
- Accessibility for children

Having a *clear mandate and power* means being established by law, preferably through a constitutional mandate. The institution should have a broad mandate to investigate, issue reports and give statements. It is a prerequisite to fulfill this mandate that the institution can access any relevant information and documentation and access institutions and other facilities for children. The mandate should be linked to monitoring the state's implementation of the CRC.

An *independent* institution is free to set its own agenda. The appointment process of the ombudsperson or commissioner must be transparent, and the institution must have financial and operational autonomy. This independence relies heavily on the professionalism and accountability of the leader and the staff.

To voice children's interests in society and have profound knowledge of children's lives and problems, it is crucial for the institution to be *accessible to children* – to be in direct contact with children through various channels. Children should influence the work and priorities of the institution, and a core value for the institution should be to bring children's experiences and views into the rooms where decisions are made.

More than 70 countries have established an independent human rights institution for children[50]. These institutions are an important resource to highlight the profound problems bullying and cyberbullying represent in children's lives, potentially causing severe damage to health, learning and children's ability to develop and reach their full potential. Besides monitoring and reporting to international bodies like the CRC, they can inspire policy-making and implementation of policies and give important support to children and families in individual cases where bullying isn't addressed by schools or responsible authorities. In the following sections we will describe how independent human rights institutions for children can work along all these lines to prevent and respond to bullying.

Handling individual cases

Some independent human rights institutions for children handle individual complaints, others do not. The ones that formally handle individual complaints can have an impact in both individual cases and more generally through their practice. The Ombudsman for Children in Norway doesn't handle individual complaints formally, but we follow many cases through the complaints system. Through advice to children, families, schools, and other relevant parties, we help in securing for children a safe school environment. This work also gives us important knowledge that can be used to improve the system that prevents, detects and stops bullying.

Many children and parents contact the ombudsman's office to ask for help in serious bullying cases. Our main task is to give them information about their rights, and through that information empower them to claim these rights. In many cases, neither the children, the parents nor the schools have sufficient knowledge about children's rights to a safe school environment, the school's obligations to secure this right and the procedural provisions that are in place to secure rule of law. In many cases, quite basic advice can make a big change for children. Here are some examples:

- Many schools fail to document their work in individual bullying cases. Helping children and parents claim documentation can make things change, and is very important if they decide to complain later.

- The Education Act obliges the school to make a written decision in individual cases. This is sometimes neglected. Informing parents and children about this right and the basic elements of a decision can have great impact on the case.

- Sometimes schools fail to inform children and families about the possibility to complain. Giving information about the complaints system and the formal steps that need to be taken before filing a complaint can be of great importance, for example by reducing the time before a complaint is filed and handled.

Some cases are very complex, and they raise more fundamental questions that need to be addressed. An independent human rights institution for children can bring such cases to the attention of relevant authorities, often with some clear recommendations about measures that need to be made to solve the case or prevent similar cases in the future.

The mandates of independent human rights institutions often grant them access to information that is not fully accessible for anyone else. This makes it possible to look into all different aspects of a case. In many cases, the ordinary complaints and monitoring system will be sectoral: one institution is responsible for complaints and monitoring in education, another in health and a third in justice. They limit their investigations to their own sector and legal framework, and are often unable to see the whole situation of the child because there is significant information that they can't access due to confidentiality rules. Looking into all aspects of a case, however, is very important to detect holes in the safety net.

Independent human rights institutions can use the insight they get from individual cases to point to more general problems or to map areas in need of further investigation. The strength of independent human rights institutions is that they can see the whole case, and that their mandate is seldom limited to one specific sector, like many other complaints' mechanisms. They can also generalize information from individual cases and use the information to raise awareness or influence policy making.

Awareness raising – making decision-makers see the challenges

In too many countries, the issue of bullying of children is not high enough on the public and political agenda. This may have several causes, the root cause probably being the issue pinpointed by the UN Committee on the Rights of the Child in general comment number 14: "Children have less possibility than adults to make a strong case for their own interests and those involved in decisions affecting them must be explicitly aware of their interests. If the interests of children are not highlighted, they tend to be overlooked."[51]

Independent monitoring mechanisms can have an important role in raising awareness about prevalence and the potentially very grave consequences of bullying both among decision makers and in the general public. Individual cases can be used to highlight the gravity of bullying; reports and results from more general monitoring work can shed light on the prevalence of bullying and on other relevant issues, like regional differences, and also highlight the specific groups of children that are more often subjected to bullying than others.

In Norway the Ombudsman for Children has been working to raise awareness about bullying for many years. We were among the institutions that initiated the "Manifesto against bullying". The first manifesto was signed by the Norwegian prime minister in 2002, and different stakeholders – municipalities, labor organizations and groups of parents co-signed. The core of the manifesto was to establish a binding cooperation in which all parties to the agreement pledged to work systematically to end all bullying in schools. The Manifesto has been revised and changed through the years, and the Ombudsman is no longer a direct party to the agreement – the effect on the prevalence of bullying is also debatable. It is not questionable, however, that the notion of a coordinated, concrete effort from several different stakeholders has been an important way of raising awareness and creating public debate about bullying and its damaging effects.

Independent human rights institutions for children can play an important role in establishing such initiatives and shared efforts. Their independent nature and the mandate to protect and promote children's rights, give them a voice different from both NGOs (dependent on donors and/or members) and the government or local authorities (that have conflicting interests, being both responsible for the children in schools, the school professionals and the balance in the budget). Independent human rights institutions can take the children's perspective and demand cooperation and joint efforts from all stakeholders with great legitimacy.

Involving children in prevention and response

Article 12 of the CRC gives all children the right to be heard and participate in decisions that affect them. The right to participation is one of the fundamental principles of the Convention. Still, in most countries, children aren't necessarily heard, and their views aren't taken into account in individual cases or in policy making.

One of the most important roles of an independent human rights institution for children, is to underline the obligation to ask children their opinions, and to give their views due weight before making a decision. Independent human rights institutions for children can play an important role in ensuring that school administrations, complaints bodies and monitoring mechanisms listen to children in their work against bullying and in developing a safe school environment.

The complaints and monitoring system for education in Norway has not been good at involving children directly. The system has gathered children's views indirectly, through parents and/or representatives of the school. In bullying cases however, as in many other cases, this will often not give a real picture of children's views or needs. There may be a conflict of interest, both between the school and the child, and between the child and the parents. In some of the cases that we have received in the Ombudsman's office, this is very clear in at least two ways:

- In serious bullying cases, the parents might at some point be so emotionally exhausted that they lose sight of the child's best interest – and instead end up in an unsolvable conflict with the school and other services that are actually there to help their child.

- In monitoring the school's work to create and maintain a friendly, positive school environment, talking directly to children is crucial. The children can provide important information that the adults usually can't, for example explain what areas in the school are safe or unsafe, where the adults can see you and where you can hide and how the social system between students is organized.

The Ombudsman's office has worked through many different channels to raise awareness of the importance of listening to children directly. We have participated at conferences for school administrators and worked systematically to ensure that children's right to participation is incorporated in legal provisions and administrative standards both on a national and a regional level.

This has resulted in more children being heard in the complaints system, and also in changes to procedural guidelines for monitoring that now stress the obligation to listen to children directly and to document children's views and take them into account. This work is at the core of what independent human rights institutions for children should do: It helps implement the fundamental principles of the CRC in the education system.

Child participation and child perspective in policy making

Independent human rights institutions for children can have an important impact on policy making, being their country's leading experts on children's rights. They have the important role of upholding a clear child perspective in policy processes where conflicting interests easily distract the decision makers from the interests of the children that are affected. Independent human rights institutions for children have a natural role in stating their opinions clearly throughout the policy making process, and in participating in public debates about important new policies for children. In the following example we want to illustrate how children themselves, through an independent human rights institution, can have an impact on policy making.

In 2013 the Norwegian Minister for Education ordered a commission to review all parts of the education system to secure for all children their right to a safe school environment. The commission gathered the views of experts and practitioners, but they had no direct information from children with experience of serious bullying. The Ombudsman's office therefore gathered a group of 23 children that had been bullied in school. We call such groups of children "young experts"[52] – they are experts on their own experiences, and they always have important knowledge that older experts tend to miss out on – simply for not being young today and being further away from the experiences of young people.

The information from the children was gathered in the report "I want to have good dreams",[53] a report that shed light on both the very serious consequences of bullying, and of some important flaws in the systems that needed to be addressed by the new policy. Nearly all the children in the expert group told us that they hadn't been heard and taken seriously when they reported bullying. Through very concrete examples they illustrated how the bullying they had experienced over time constituted serious breaches of their basic human rights – like the right to protection against violence and the right to education. The commission took the children's views very seriously, and proposed many changes that were in line with the recommendations made by the children, for example continuous work on prevention in all schools, and including the children's right to be heard explicitly in the Education Act.

The group of young experts also met with the Minister of Education. One of the issues they raised most loudly and insistently was the fact that children aren't taken seriously when they complain. At first the Minister told the children that the adults in their schools were taking them seriously – but listening to the children's stories, he eventually understood that not all the adults were doing this.

Policy makers need to listen to children. The young experts have had a great impact on the proposed policy changes in Norway on bullying in schools and kindergartens. This year, the Norwegian Parliament will pass legal and other measures to make the complaints system more child friendly and accessible to children, to raise awareness and knowledge among teachers and other school professionals, and to impose sanctions on schools who don't comply with their legal obligation to prevent and stop bullying.

Demanding accountability

To address bullying – both online and in schools, the responsible authorities need basic information about for example the prevalence of bullying, especially involving vulnerable groups, and of the differences related to age and gender. They also need information about effective policies, methods, and programmes to reduce bullying behaviour. Too often, schools have been laboratories for methods with poor or no real evidence based effect. Responsible authorities, eager to act, can easily be tempted into implementing comprehensive, and often expensive, universal programmes or action plans without a proper plan for implementation and without drawing on evidence based effect.

Independent human rights institutions for children can demand that governments and local authorities gather the information they need as a basis for policy making and budgeting. Asking the right questions, to the right people, at the right time can have great impact on accountability.

Another important aspect of accountability is to secure efficient budget tracking. It is important that the funds allocated to preventing and stopping bullying are in fact used for that purpose. Using funds meant for bullying prevention for other good causes might be tempting. In many countries, responsibility for education is placed at the local or regional administrative levels. This means that funds allocated by parliament in the state budget are transferred to the local or regional level, and that the parliament to a certain extent loses some control over the funds.

Bullying is often seen as mainly a challenge for the education sector. The responsibilities of other sectors, such as the justice or health sectors, can be more unclear. Independent human rights institutions can pinpoint the problems generated by silos and these unclear lines of responsibility. By highlighting such problems from the child's perspective, the human rights institution can help build important bridges between sectors, and make politicians see the importance of commitment to cross-sectoral responses to bullying both at the national and regional levels.

NGOs and other stakeholders also have an important role in demanding accountability, but the specific mandate of monitoring mechanisms give them both authority and an obligation to demand that responsible authorities gather the knowledge needed for accountable policy making and budgeting. Being completely independent is important in this respect – the independent institutions can have a clear child perspective, without regard to what donors, members or partner organizations think.

Monitoring and reporting

Most independent human rights institutions have an explicit obligation in their mandate to monitor the state's implementation and compliance with one or more international conventions, or in the case of children, the CRC. This responsibility includes monitoring the situation for children, and reporting, both nationally (typically to the parliament) and to relevant international bodies. These core activities are of course great opportunities to highlight the holes in the safety net for children when it comes to bullying. Each country has a different context, and the way institutions report vary significantly. Here are some examples of how we have reported on bullying to both national authorities and to the UN Committee on the Rights of the Child.

Reporting to the UN CRC Committee

In 2009 Norway submitted its fourth report on the implementation of the CRC. The Ombudsman for Children in Norway submitted a supplementary report[54] highlighting issues that were not discussed in the state party's report. Among the issues included in the supplementary report, was bullying in schools. The Ombudsman for Children's main concern was that the system that should guarantee the children's rights to a safe school environment didn't have measures to enforce their decisions. If a child experienced an unsafe school environment, the family could issue a complaint to the County Governor. The County Governor would then investigate the case and make a decision. If the decision were that the school and/or municipality hadn't acted according to the law, there were no real sanctions available for the County Governor to enforce the law. The Ombudsman had received individual cases from families that, even though the decision of the County Governor was in favor of the child, had resulted in no real change in the way the school and/or municipality handled the case.

In 2010, after the examination of Norway by the UN CRC Committee, the committee issued its concluding observations.[55] The committee was concerned about the high numbers of bullying cases reported in schools, and recommended the state party to strengthen its efforts to combat bullying in kindergartens and schools.

Clear recommendations from the UN Committee provide forceful arguments that both independent human rights institutions, civil society and other stakeholders can use in order to make decision makers give the necessary priority to such issues as bullying.

Reporting to the national authorities

In 2009, at the same time as the Ombudsman reported concerns about the complaints system for children who experienced bullying to the UN, we also reported more extensively on the issue to national authorities in Norway. The report "The difference between having rights and the fulfilling of rights"[56] was based on information from interviews with representatives of the complaints mechanism for children, with children and families and on documentation from individual cases. It showed a monitoring and complaints system that was not child sensitive, received few complaints and was inefficient because it had no real possibilities of sanctioning its decisions.

The report was sent both to the Ministry of Education and distributed generally through the media. It sparked a debate on the real access to justice for children, and was the first, important step towards the acknowledgement among politicians that there was a need for policy changes and changes in the legal framework to make the system child friendly and able to secure children their rights. After many debates, a two-year national inspection of safe school environments, and one more report from the Ombudsman for Children in 2012, the Minister for Education in 2013 ordered a commission to review all parts of the system to create safe school environments and to prevent and stop bullying.

The combined reporting to national authorities and to the UN Committee on the Rights of the Child were important steps on the way to initiate the important work on policy and legislation that we have described above. In 2009, at the time of the first reports, no other organizations or bodies were really concerned about the problems in the system that was supposed to protect children from bullying. Had it not been for the independent human rights institution for children, the problems might have persisted even longer.

Conclusions

There are three features of independent human rights institutions for children that make them especially important in this work. The first is the pure, child rights perspective. While NGOs and official bodies may need to balance different interests, an independent human rights institution can build on a solid child rights perspective. This gives both legitimacy and impact. The second is the insight they can have into individual cases, and the ability to investigate the whole case, rather than being limited to one sector or legal framework. The third is their role as a spokesperson for children, both indirectly, but also directly, through gathering information from children themselves and thus bringing them to the decision-making table.

Independent human rights institutions for children can have many roles in preventing and responding to bullying. Through addressing individual cases, raising awareness, contributing to policy making, demanding accountability, monitoring, and reporting human rights issues, institutions can have a significant impact in protecting children against bullying and cyberbullying.

Endnotes

48 The UN Principles Relating to the Status of National Institutions, Adopted by General Assembly resolution 48/134 of 20 December 1993.
49 CRC General Comment No 2, CRC/GC/2002/2.
50 UNICEF (2012), Championing Children's Rights: A global study of independent human rights institutions for children. Florence, UNICEF Innocenti Research Centre.
51 UN Committee on the Rights of the Child: General comment No. 14 (2013), CRC/C/GC/14.
52 The Ombudsman for Children in Norway (2011): The Expert Handbook. http://barneombudet.no/english/publications/the-expert-handbook/
53 The Ombudsman for Children in Norway (2014). I want to have good dreams. http://barneombudet.no/wp-content/uploads/2015/10/Good-dreams.pdf
54 The Ombudsman for Children in Norway (2009). Supplementary Report to the UN Committee on the Rights of the Child. http://barneombudet.no/wp-content/uploads/2013/09/suplementary-report-to-the-un_english.pdf
55 Committee on the Rights of the Child (2010). Concluding observations: Norway. CRC/C/NOR/CO/4 http://tbinternet.ohchr.org/_layouts/treatybodyexternal/Download.aspx?symbolno=CRC/C/NOR/CO/4&Lang=En
56 The Ombudsman for Children in Norway (2009) "Forskjellen på å ha ret tog å få rett" (Norwegian only) http://barneombudet.no/wp-content/uploads/2013/09/tilsyns-og-klagesystem-innen-skole-web-.pdf

Teachers assisting children, Haiti.
© UNICEF/UNI121148/Dormino

Chapter II. Legislation and Public Policies

4. A national multi-facetted approach to prevent and address bullying and cyberbullying

Brian O'Neill

Introduction

Since the first efforts to systematically study children's experiences of bullying and harassment, particularly in school settings, it is now recognized that bullying is a complex problem that takes a variety forms and occurs in multiple locations including on new communications platforms. For this reason, the benefits of a multi-facetted approach at the national level are widely advocated to ensure that individual actors, such as schools, are not left isolated in their efforts to combat a phenomenon that appears to grow ever more prevalent. National responses to complex social issues such as bullying are required to ensure a coherent, consistent and holistic approach and to optimize resources and expertise for the widest benefit. This chapter profiles the example of Ireland and in particular the work that contributed to the development of a national *Action Plan on Bullying*[57] in 2013 as a case study to illustrate the challenges facing policy makers in responding to a major issue of public concern. The lessons learned from this and other equivalent examples point to the need for an overarching and comprehensive framework to sustain effective strategies in tackling and preventing bullying.

Guiding framework for a national response

Multi-stakeholder action to combat bullying and violence in schools has been a feature of many national responses towards an issue that has gained in international research and public policy prominence. Ireland published its *Action Plan on Bullying* in 2013 joining a number of its closest neighbors in developing cross-sectoral, collaborative responses to supporting better outcomes for children. The Northern Ireland Anti-Bullying Forum (NIABF) was formed in 2004 by Save the Children, at the request of the Department of Education, bringing together 25 regional statutory and voluntary sector organizations in a joint effort to combat bullying of children and young people in schools and in the wider community.[58] The NIABF is also a constituent member of the British and Irish Anti-Bullying Forum (BIABF) where government and non-government agencies across the five jurisdictions (i.e. Northern Ireland, Republic of Ireland, England, Wales and Scotland) meet twice yearly to share information and best practice in the area.[59]

A similar collaborative approach to anti-bullying was also sponsored by the Scottish government and a national strategy developed by the Scottish Anti-Bullying Steering Group following consultation with a wide range of stakeholders. The objective of government was therefore to build a consensus around what the approach to anti-bullying measures should be: to communicate and promote a common vision; and to ensure effective joint action between relevant agencies and communities in support of a holistic approach towards anti-bullying in Scotland.[60]

What such initiatives share in common is a recognition that individual efforts by schools on their own are not enough to counteract bullying and violence in schools and that unified and coordinated action is needed to address what is a wider societal problem. Such efforts also bear out the increasing recognition given to bullying as a priority for public policy as a public health issue[61] – as supported by the weight of international evidence on bullying behaviour and the seriousness with which it is viewed by educational and health professionals.

As defined by Jenkins, public policy refers to the "set of interrelated decisions taken by a political actor or group of actors concerning the selection of goals and the means of achieving them within a specified situation where these decisions should, in principle, be within the power of these actors to achieve".[62] Policy is thereby tied to the availability of resources as well as the distinct contexts within with which policy actions are implemented with the aim of achieving targeted solutions. Policy literature typically points towards the distinct stages of a policy making process, setting out, for example: the triggers and agenda setting that defines the policy goals; the policy formulation process itself and its legitimization within a social context; the stage of policy implementation; and ultimately the evaluation of policy programme and its success in achieving its goals.[63] The literature on the policy process offers a useful guide towards understanding what policy is and how it is developed. There is less consensus, however, on what makes for good public policy or indeed the requirements for an effective or promising public policy intervention.

A sample guiding framework for a national approach to bullying has been developed by O'Moore.[64] Drawing on the recommendations of the WHO *World Report on Violence and Health* (2002), she characterizes the requirements of an effective national response to bullying as a series of steps, each of which add essential capacity and direct targeted attention to key stakeholder obligations and requirements.[65] The distinct stages are summarized in Table 1.

Table 1:
Features of a National Response to Bullying[66]

Step	Description
1	Draw up, implement and monitor a national plan of action to prevent school bullying and violence.
2	Enhance the capacity to collect data on school bullying and violence.
3	Define priorities for, and support research on, the causes, consequences, costs and prevention of school bullying and violence.
4	Develop a national strategy to assist schools to prevent and reduce school bullying and violence.
5	Promote a media campaign to promote non-violent values, attitudes and behaviour.
6	Integrate School Bullying and Violence Prevention into teacher education at both pre-service and in-service levels.
7	Establish an advisory body for partners in education.
8	Contribute to an international research network.
9	Promote legislation to deal effectively with school bullying and violence.

The framework, as outlined by O'Moore, sets out the key elements of a coordinated national response to the problem of school bullying and violence. The framework encompasses multi-stakeholder collaboration and coordination; leveraging of multi-disciplinary expertise, including state agencies, to deal with different dimensions of bullying; the building of research capacity to underpin evidence-based policy making; and the use of the media for awareness-raising and attainment of public support. Inspired by the WHO framework for mobilizing action in response to violence, it models the necessary conditions and the actions to be addressed by different stakeholders if the strategy is to be effective and sustainable.

Brief background: bullying in Ireland

In Ireland, as elsewhere, policy interest in the subject of bullying in schools came to prominence in the late 1980s and early 1990s as countries ranging from Great Britain, Australia, Japan, Canada and the United States began to pay serious attention to a phenomenon that up to then had neither been well-researched nor understood. Prior to this time, attention to the issue was largely confined to Scandinavian countries where, through the pioneering work of Dan Olweus,[67] efforts to develop a more systematic understanding of bullying took root. There, for instance, through the use of the Olweus Bully/Victim Questionnaire, it was estimated that in 1983 some 15% of children aged 7 to 16 years in Norway and Sweden were involved in bullying either as victims or perpetrators.[68] The development of the Olweus anti-bullying prevention and intervention strategy in the 1980s and 1990s provided the model for most subsequent school-based programmes and continues to exert significant influence on the field today.[69]

Attention to the subject of bullying in Ireland was until the mid-1990s sporadic.[70] 1993 marked something of a turning point, however, with a national conference devoted to the subject[71] and the publication of national guidelines for schools to deal with bullying at both primary and post-primary level.[72] More extensive research followed with the first nationwide survey of bullying behaviour in schools funded by the Department of Education in 1993-4. Based on a nationally representative sample of 20,422 pupils aged 8 to 18 years, drawing on 10% of all primary schools and 27% of all post-primary schools, this was, to that point, the largest sample to date in the UK or Ireland and the only national study of bullying behaviour outside of the landmark Olweus nationwide study in Norway.[73]

By way of context, corporal punishment in Irish schools had been abolished in Ireland in 1982 by order of the Minister for Education, and was accompanied by an overhaul of classroom discipline measures and implementation of a more child-centered curriculum. Research conducted by the Department of Education indicated that while the level of classroom indiscipline remained low, a level of school-based violence was prevalent particularly in urban, economically disadvantaged schools.[74]

Findings from the 1993-94 survey found that 32.1% of primary school pupils and 15.6% of secondary school students reported having been bullied. Accordingly, O'Moore, founding Director of the National Anti-Bullying Research Centre and Rapporteur for the first Council of Europe-sponsored European seminar on school bullying in 1987, estimated that nearly one in four school children in Ireland were at risk of bullying either as bully or as victim.[75] An anti-bullying programme, the Donegal Primary Schools Anti-Bullying Programme, following the Norwegian 'whole school' approach, with simultaneous engagement with each of the different groups within the school community: school management, teachers, parents and pupils, was found to be effective at a regional level.[76] However, a subsequent intervention, the 'ABC' programme, while contributing important expertise and resources at the national level, struggled to achieve the same impact. Follow-up research in 2004-5 found, despite the introduction of such programmes and the implementation of the 'Guidelines on Countering Bullying Behaviour in Primary and Post-Primary Schools', a higher incidence of victimization among both primary and secondary schools with risks of involvement in bullying among post-primary pupils rising from 26.5% in 1993-4 to 36.4% in 2004-5.[77]

The insidious effects of school-based bullying were echoed in a national consultation with children and young people, coordinated by the Ombudsman for Children's Office (OCO).[78] Noting that bullying was among the top five issues raised most frequently in education-related complaints, the Ombudsman recommended that future efforts be supported by the education system as a whole and be "reinforced by wider community/societal initiatives that combat discriminatory attitudes and promote a culture of respect for human rights".[79]

Towards a national approach

Responding to what was perceived as a serious problem of bullying in schools as well as a wider societal phenomenon of gender-based violence, the coalition government established by the political parties of Fine Gael and Labour included in their Programme for Government a commitment "to encourage schools to develop anti-bullying policies and in particular, strategies to combat homophobic bullying".[80] A national Anti-Bullying Forum was convened in May 2012, jointly sponsored by the Department of Education & Skills and the newly established Department of Children & Youth Affairs.[81]

At the same time, the Minister for Education & Skills also established a Working Group to tackle bullying, including homophobic bullying, cyberbullying and racist bullying. The Minister also launched a national consultation, inviting submissions from relevant stakeholders as well as members of the public on the options available and actions required. The outcomes and recommendations from both the consultation and the national Forum were assessed by a multi-stakeholder Working Group which included relevant government departments and state agencies, NGOs and representative student and youth groups. Following further consultation with experts and relevant sectoral groups, the Working Group produced its new Action Plan on Bullying, launched jointly in January 2013 by the then Ministers for Education and Skills and Minister for Children and Youth Affairs.[82]

The Action Plan on Bullying presents a national, government-backed approach to tackling bullying in schools while promoting an anti-bullying culture based on diversity and inclusiveness. The plan offers a revised and updated definition of bullying to ensure that all forms are captured and outlines twelve action points, including new anti-bullying procedures, training supports for schools, evaluation mechanisms, measures to promote awareness-raising and new research initiatives.

The key features of the plan may be summarized as follows:

1. **New national anti-bullying procedures for schools**

    A significant feature of the approach is the updating of the original 1993 guidelines issued to schools as well as the template, published in 2006, to assist schools in drafting Anti-Bullying Policies.[83] New policies must now be integrated into the school's Code of Behaviour whilst schools are encouraged to adopt a school-wide approach, displaying a positive school culture climate that is welcoming of difference and diversity. All grounds of harassment and discrimination (as recognized under Equal Status legislation) are to be included in schools' anti-bullying policies (e.g. gender including transgender, civil status, family status, sexual orientation, religion, age, disability, race and membership of the Traveller community). Policies must also set out the school's procedures for investigating and dealing with bullying and the procedures for the formal noting and recording of bullying behaviour on a standardized template.

2. **Training and teacher education support services**

   Recognizing the extensive training needs to ensure consistent and effective implementation of anti-bullying policies, the plan provides for the provision of Continuous Professional Development (CPD) to support teachers' capacity to deal with all forms of bullying, including identity based bullying, including homophobic bullying, and cyberbullying. Education support services as a result have been tasked with developing a comprehensive CPD response to equip managers and teachers on implementation strategies and methodologies with sample materials and resources relevant to the national context. The plan also envisages a coordinated approach towards training and awareness-raising for Boards of Management and parents' councils building on existing initiatives to develop guidelines for boards of management on supporting LGBT young people.[84]

3. **Awareness-raising initiatives and development of resources**

   Much emphasis is given in the Action Plan towards building awareness of the diverse forms of bullying, in particular homophobic and transgender bullying, and the increasing prevalence of cyberbullying. The plan includes support for the Stand Up! Against Homophobic and Transphobic bullying campaign, organized by BeLonG To Youth[85] Services. A media campaign focused on cyberbullying was implemented as part of Safer Internet Day 2013, encouraging secondary schools pupils to positively intervene as 'bystanders' when they see cyberbullying in an effort to show solidarity with victims and stamp out cyberbullying.[86] A national anti-bullying website was also developed to provide information for parents, young people and school staff on types and methods of bullying and how to deal with bullying behaviour.[87]

4. **Evaluation mechanisms**

   The Action Plan encompasses a variety of evaluation mechanisms. Firstly, the plan adapts methods for whole school evaluations (WSEs) by amending questionnaires and by other means to include more evidence gathering concerning the effectiveness of the school's anti-bullying policies. Secondly, a thematic evaluation of bullying in schools is to be carried out by the Schools Inspectorate to take account of the effectiveness of schools' actions to create a positive school culture and to prevent and tackle bullying. Thirdly, schools are to be assisted in the development of self-evaluation mechanisms to assess the effectiveness of their policies with guidance and criteria aimed at management level and student support services.

5. **Support for further research**

   Finally, a number of measures to stimulate further research to support anti-bullying measures are included in the plan. A study on good practice and effective interventions in Irish schools for the prevention of bullying of children with special educational needs was commissioned as part of the plan.[88] Research on the prevalence and impact of bullying linked to social media on the mental health and suicidal behaviour among young people was also commissioned.[89] The national Anti-Bullying Research and Resource Centre at Dublin City University also received support under the plan as a means of building national research capacity.[90]

Reception and implementation

The *Action Plan on Bullying* has been positively received in Ireland as a long overdue revision of the approach to tackling and preventing bullying in schools. Its strategy in tackling bullying in a holistic way, which views schools as pivotal but places the issue within a much wider social context, is a noteworthy feature of the national framework. The support for policies of inclusiveness and diversity and the special attention to issues of homophobic, transgender and identity-based bullying has likewise been welcomed as a breakthrough, aligning educational policy with the broader project of legislative reform that culminated in the successful referendum campaign to extend civil marriage rights to same-sex couples in 2015. Furthermore, the inclusion of cyberbullying within the terms of reference for schools' anti-bullying policies is also significant in removing ambiguity regarding schools' responsibilities in this area and ensuring better linkage with efforts to support internet safety and digital citizenship in the classroom.

The updating of schools' anti-bullying policies and procedures for dealing with incidences of bullying is one of the most tangible achievements of the Action Plan. As a result of the plan, the Department of Education and Skills issued new anti-bullying procedures for the sector as a whole.[91] Boards of Management in the 4000 primary and post-primary schools in Ireland have adopted an anti-bullying policy in line with the new arrangements and they are required to comply with best practice in tackling and preventing bullying. Many have also followed with targeted measures towards cyberbullying such as the development of a specific Anti-Cyberbullying Policy as an addendum to the school's anti-bullying policy. Additional measures have included appointing a staff member to act as a dedicated Cybersafety Officer, and training staff to identify signs of cyberbullying and deal with incidences as they occur. Guidelines for preventing cyberbullying in the school environment have been widely disseminated and supported.[92]

When viewed against a model national framework, some shortcomings are also evident. While 0.5 million was initially earmarked to support implementation of specific initiatives within the plan, this has coincided with underinvestment in the sector as a whole with educationalists pointing to the many economic challenges facing schools and school staff.[93] Schools are granted the autonomy to develop or select their own anti-bullying programme and while this has the positive feature of empowering schools to be innovative in implementing initiatives tailored to their specific context, it also has the potential for inconsistent engagement and uneven provision. A single national action plan in other words is not the same as a single coordinated national programme.

Concern has also been expressed about the failure to develop a more robust legal framework to combat bullying and harassment, particularly in relation to online bullying and harassment and against a background of increased incidence of cyberbullying threats and apparent lack of industry engagement.[94] The Working Group on Bullying was explicit in its view that it did not regard punitive legislation as desirable, and favored instead securing the implementation of existing legislative requirements, supporting further inclusiveness measures and assisting in developing more effective complaints handling mechanisms. In this, it recommends better partnership with industry, specifically social media companies, to raise awareness of cyberbullying and how it can be dealt with. How to achieve effective, successful partnerships is less clear and points to the need for more formal arrangements between the education system and industry in handling the most severe incidences of cyberbullying.

The recommendation to establish an implementation group is seen as vital to the success of the programme as is the commitment to its long-term evaluation.[95] Schools themselves play a pivotal in the evaluation of their individual anti-bullying initiatives while further research on the effectiveness of the programme as a whole is envisaged.

Conclusion

The recognition given to a whole school and community approach to bullying, locating the school within a wider societal context and emphasizing a positive culture of inclusion and respect for diversity, is an important contribution to framing a national response to the persistent and challenging problem of bullying. The measures included in the example of Ireland's Action Plan on Bullying should, when implemented throughout all schools, lead to a significant reduction in the level of bullying and serve to heighten awareness of what bullying is, better equip schools to deal with its many forms and address gaps in public policy provision. Equivalent national initiatives share many of the same features and concerns: monitoring and evaluation remain particular requirements with the need for sustained governmental involvement as well as extensive research to know what is working. The notion of a national response as discussed in this chapter also points to the complex interaction between policies that frame the overall response and the individual programmes which implement and seek to achieve particular outcomes. Neither on their own is recognized to be sufficient and more research is needed to better understand the relationship between them.

Endnotes

57. Anti-Bullying Working Group (2013). *Action Plan On Bullying. Report of the Anti-Bullying Working Group to the Minister for Education and Skills.* Dublin: Dept. of Education and Skills.
58. See: http://www.endbullying.org.uk/
59. Mc Guckin, C (2013). *School bullying amongst school pupils in Northern Ireland: How many are involved, what are the health effects, and what are the issues for school management?* Cork, Ireland: Cork University Press.
60. Scottish Government (2010). *A National Approach to Anti-Bullying for Scotland's Children and Young People.* Retrieved from: http://www.gov.scot/Publications/2010/11/12120420/0
61. Feder, L (Ed.) (2007). Bullying as a public health issue. *International Journal of Offender Therapy and Comparative Criminology,* 51(5): 491–494.
62. Jenkins, WI (1978). *Policy analysis: A political and organisational perspective.* London: M. Robertson (p.31).
63. Sabatier, PA, & Weible, C (2014). *Theories of the Policy Process.* US: Westview Press.
64. Krug, EG et al. (Eds). (2002). *World report on violence and health.* Geneva: World Health Organization.
65. O'Moore, M (2005). A Guiding Framework for Policy Approaches to School Bullying & Violence. In *A report from the conference 'Taking Fear Out of Schools'* (pp. 38–51). Retrieved from http://www.oecd.org/education/skills-beyond-school/33866844.pdf
66. Adapted from O'Moore, M (2005). Op. cit.
67. Olweus, D (1978). *Aggression in the schools: Bullies and whipping boys* (Vol. xiii). Oxford, England: Hemisphere. Also, Olweus, D (1994). Bullying at School. In L. R. Huesmann (Ed.), *Aggressive Behavior* (pp 97–130). Springer US.
68. Olweus, D (1995). Bullying or Peer Abuse at School: Facts and Intervention. *Current Directions in Psychological Science* 4(6): 196–200.
69. Limber, SP (2011). Development, Evaluation, and Future Directions of the Olweus Bullying Prevention Program. *Journal of School Violence* 10(1): 71–87.
70. Mc Guckin, C (2011). *Cyberbullying: The research situation in Ireland.* Verlag Emprische Padagogik. See also W Core (2012). *An evaluation of an anti-bullying intervention in a second level school.* Dept. of Psychology, Dublin Business School, Dublin.
71. O'Donnell, V (Ed.) (1993). *Proceedings of the First National Conference on Bullying in Ireland.* Dublin: Campaign Against Bullying. Dublin: Campaign Against Bullying.
72. Department of Education and Science (1993). *Guidelines on Countering Bullying Behaviour in Primary and Post-Primary Schools.* Dublin: The Stationery Office.
73. O'Moore, AM, Kirkham, C & Smith, M (1997). Bullying behaviour in Irish schools: A nationwide study. *The Irish Journal of Psychology* 18(2): 141–169.
74. O'Moore, M & Minton, S (2003). Tackling Violence in Schools: A report from Ireland. In PK Smith (Ed.), Violence in Schools: *The Response in Europe.* London: Routledge and Falmer.
75. O'Moore, M (2000). Critical issues for teacher training to counter bullying and victimisation in Ireland. *Aggressive Behavior* 26(1): 99–111.
76. O'Moore, AM & Minton, SJ (2005). Evaluation of the effectiveness of an anti-bullying programme in primary schools. *Aggressive Behavior* 31(6): 609–622.
77. Minton, SJ & O'Moore, AM (2008). The effectiveness of a nationwide intervention programme to prevent and counter school bullying in Ireland. *International Journal of Psychology and Psychological Therapy* 8(1): 1–12.
78. Ombudsman for Children's Office (2012). *Dealing with Bullying in Schools: A consultation with children & young People.* Dublin: Ombudsman for Children's Office.
79. Ibid. p.13
80. Programme for Government 2011-16. Retrieved from: http://www.taoiseach.gov.ie/eng/Work_Of_The_Department/Programme_for_Government/Programme_for_Government_2011-2016.pdf
81. 'Anti-Bullying Forum'. Retrieved from: http://www.education.ie/en/Press-Events/Events/cp_anti_bullying/
82. See: http://www.education.ie/en/PressEvents/Events/cp_anti_bullying/#sthash.Dmc2lgEM.dpuf
83. Department of Education and Skills (2013). Circular 0045/2013: Anti-Bullying Procedures for Primary and Post-Primary Schools. Retrieved from http://www.education.ie/en/Circulars-and-Forms/Active-Circulars/cl0045_2013.pdf
84. *"Being LGBT in School" A Resource for Post-Primary Schools to Prevent homophobic and Transphobic Bullying and Support LGBT Students* is a resource developed by the Gay and Lesbian Equality Network (GLEN) as part of the implementation of the Action Plan on Bullying. Retrieved from: https://www.education.ie/en/Publications/Education-Reports/Being-LGBT-in-School.pdf
85. See http://www.belongto.org/
86. 'Safer Internet Day 2013 – Connect with Respect'. Retrieved from: http://www.webwise.ie/news/safer-internet-day-2013-connect-with-respect-2/
87. See http://www.tacklebullying.ie/
88. National Disability Authority (2014). *Preventing school bullying of children with Special Educational Needs or Disability. National Disability Authority.* Retrieved from http://nda.ie/nda-files/Preventing-School-Bullying1.pdf
89. Gleeson, H (2014). *Literature Review: The prevalence and impact of bullying linked to social media on the mental health and suicidal behaviour among young people.* Department of Education and Skills. Retrieved from http://www.hse.ie/eng/services/list/4/Mental_Health_Services/NOSP/Research/bullyingimpact.pdf
90. See http://www4.dcu.ie/abc/index.shtml
91. Department of Education and Skills (2013). *Anti-Bullying Procedures for Primary and Post Primary Schools.* Dublin: Department of Education and Skills. Retrieved from http://www.education.ie/en/Publications/Policy-Reports/Anti-Bullying-Procedures-for-Primary-and-Post-Primary-Schools.pdf
92. *Guidelines for preventing cyber-bullying in the school environment: a review and recommendations.* (2012) Retrieved from: https://sites.google.com/site/costis0801/guideline
93. "IGC Response to Action Plan on Bullying". Retrieved from: http://www.igc.ie/Events_Publications/IGC-Press-Releases/IGC-Response-to-Action-Plan-on-Bullying

94 "Children 'being failed' by lack of cyber bullying controls" (2016, March 6). *The Irish Times*. Retrieved from http://www.irishtimes.com/news/social-affairs/children-being-failed-by-lack-of-cyber-bullying-controls-1.2562134

95 "Mona O'Moore: Anti-bullying plan is well timed and welcome – now let's implement it" (2013, January 30). *The Irish Independent*. Retrieved from http://www.independent.ie/opinion/analysis/mona-omoore-antibullying-plan-is-well-timed-and-welcome-now-lets-implement-it-29025065.html

Two girls outside a house in a refugee camp, the West Bank.
© UNICEF/UNI9386/Pirozzi

5. Combating bullying in schools: changing perceptions to change public policies
Eric Debarbieux

Introduction

Those dealing with harassment at school (the term now used in France to refer to school bullying) know how difficult it can sometimes be to raise awareness of how widespread it is and of its impact on the lives and mental health of victims. With the exception of very serious cases, highlighted by the media, the tendency is to consider such occurrences as trivial, a commonplace of school life. The narrative is still "it is not serious", and "you have to put up with it", making the victims responsible for their suffering.[96] Sufficient credible research now exists for minor episodes of violence to be taken seriously: the cumulative, repetitive effect is to cause significant suffering, leading to long-term depression, dropping out of school, and various psychological problems, possibly even attempted suicide.

There is another reason for this inability to see the reality, inasmuch as in the view of the public, as well as political figures, violence in schools essentially involves dramatic episodes of violence by external perpetrators, which are bound to increase in times when terrorist threats dominate debate on political and security questions. By presenting here the case of France, we want to show that it is, nonetheless, possible to rationalize the debate, to change the paradigm in terms of action by the authorities to counter harassment by peers, even if much remains to be done and backsliding is always possible.

Ideology and powerlessness to act

In political terms, in the 1990s and the 2000s the problem of violence in schools became an occasion for major ideological confrontation. The fault lines reflected political debate and various changes in government. Public declarations mirrored the tussles over security, in which left-wing government was constantly accused of permissiveness, while solutions were put forward aimed at "protecting" the school environment, at "eradicating" violence.

Violence in schools has long been perceived in France[97] purely as convulsions of violence by external perpetrators. The media focus on the spectacular highlights such violence. It has mostly been analysed in terms of crime originating outside the school, and as a result suggested solutions have mostly been in terms of the police and the judicial system, or support by specialized teams for institutions in difficulty. There has also been massive investment by local authorities in such equipment as security cameras, in theory allowing these intrusions to be dealt with. For twenty years the problem has primarily been approached as a public security issue, which, of course, at times it is.

Unsurprisingly, this analysis is coupled with calls for external means of dealing with the problem. To the extent that the problem is external, the system of education does not offer a solution: the school environment must be closed off and protected against intrusions, which are seen as largely accounting for violence in the school environment. Hence the advocacy of agreements with the national police, for closer working relationships with police officers, as well as technical solutions, of which security cameras are the most visible. A striking summation of this type of approach is to be found in the presidential statement: "Making schools safe". On 28 May 2009, at a meeting with the principal actors in security, the criminal justice system and national education, Nicolas Sarkozy, then President of the Republic, said: "Security in educational institutions, in whatever district, offering whatever kind of education, is an absolute prerequisite for the equality of opportunity that the Republic must guarantee. Educational institutions must be made safe, protected against any form of violence. This is an absolute priority for government authorities."

The following list was drawn up at the meeting:

In order to make schools safe, the following principal measures are announced:

- A security assessment at 184 sensitive educational institutions;

- Authorization of teaching staff to inspect school bags and packs;

- Installation, on a case-by-case basis, where needed, of detection portals;

- Under each chief education officer, setting up of a mobile team, able to provide reinforcement for school principals;

- Posting of referring police officers in all schools, establishment of arrangements allowing quasi-instantaneous intervention in schools by the police;

- Initiation of recruitment of volunteer reservists in the national police, so as to strengthen security in schools.

Paradoxically, however, this analysis ascribing violence in schools to external factors points to the futility, or impossibility, of dealing with the problem internally, and the irrelevance of neomarxist theories that see such violence as the outcome of ultraliberal policies. A summation of this argument may be found in an article in Le Monde diplomatique in which the authors roundly reject the notion that violence in schools might be caused by the methods used by educational practitioners and might thus be tackled by training these practitioners or by education reform:

> This analysis, ascribing 'violence in schools' to the institution and the practices of its staff, leads to exoneration of politicians and concealment of the violence afflicting the workplace, in particular the dismissal of the 'lower classes' to the fringes. [...] as if it were equally possible for the school to neutralize the violence by means of which part of the underclass responds to the violence of their social relegation – this violence that educators are unjustifiably called upon to defuse, to cushion against or to contain by recourse to the forces of law and order. Making schools responsible for maintaining a social cohesion which the State no longer guarantees can only lead to failure to achieve that end.[98]

In short, the education system is the superficial fix that contributes to leading us away from a more relevant analysis of social relationships.

If for these authors the education system is an irrelevance, for the other end of the political spectrum it is frankly a danger. Thus, far from being part of the solution, for Luc Ferry, appointed Minister of Education in 2002, it is one cause of violence. In a speech on 22 October 2002 he said:

> I would simply like to say that for the past 30 years an excessive focus on creativity, on the spontaneity of students, has not only worked to the detriment of acquiring knowledge, but also of those attributes that necessarily involve respect for tradition. There are two traditions in education that must be respected: language, for we do not invent language ourselves, we receive it from outside, and civility [...]. And one of the reasons why these two essential elements of culture are today in crisis is that teaching methods have emphasized exercises that promote spontaneity and creativity [...].

This opposition to the education system will inform the approaches of several ministers and public discourse for many years: the metaphor of the school under siege is readily associated with the enemy within in the form of "child-centred education", offering a convenient, but for some heartfelt, pretext for eliminating teacher-training institutions, and reducing by half the years spent in training.

In short, apparently irreconcilable ideologies converge to make victims invisible and helping them impossible. As a result, in France there was no public policy against harassment until 2011: no real awareness, other than on the part of a few researchers, the occasional non-governmental organization (NGO), or, in confidence, in psychologists' consulting rooms. Subsequently, significant measures – though certainly never enough – have been put in place; a real policy has been outlined, transcending the deeply rooted traditional political divides characterizing the French landscape. How is it that this situation did not simply develop but apparently became unstuck so quickly?

Research, campaigners and practitioners: towards a reorientation of public policy[99]

The question of school bullying was posed for the first time in France in 1997 as work was under way by a group of researchers at the University of Paris X Nanterre, led by Jacques Pain,[100] which led to the translation and publishing in 1999 of a work by Dan Olweus.[101] Meanwhile a special edition appeared of the leading French publication on education questions – edited by Eric Debarbieux – with, in particular, a synopsis on school bullying.[102] In the same edition another synopsis, covering all the work on violence in schools carried out in France over 30 years, showed that while the question of harassment had been ignored, a new model was emerging, one that sought to give the victims themselves a voice. Research into victimhood was already focusing on the significance of repetitive violence, suggesting the need to take into account the impact of repeated instances of low-level violence targeting heavily victimized students.

A degree of political interest in this research was already apparent. Thus, the establishment in October 2000 of a National Committee on Violence in Schools, headed by schools inspector Sonia Heinrich, was a follow-up to various recommendations emerging from research: stabilization of teams, training of heads of institutions, work on school disciplinary machinery. Acceptance of the reasoning underlying the research would result in support by the Ministry for the holding of the first world conference on the subject, held in March 2001 at the United Nations Educational, Scientific and Cultural Organization (UNESCO) by the European Observatory of Violence in Schools, with participation by some ten countries[103] and, in particular, a notable keynote address on bullying by Peter K. Smith.[104] However, this momentum was checked by changes in the political landscape, limited in scope but still having an impact, so that solutions focusing exclusively on security were again advocated (see for example, supra, the speech and pronouncements by the President of the Republic in 2008, typical of societal thinking at the time).

Nevertheless, the research had largely resolved a number of fundamental questions and invalidated treatment of violence at school exclusively as an external, security-related matter. In particular, surveys of victims in France, as well as surveys of incidents by the national education authorities, showed that school violence was not primarily by external perpetrators but was repetitive violence among peers, and that students were first and foremost the victims of other students. The same was true of teachers and other staff. There is consistent research, both American[105] and French[106]: less than 5% of school violence is by external perpetrators. This does not, of course, mean that violence from external sources can be overlooked or that it must not be averted, or in particular that there should not be a partnership with the police and gendarmerie. Despite all these obvious factors, public policy between 2003 and 2010 continued to be ill-founded, and represented a step backwards given the research findings. Research in France, frequently backed up by the media, but neglected by the political class, gained broad international standing with the creation of a federation of researchers in an International Observatory of Violence in Schools, which, since the inaugural conference in 2001 in Paris, has held five world conferences, bringing together researchers from over 52 countries, generally without significant public funding (Québec, 2003, Bordeaux, 2006, Lisbonne, 2009, Mendoza, 2011, Lima, 2015). This internationalization of French research has had two main consequences: reinforcement of new paradigms, in particular through access to and participation in comprehensive literature on bullying and its consequences, and the increased credibility of the research.

This is why, contrary to all expectations, when a dramatic news story shook the self-assurance of the Government in power, the place of research suddenly became more significant. The death of a student in an Ile-de-France high school: Hakim, 18 years old, stabbed by another student on 8 January 2010, was an eye-opener for the then Minister of Education, Luc Chatel, and his office. The institution was highly secure, with video protection, and a press campaign weakened the Minister's position. Undoubtedly in an endeavour to understand, certainly to counter the press campaign, it was decided to hold a "States-General on Security at School", the scientific presidency of which was entrusted to the writer of these lines, and who very publicly has consistently assumed the mantle of opposition to the security-related ideology of violence in schools. Rejection of this ideological approach means adopting a scientific approach based on international research, and the States-General, held in the prestigious setting of the Sorbonne in April 2010, were the occasion for robust ideological challenges. A single example, without going into detail: a lecture given by Russel Skiba, one of the world's leading experts on policies of zero tolerance[107] who demonstrated their harmful nature before various political leaders were drawn to such policies. While, disappointingly, the Minister's final statement reflected his party's thinking more than it did scientific findings, a group (and to a great extent societal) consensus developed regarding the unsuitability of punitive policies alone, and the importance of also adopting a pedagogical approach to these issues.

The real ideological shift was to take place the following year, as the direct outgrowth of the research, backed by and relying on mobilization by the professional community and the media. This change in paradigm was marked by the passage from a focus on security in the school to a "National Conference on Harassment at School", held in Paris on 2 and 3 May 2011. The change may be summed up as follows: an awareness that violence at school is not fundamentally violence by external perpetrators, but repetitive violence, part and parcel of the day-to-day functioning of school institutions, which can only really be forestalled and dealt with through ongoing pedagogical action and the establishment of a receptive school environment, and an awareness of the academic, psychological and security-related aspects of harassment at school. Several factors led to this development: publication of a survey of victimhood carried out with the assistance of the United Nations Children's Fund (UNICEF)[108] by eight university teams working in this area, the results of which would be broadly reproduced; publication of an open letter written by NGOs and therapists; and, less well known, a meeting between the Minister and victims and parents of victims which convinced him, with no involvement by the press, of the reality of the problem. Above all the Conference would provide an opportunity for politicians of all stripes and for public opinion to assimilate the principal lessons of the international research on the consequences of bullying.

This understanding is based on various elements: surveys consistently find that violence is directed against a limited number of individuals. The personal experience of victimization, for students and teachers alike, is linked to minor incidents, serious victimization being rare.[109] This is borne out by the survey referred to above, of a random national sample of 12,326 students between 8 and 11 years old, at 162 primary schools,[110] and subsequently confirmed by other surveys, for example that of 18,000 middle-school students.[111] Of note is the concentration of the incidence of victimization on a limited number of students: 6.3% of middle-school students and 5.1% of children finishing primary school may be considered victims of severe or very severe harassment, with around 10% of students, at both the primary and secondary levels, suffering most of the victimization recorded.

It is true that minor incidents are not, if viewed in isolation, dramatic (which does not mean that they are acceptable). But it is very different when these minor acts of aggression are repeated, when it is always the same persons who are the victims or perpetrators. This is repeated violence – verbal, physical or psychological – perpetrated by one or several students against a victim who, in a position of weakness, has no defence against an aggressor bent on harming the victim.[112] Worldwide research conducted over long periods was needed for the ideological focus to move beyond the emotional and centre around a coherent rational viewpoint. Each cohort concerned is sensitive to different arguments, and it is the convergence of these arguments that ultimately proves convincing.[113]

Firstly, and of primary importance to educators, the academic consequences of harassment must be considered. The relationship between violence and learning has been the subject of numerous studies and it has been demonstrated that regular exposure to violent behaviour modifies such cognitive functions as memory, concentration and capacity for abstract thought. Children who are victims of ostracism have a more negative view of school, adopt avoidance strategies and thus are absent more often, with below-average academic performance.[114] Aggressors, too, have serious problems, with a significant percentage of students underperforming. The harassment suffered by "good students" owing to their difference from the group is a factor winning over educators.

For parents and public opinion, the psychological consequences are the most significant. This kind of victimization induces an erosion of self-esteem that leads victims to bear their suffering in silence. They develop symptoms of anxiety, depression and suicidal ideas, problems that may persist long term. At the age of 23, males who have been victims still present with problems of depression and low self-esteem, while harassment has been identified as one of the stressors most closely identified with suicidal behaviour among teenagers.[115]

For those with a "security" focus, the National Conference simply confirmed that, with regard to the most serious violence, to which the problem of violence at school – indeed, crime and insecurity – is often reduced in the popular mind, the research strongly suggests that there is a link between repeated early aggression and subsequent criminality, even in some cases lethal violence. Young males who are victims are more likely than others to use weapons, and themselves to engage in violent behaviour, independently of familial and social factors. In short, being a victim of harassment at school is an important factor in school shootings, as shown by research in the USA. This research, published in a report by the Federal Bureau of Investigation[116] related to lethal shootings in schools between 1974 and 2000, and showed that 75% of school shooters had been victims of abuse by other students. The report stated that the shooter often felt persecuted, harassed, humiliated, attacked or harmed before the incident: "Many had suffered severe bullying over a long period and had been harassed, which several aggressors described as torment."

Conclusion: change in outlook

Thus in France recently there has been a change in outlook, in which the research has played a major role. It has not been the only factor, the role of NGOs and prominent figures should be kept in mind.[117] Media coverage of very distressing cases of youngsters who fall victim to harassment has also played in important role, highlighting the inadequacy of public policy in this area. A new awareness has emerged, and will undoubtedly develop further.

The National Conference on Harassment, held at a time of electoral turmoil when issues relating to public security loomed large, interestingly, forged a national, multiparty consensus. January 2012 saw the creation of the first website and first videos on the subject, the first helpline and the first courses.[118] The risk was that with the political changeover that saw the arrival at the Ministry of Education of a new Minister of a different political outlook these initiatives would be consigned to oblivion; however, this is far from having been so. Thus, an interesting indication of continuity, notwithstanding partisan differences, was the creation by the new Minister of a ministerial commission charged with prevention and countering of violence in schools – which, again, was entrusted to the author of these lines: that is to one having agreed to working with the "political opposition". My personal involvement is irrelevant,[119] but a strong message was sent of the political will to take action over the long term on the basis of the research, rather than being swayed by ideology and short-term considerations.

This shift in public policy reflects two changes – theoretical and ideological. The first change is the taking into account of repeated incidents, within the school, and relationships in schools, which could never be encompassed by a simplistic focus on security. The second change is a rethinking of relationships of "dominance". In France, we tend to think of this dominance solely in terms of economic inequality, which cannot be overlooked here. Yet we must also think of dominance as a phenomenon that can affect "equals", in the same social class: the small, the big, the strong, the puny, the different, which is not exclusive to education. The geography of violence in schools cannot be reduced to certain urban areas. It constitutes conformist oppression which, everywhere, rejects diversity.

Endnotes

[96] Which does not mean that assertiveness training for victims and reinforcing the ability to say "no" are of no use.

[97] Debarbieux, É (2006). Violences à l'école: un défi mondial? Paris: Armand Colin.

[98] Garcia, S, Poupeau, F (2000/10). "L'enseignement pris en otage. Violences à l'école, violence de l'école", Le Monde diplomatique, pp. 4-5.

[99] As an author closely identified with the process to be described, the writer of these lines wishes them not to be seen as a narcissistic defence. It suffices that lengthy altercation has had some impact, however limited.

[100] The research was conducted further to an official invitation to apply for funding that resulted in the financing of a dozen or so teams on the broader issue of violence in schools. In Charlot, B, Émin, JC (Eds) (1997), Violences à l'école. État des savoirs. Paris: Armand Colin.

[101] ESF, (1999).

[102] Peignard, E, Roussier-Fusco, E, Van Zanten, A (1998). La violence dans les établissements scolaires britanniques: approches sociologiques. In Revue Française de Pédagogie 123: 123-151

[103] Debarbieux É, Blaya C (2001), Violences à l'école et politiques publiques. Paris, ESF (trad. anglaise Elsevier, Paris, 2001, et portugaise, UNESCO, Brésil, 2003).

[104] Smith, PK in Debarbieux, É, Blaya, C (2001). Op. cit.

[105] Gottfredson, DC (2001). Schools and delinquency, Cambridge, University Press.

[106] Carra, C & Sicot, F (1996). Une autre perspective dur le violences scolaires: l'expérience de victimation. In B Charlot and JC Émin (Eds). Violences à l'école: Etat des savoirs. Paris: Armand Colin.

[107] Skiba, RJ, Arredondo, M & Williams, NT (2014). More than a metaphor? The contribution of exclusionary discipline to a School-to-Prison Pipeline. Equity and Excellence in Education 47: 546-564.

[108] Debarbieux É (2010). À l'école des enfants heureux... enfin Presque. Rapport de l'Observatoire international de la violence à l'école pour l'UNICEF, France, 2010.

[109] Gottfredson, DC (2001). Op. cit.

[110] Debarbieux É (2010). Op. cit.

[111] DEPP-MEN (2012), "Les actes de violences recensés dans les établissements publics du second degré en 2011-2012", Note d'information téléchargeable sur: www.education.fr

[112] Smith, PK and Sharp, S (Eds) (1994). School Bullying. Insights and Perspectives. London: Routledge.

[113] Debarbieux, E. (2011). Refuser l'oppression quotidienne : la prévention du harcèlement à l'école. Rapport au ministre de l'éducation nationale. Paris : MEN. En ligne: www.education.fr/cid55897/refuser-l-opression-quotidienne-la-prevention-du-harcelement-a-l-ecole-rapport-d-eric-debarbieux.html

[114] Smith, PK & Sharp, S (Eds) (1994). Op. cit.; DeRosier, ME, Kupersmidt, JB & Patterson, CJ, (1994). Children's academic and behavioral adjustment as a function of the chronicity and proximity of peer rejection. Child Development, 65(6): 1799-813.

[115] Olweus, D (1993). Bullying in schools: what we know and what we can do. Oxford: Blackwell.

[116] Vossekuil, B, Fein, R, Reddy, M, Borum, R, & Modzeleski, W (2002). The final report and findings of the Safe School Initiative: Implications for the prevention of school attacks in the United States. Washington, DC: U.S. Secret Service and U.S. Department of Education.

[117] The text of the open letter of January 2011 may be downloaded at http://www.ecolechangerdecap.net/IMG/article_PDF/article_a172.pdf.

[118] http://www.nonauharcelement.education.gouv.fr/ The site has all the "official" actions, to which, of course, action to counter harassment is not limited: students and staff at schools, NGOs, practitioners and parents remain, and will remain, the most important actors in countering harassment.

[119] Clarification: I resigned my duties in September 2015 in order to initiate action at 30 highly disadvantaged locations in France. The ministerial commission is still in existence.

Having escaped child labour and then child marriage, 15-year-old is pictured with a friend, India
© UNICEF/UNI88839/Macfarlane

6. Poverty and inequity: multi-country evidence on the structural drivers of bullying
Kirrily Pells, María José Ogando Portela and Patricia Espinoza

Introduction

The majority of research into peer bullying has focused on children's individual psychological characteristics or psychosocial well-being, both to identify the predictors of who gets bullied, as well as the effects of bullying on children. Less attention has been given to how structural factors, such as poverty and inequality, shape the contexts within which children interact and where bullying occurs.[120] This chapter uses data from the Young Lives[121] longitudinal study of childhood poverty in Ethiopia, India (the states of Andhra Pradesh and Telangana), Peru and Viet Nam to explore how children's experiences of being bullied occur within the context of wider economic and social inequalities, such as poverty and gender norms. We address two questions. First, which children are at greater risk of being bullied, and how, at age 15? Second, why are certain groups of children bullied?

Peer bullying: the structural drivers

Bullying is usually defined as the systematic abuse of power involving the repeated infliction of negative actions intended to cause harm or discomfort, over time.[122] We adopt this definition of bullying to highlight inequalities of power, rather than to pathologize children and young people as aggressive.[123] Different groups of children may experience different types of bullying depending, for example, on their age and gender.[124] There are multiple forms of bullying, including direct attacks, either *physical* (such as hitting or kicking) or verbal (name-calling, nasty teasing, issuing verbal threats etc.) or *indirect* actions[125] intended to damage social relationships, self-esteem and/or social status, such as by spreading rumours or socially excluding others.[126] Attacks on property, such as vandalism or theft of personal items sometimes feature in research as another type of bullying.[127] In this chapter we focus on these four different types of bullying.

Within existing research there has been a greater focus on individual and interpersonal factors that may predict bullying rather than the dynamic relationship between structural determinants and the ways in which peers interact. Structural determinants are factors arising from the ways in which societies (and institutions, such as schools) are organized politically, economically and socially that create inequalities in power, wealth, status and access to resources and information.[128] Inequalities in income, education status or norms relating to gender, sexuality and ethnicity in part shape school and community environments and interpersonal relationships and may combine with individual characteristics to render some children more vulnerable to bullying than others. Children may be bullied because they are poor or disadvantaged, being marked out as different from other children or because of stigma towards certain social groups. The evidence on bullying and poverty is mixed, with some studies finding children from poorer households were not at greater risk of being bullied[129] whereas others found that children from poorer families, with parents with low levels of education as well as children of immigrants, were all more likely to be bullied at school.[130]

Structural inequalities may contribute to bullying through the creation of stressful living environments with poor social connectedness that contribute to higher levels of bullying overall. Here a number of other studies have found income inequality rather than individual socio-economic status to be predictive of bullying.[131] For example, higher income inequality was associated with greater bullying among 11-year-old boys and girls across 37 countries.[132] The percentage of children who reported bullying other children was four to five times greater in countries with high income inequality.

In resource-poor settings, especially in low- and middle-income countries where education systems have undergone rapid expansion and classroom overcrowding and inadequate teacher supervision are common, these pressures may contribute to bullying.[133] In addition, the ways in which schools are organized and the norms and values promoted, especially through disciplinary practices, can give rise to increased levels of bullying. For example, a study into violence in schools in Zimbabwe, Malawi and Ghana highlighted how gender-based violence occurred against the backdrop of high levels of corporal punishment and bullying.[134] The actions of teachers can therefore shape the behaviours and responses of children and reinforce gender norms. It is also documented that teachers sometimes verbally abuse, ridicule and humiliate children or incite students to bully others.[135]

Research on bullying comes predominantly from high-income countries and far less is known about the predictors associated with bullying in low- and middle-income countries. Studies are hampered by both a scarcity of data and also the lack of comparable data across different contexts.[136] Using Young Lives survey data we are able to start to build a picture on the predictors of children being bullied in four low- and middle-income countries and through qualitative analysis explore the social context in which bullying occurs.

Young Lives

Young Lives is a two-cohort longitudinal study of childhood poverty, which has been following approximately 12,000 children in Ethiopia, India (Andhra Pradesh and Telangana), Peru and Viet Nam since 2002. Using a multi-stage sampling procedure, children of the right age and their households were randomly sampled within 20 selected sites.[137]

Which children are bullied and how at age 15?

Indirect bullying is the most prevalent type of bullying across three of the countries (see Table 1) and physical bullying is the least prevalent type across all of the countries. Verbal bullying is also common, and in India and Peru attacks on property are also at similar levels as verbal and indirect bullying. This highlights not only the prevalence of bullying across the four countries but also the importance of looking beyond just physical bullying to examining emotional and psychological forms of bullying.[138]

Table 1.
Prevalence of acts of bullying, experienced twice or more in the last year by 15-year-olds (percentage)

Type of bullying	Ethiopia	India	Peru	Viet Nam
Child experienced physical bullying	5.4	22.4	8.2	7.0
Punched, kicked or beaten you up	4.9	17.5	4.0	5.3
Hurt you physically in any other way	1.5	12.2	6.6	3.9
Child experienced verbal bullying	14.2	26.5	33.8	20.3
Called you names or sworn at you	7.7	16.9	28.5	7.2
Made fun of you for some reason	9.4	14.5	14.5	17.7
Child experienced indirect bullying	15.0	28.1	31.9	27.4
Tried to get you into trouble with your friends	9.6	15.5	17.2	8.9
Made you uncomfortable by staring at you for a long time	5.9	9.0	15.1	21.0
Refused to talk or made other people not talk to you	5.8	14.9	14.8	5.0
Child experienced attacks on property	10.5	27.2	31.9	9.0
Tried to break or damaged something of yours	2.5	12.3	11.3	5.1
Took something without permission or stole from you	9.8	22.1	28.7	6.1
Observations	971	958	614	958

The following sections explore which children are more likely to experience different types of bullying by examining the associations between bullying and a range of child and household characteristics. We report on the principal patterns.[139]

Bullying and gender

Boys are significantly more likely than girls to report experiencing physical bullying in Ethiopia, India and Viet Nam. In India, 26% of boys reported physical bullying compared to 19% of girls. Boys also report higher levels of experiencing verbal bullying in Ethiopia and India, in each case girls were about half as likely to report verbal bullying as boys. In contrast, girls are more likely to report experience of indirect bullying in India and Peru. These general patterns mirror findings from high-income countries which have found that while boys experience more physical and verbal bullying, girls are at greater risk of being bullied indirectly.[140]

Bullying and children's physical characteristics

Children's physical characteristics have often been associated with being bullied.[141] While much of the literature has focused on obesity and being overweight as predictors of being bullied, these factors do not present clear differences in the prevalence of being bullied in any of the four Young Lives study countries. Instead, thinness (low weight-for-age) in India is associated with a greater risk of being physically or verbally bullied (33% of children with a low weight-for-age reported being physically bullied, compared to 19% of their peers). Stunting (that is having a low height-for-age) is a risk factor for being physically bullied in India and Peru, but not for other forms of bullying.

Bullying and enrolment status

The majority of studies examining bullying have been conducted in a school setting and so exclude from the analysis those children who do not attend. However, emerging from the qualitative data was a strong divide between children attending school and children out-of-school, which manifested in experiences of being bullied. We examined the differences between these two groups in being bullied and found that in general children who are out-of-school report higher levels of bullying though differences are often not significant. The most clear cut evidence comes from Viet Nam, where out-of-school children are significantly more likely to be bullied across all four types of bullying. In addition, in Ethiopia and India out-of-school children are significantly more likely to be made fun of by their peers. Out-of-school children in Ethiopia are also significantly more likely to report being physically bullied and in India being verbally bullied. These new findings highlight the importance of researching bullying as a phenomenon which does not only occur in schools.

Bullying and economic status

Poor children were significantly more likely to report being bullied across all four types in India and by some types (physical and property attacks) in Viet Nam.[142] In India poorer children were 12 percentage points more likely to be physically bullied and 19 percentage points more likely to be verbally bullied than the least poor children.

By contrast in Ethiopia, where the results are significant these suggest that the poorest children reported less bullying than the least poor children. For example, poor children were 10 percentage points less likely to report verbal bullying. This may be a true finding, as the literature review suggests mixed evidence on the relationship between poverty and bullying, but we are cautious since the sample size of children in Ethiopia reporting bullying is much lower and therefore there is a greater probability that cases exist within the data that are not representative of the whole population. The small sample size may be a result of the challenges of using a self-administered questionnaire in contexts of low literacy. Moreover, in the qualitative interviews discussed below the links between poverty and bullying emerged as a strong theme.

Summary

The predictors of being bullied are mixed and often specific to the country and context.[143] Young Lives data suggest that boys are at greater risk of physical and verbal bullying and girls are more likely to be bullied indirectly. Poorer children are consistently more likely to be bullied in India and experience some types of bullying in Viet Nam. Out-of-school children are more likely to be bullied by types of verbal bullying (Ethiopia, India and Viet Nam), physically in Ethiopia and Viet Nam, and by types of indirect bullying in India and Viet Nam.

Why are certain groups of children bullied?

Moving to our second question we use qualitative data to examine how the contexts in which children are growing up and wider inequalities of poverty, ethnicity/caste and gender norms shape children's experiences of being bullied.

Poverty, status and markers of difference

Poverty featured heavily, as a key factor in children's accounts of being bullied, particularly in Ethiopia and India. Children described verbal bullying that made direct reference to their impoverished circumstances, whether through name-calling and insults such as "child of a destitute" or through making fun of the poor quality of their clothing or their lack of shoes. In Ethiopia, clothes serve as an obvious indicator of children's economic status and attract insults to the extent that children missed school rather than be bullied. For instance, 12-year-old Kebenga,[144] living in rural Oromia, Ethiopia, described being absent from school for three days because of not having clothes after having been insulted by peers previously:

> I went to school barefoot because my shoes were torn apart. Then students laughed at me, and some of them insulted me calling me a "poor boy". It was last year. I informed my parents of the problem I faced and they bought me new shoes the next day.

Conversely, children remembered the occasion of getting new clothing as one of the happiest events in their life because it gave them dignity, security and protection from insults from their peers. Poverty also contributed as an indirect factor in children being bullied by other children. For example, children explained how others would exclude them from social activities because they had to care for family members or undertake work.

A similar dynamic of being marked out as different and so bullied, often by name-calling, being socially excluded or by being treated with a lack of respect was reported by children from ethnic minority or disadvantaged caste backgrounds in mixed communities. For example, Y Thinh was 16-years-old and from the Cham H'roi ethnic minority group in Viet Nam. At the end of seventh grade he got into many fights with other children who bullied him because of his ethnicity. Y Thinh described how another boy "mocked me" for being "an ethnic"' and then "punched me with his fist". He could not endure the continued bullying and added, "I couldn't digest the lessons. So I felt tired of learning". He left school and worked on the family farm.

Children's interactions, including bullying towards peers therefore do not take place in a vacuum but may be shaped by wider inequalities that discriminate against certain groups. Not all contributory factors to bullying are necessarily linked with structural factors, however, a common thread across these accounts is a tendency to view difference negatively, that takes specific forms depending on what is "different" for specific contexts.

Social and institutional contexts

The accounts also raise questions about the social and institutional contexts which give rise to bullying and the social norms which both shape bullying and are reinforced by it. Within the qualitative analysis that follows we see how peer bullying can be a reflection of wider violence, specifically harsh disciplinary practices by teachers and by parents. Bullying reproduces hierarchies of power and is used to reinforce conformity with social or gender norms. This is illustrated by the following three examples.

Disciplinary practices and violent environments

Across the four countries many children in the qualitative interviews described being hit by parents and teachers, as well as experiencing fighting or bullying between peers, so experiencing multiple forms of violence in different locations. Within schools bullying is often part of a wider violent environment, where harsh disciplinary practices such as corporal punishment serves to normalise violence. Corporal punishment is also used to reinforce gender norms and affects different groups of children disproportionately, particularly poorer students and children from other disadvantaged groups.[145]

The use of corporal punishment by teachers and violent behaviour between peers are linked as children may draw on similar strategies in interacting with peers. In Peru, adolescents justified the use of physical violence against peers using the same argument made by teachers to justify corporal punishment, namely the need to teach a lesson and change behaviour.[146] Boys also identified "negative" behaviours, such as other boys reporting violence to teachers as exhibiting feminine behaviour and in need of punishment through being hit. In this way peer relations end up reproducing the authoritarian and masculine system of the school, where power relations are closely associated with control through physical strength.[147] In contrast girls may be expected to conform to gender norms of being gentle and well-behaved, be more likely to be punished for transgressing these norms and so adopt indirect methods to bully others.

Social norms and out-of-school children

Relationships between children who attend school and those who are out-of-school reflect pervasive social norms. This theme emerged most clearly in Ethiopia and India where powerful discourses exist over who is considered a "good child", usually one who studies hard, is clean and neatly dressed and who is well-behaved. Children who cannot attend school whether because of poverty, the need to work to support the household or who have been alienated from the school environment are not able to conform to these norms. Considerable stigma is attached to children who are out-of-school and both teachers and caregivers warn against the dangers of enrolled children becoming corrupted by their out-of-school peers. As Kebenga (age 12, rural Oromia, Ethiopia) explained:

> They [his parents] advise me not to have friends who are out-of-school. They advise me to have children who are learning. They believe that those who are out-of-school can spoil my behaviour. As a result, I stopped relationship with friends who are not learning.

Caregivers and teachers describe children out-of-school as being undisciplined. For example in India, children recounted how teachers beat children who were "dirty" or irregular in attending school. Children adopted and replicated a similar discourse of wanting to beat children who were not in school.

Consequently, there exists a big divide between children who attend school and those who do not, which results in what can be conceived as bullying behaviours on both sides. We saw in the survey findings that out-of-school children in Ethiopia, India and Viet Nam were at greater risk of experiencing at least one type of bullying. Mikitu, aged 12 from rural Oromia, Ethiopia captures the mutual apprehension and misunderstanding between school children and those children who are out-of-school: "Those who are at school have better behaviours as compared with those who are outside school. Those who are out of school fight with each other. They are not disciplined". These two groups of children seem to constitute two camps, which at times might be afraid of each other, might be mocking each other and even bullying one another. Children who did not attend school discussed not being liked by children who were in school, who did not socialize with them or treat them with respect. On some occasions this led to retaliation by children not in school, such as verbally or physically threatening or bullying their peers, including on their way to school.

Gender norms and bullying

While evidence from the survey data pointed to the greater vulnerability of boys in general to physical and verbal bullying, girls were found to be at higher risk of experiencing indirect bullying. In the qualitative interviews a more subtle picture was revealed of some of the bullying experienced by girls, which reflected unequal gender norms and overlap with gender-based violence by encompassing harassment and intimidation of a sexual nature or related to gender norms and stereotypes. Adolescent girls in both Ethiopia and India experience being intimidated on the way to and from school. For example, Harika, aged 14, described the difficulties that girls faced on the journey to and from school in rural Andhra Pradesh and the fear of bullying and harassment from boys. This has led to some girls dropping out of school and for others it has caused difficulties in studying. She explained:

> Earlier we used to be in school [doing homework] but now no one stays back after school... we all decided now in 10th class we return home fast. [...] Big boys used to come and sit there, at the school... Because other boys come to the school, so they [the girls] don't come now.

Gender-based bullying occurs also within schools affecting girls' capabilities to engage with schooling. In Ethiopia and Andhra Pradesh girls described fear of using the toilets, which are often not gender-segregated and so the girls feel unsafe and concerned about bullying and harassment from boys.

Summary

In summary, as found in the survey, children described being bullied on account of factors which marked them out as different, such as by having poor quality clothes, being from an ethnic minority or having physical characteristics that are considered to deviate from the norm. Moreover, qualitative analysis illustrates how children's experiences of being bullied are often therefore a reflection of disadvantage, stigma and discrimination within wider society towards certain groups, as children's interactions replicate and reinforce wider power dynamics and social norms related to the privileged position within wider society of certain groups as opposed to others.[148] This has the potential to compound existing disadvantage, such as when children are absent or leave school, or live in fear as a result of being bullied.

Conclusions

Within this chapter we have undertaken exploratory analysis on the predictors of bullying in adolescence in four low- and middle-income countries. In this section we consider the ways in which our analysis contributes to a nascent evidence-base on bullying in low- and middle-income countries and to identify the implications for research and policy.

First, the role of poverty and inequality in driving bullying has been relatively underexplored and the literature review revealed that the limited survey evidence in this area is mixed. Within Young Lives survey data we find that poorer children are consistently more likely to be bullied in India and experience some types of bullying in Viet Nam. In the qualitative interviews, particularly from Ethiopia and India, children describe the multiple ways in which poverty marks them out as different to their peers, whether by the lack of clothes or indirectly, such as necessitating that children work and so are excluded by peers from social activities.

Structural disadvantages such as poverty or unequal power relationships that underpin entrenched discriminatory norms can therefore put different groups of children at risk of being bullied, but the form these markers of difference take is often shaped by context. This includes the capacities of institutions and services, as well as the pressures put upon them. Children do not go to school for fear of being bullied by peers and punished by teachers for lacking materials or because of stigma associated with poverty or other socially disadvantaged groups. Typically research on peer bullying has focused on bullying within schools, yet we find that out-of-school children are more likely to be verbally bullied in Ethiopia, India and Viet Nam, physically bullied in Ethiopia and Viet Nam and indirectly bullied in India and Viet Nam. In the context of low- and middle-income countries where large numbers of adolescents are no longer in school, better understanding of how institutional and interpersonal forms of exclusion intersect is important in designing policies and programmes to reach all children, especially those not in school.

Second, children's experiences of bullying are also shaped by age and gender. We have observed how boys and girls often experience different types of bullying with boys at greater risk of experiencing physical and verbal bullying, whereas girls are at greater risk of bullying by more "hidden indirect means. This is consistent with general trends observed in the literature. The types of bullying experienced may also vary by age. For example, during adolescence, girls report greater harassment from boys, shaped by wider gender inequalities.

Third, this highlights the importance of a mixed methods approach to bullying, bringing together survey data with qualitative research to explore the more subtle, less observable or easily measurable forms of bullying and the ways in which markers of difference play out in different contexts. This is particularly important in understanding forms of emotional violence, such as verbal or indirect bullying, which may take different forms in different contexts.

Schools offer an important platform for teaching the values of tolerance and diversity.[149] To do so this means addressing wider cultures of violence in school (as well as within communities and the home), of which bullying is both a part and a reflection. In particular, this means addressing institutional cultures that permit corporal punishment and other forms of harsh discipline and which dissuade children from seeking help. However, our findings illustrate that not all children affected by bullying are in school and there are also links between what happens at home, in the community and in schools.

Lastly, efforts to tackle peer bullying have often lagged behind those directed at other forms of violence affecting children but have been rising up the international policy agenda, as indicated by the United Nations General Assembly Resolution on protecting children from bullying.[150] Both the UN Resolution and the Global Goals, which include targets and indicators on the protection of children from violence, abuse and exploitation are important opportunities to stimulate greater international and national attention to violence affecting children more generally, as well as the specific dynamics of bullying, including better data collection and increased resource allocation to violence prevention.

Endnotes

[120] Elgar, FJ, Craig, W, Boyce, W, Morgan, A, and Vella-Zarb, R (2009). Income Inequality and School Bullying: Multilevel Study of Adolescents in 37 Countries. *Journal of Adolescent Health*, 45(4): 351–359; Hong, JS and Espelage, DL (2012). A review of research on bullying and peer victimization in school: An ecological system analysis. *Aggression and Violent Behavior*, 17(4): 311–322; Horton, P (2016). Portraying monsters: framing school bullying through a macro lens. Discourse: *Studies in the Cultural Politics of Education*, 37(2): 204-214.

[121] Young Lives is is core-funded from 2001 to 2017 by UK aid from the Department for International Development (DFID) and co-funded by the Netherlands Ministry of Foreign Affairs from 2010 to 2014, and by Irish Aid from 2014 to 2015. This chapter reproduces text and findings from the following paper: Pells, Kirrily; Ogando Portela, Maria Jose; Espinoza Revollo, Patricia (2016) Experiences of peer bullying among adolescents and associated effects on young adults' outcomes: Longitudinal Evidence from Ethiopia, India, Peru and Viet Nam. Innocenti Discussion Paper no. IDP_2016_03, UNICEF Office of Research – Innocenti, Florence. The paper was funded by the UNICEF Office of Research as part of The Multi-Country Study on the Drivers of Violence Affecting Children.

[122] Rigby, K (2002). *New perspectives on bullying*. London and Philadelphia: Jessica Kingsley.

[123] Horton, P (2016). Op. cit.

[124] Carbone-Lopez, K, Esbensen, F-A, Brick, BT (2010) Correlates and consequences of peer victimization: Gender differences in direct and indirect forms of bullying. *Youth Violence and Juvenile Justice* 8(4): 332-350.

[125] Indirect bullying is sometimes referred to as social or relational bullying.

[126] Björkqvist, KL, Lagerspetz, KMJ and Kaukiainen, A (1992). Do girls manipulate and boys fight? Developmental trends in regard to direct and indirect aggression. *Aggressive Behaviour* 18(2):117-127; Smith, PK (2004). Bullying: Recent Developments. *Child and Adolescent Mental Health* 9(3): 98–103.

[127] Mynard, H and Joseph, S (2000). Development of the Multidimensional Peer-Victimization Scale. *Aggressive Behavior* 26(2): 169–178; Ponzo, M (2013). Does bullying reduce educational achievement? An evaluation using matching estimators. *Journal of Policy Modelling* 35(6): 1057-1078.

[128] Viner, RM, Ozer, EM, Denny, S, Marmot, M, Resnick, M, Fatusi, A, and Currie, C (2012). Adolescence and the social determinants of health. *The Lancet* 379(9826): 1641–165.

[129] Brown, S and Taylor, K (2008). Bullying, Education and Earnings: Evidence from the National Child Development Study. *Economics of Education Review* 27(4): 387-401.

[130] Ponzo, M (2013). Does bullying reduce educational achievement? An evaluation using matching estimators. *Journal of Policy Modelling* 35(6): 1057-1078.

[131] Hong, JS and Espelage, DL (2012). Op. cit.

[132] Elgar *et al*, (2009). Op. cit.

[133] Plan International (2008). *Learn without fear: The global campaign to end violence in schools*. Woking: Plan International.

[134] Leach, F (2003). Learning to be Violent: The Role of the School in Developing Adolescent Gendered Behaviour. *A Journal of Comparative and International Education*, 33(3): 385-400.

[135] Pinheiro, PS (2006). *World Report on Violence against Children, UN Secretary-General's Study on Violence against Children*. New York: United Nations; Horton, P (2011). School Bullying and Social and Moral Orders. Children and Society, 25(4): 268-277; Bhatla, N, Achyut, P, Khan, N and Walia, S (2014). *Are Schools Safe and Gender Equal Spaces? Findings from a baseline study of school related gender-based violence in five countries in Asia*. International Center for Research on Women and Plan International.

[136] Pinheiro, PS (2006). Op. cit.; Plan International (2008). Op. cit.; Office of the Special Representative of the Secretary General (SRSG) on Violence against Children (2012). *Tackling Violence in Schools: A global perspective. Bridging the gap between standards and practice*. New York: United Nations; UNESCO (2015). *School-related gender-based violence is preventing the achievement of quality education*. Policy Paper 17. Paris: UNESCO.

[137] For detailed information on the design and methods of Young Lives please see http://www.younglives.org.uk.

[138] UNESCO (2015). Op. cit.

[139] Full tables are available in Pells, Ogando Portela and Espinoza, forthcoming, op. cit.

[140] Björkqvist, KL, Lagerspetz, KMJ and Kaukiainen, A. (1992). Op. cit.; Rivers, I and Smith, PK (1994). Types of bullying behaviour and their correlates. *Aggressive Behavior* 20(5): 359–368.

[141] Janssen, CWM, Boyce, WF and Pickett, W (2004). Associations between overweight and obesity with bullying behaviors in school-aged children. *Pediatrics* 113(5): 1187-94.

[142] Children's economic circumstances are measured by household wealth, which is an index containing three equally weighted components: housing quality, service quality and consumer durables.

[143] UNESCO (2015). Op. cit.

[144] Names have been changed to protect the identity of the children.

[145] Morrow, V and Singh, R (2014). *Corporal Punishment in Schools in Andhra Pradesh, India. Children's and Parents' Views*. Working Paper 123, Oxford: Young Lives; Ogando Portela, MJ and Pells, K (2015) *Corporal Punishment in Schools: Longitudinal Evidence from Ethiopia, India, Peru and Viet Nam*. Discussion Paper 2015-02. Florence: UNICEF Innocenti Research Centre.

[146] Rojas, V (2011). *'I'd rather be hit with a stick… Grades are sacred': Students' Perceptions of Discipline and Authority in a Public High School in Peru*. Working Paper 70. Oxford: Young Lives.

[147] Ibid.

[148] Pinhero (2006). Op. cit.; Bhatla (2014). Op. cit.; UNESCO (2015). Op. cit.

[149] Office of the Special Representative of the Secretary-General (SRSG) on Violence against Children (2012)."Op. cit.; United Nations General Assembly (2014). Protecting Children from Bullying. Resolution A/RES/69/158 New York: United Nations.

[150] United Nations General Assembly (2014). Op. cit.

Students spread out in a circle, outdoors at the primary school, Rwanda
© UNICEF/UNI48305/Pirozzi

7. Promoting an inclusive and equitable education for all learners in an environment free from discrimination and violence: Ministerial Call for Action

Christophe Cornu and Yongfeng Liu

Introduction

On 17-18 May 2016 the United Nations Educational, Scientific and Cultural Organization (UNESCO) convened an international ministerial meeting on education sector responses to violence based on sexual orientation and gender identity/expression[151].

The meeting brought together 250 participants from 67 countries including 54 countries represented at governmental level and 15 at ministerial level, together with representatives from civil society, United Nations (UN) agencies and bodies, and other multilateral organizations. The event featured the launch of the first UN Global Report on violence based on sexual orienation and gender identity/expression,[152] which provides the first ever overview of the most up-to-date data on the nature, scope and impact of, as well as current actions to address, homophobic and transphobic violence in educational settings worldwide. It also provides education sector stakeholders with a framework for planning and implementing effective responses as part of wider efforts to prevent and address violence in schools. At the conclusion of the meeting, a group of countries affirmed a *Call for Action by Ministers for an inclusive and equitable education for all learners in an environment free from discrimination and violence,* including discrimination and violence based on sexual orientation and gender identity/expression (see text below). Other countries have joined to support the *Call for Action by Ministers* since the ministerial meeting, totalling 44 countries from Africa, Asia Pacific, Europe, Latin America and North America (the complete list of countries that support the *Call for Action by Ministers* is included at the beginning of the text below).[153]

It is the first time in the history of the United Nations that governments from so many countries agreed to a political statement where they commit to "developing and implementing responses to prevent and address discrimination and violence in all educational settings". Even more exceptionally, the *Call for Action by Ministers* refers explicitly to discrimination and violence based on sexual orientation and gender identity/expression. It is also worth noting that it has been affirmed by governments from countries with very different sociocultural contexts, including countries where the mention of sexual orientation and gender identity/expression in policy documents still remains challenging for cultural reasons, particularly in relation to education. This applies for example to most countries located in Sub Saharan Africa, Central America and Eastern

---

What is violence based on sexual orientation and gender identity/expression?

Violence based on sexual orientation and gender identity/expression in educational settings targets students who are, or who are perceived as lesbian, gay, bisexual and transgender (LGBT); and others whose gender expression does not fit into binary gender norms (masculine and feminine) such as boys perceived as 'effeminate' and girls perceived as 'masculine'. Violence based on sexual orientation and gender identity/expression is often referred to as homophobic and transphobic violence as it is grounded in: the fear, discomfort, intolerance or hatred of homosexuality and sexually diverse people – lesbian, gay, and bisexual –(homophobia); and transgender people (transphobia).[154]

Homophobic and transphobic violence in educational settings is a form of school-related gender-based violence, since it is clearly perpetrated as a result of existing gender norms and stereotypes.

Homophobic and transphobic violence can involve: physical violence; psychological violence, including verbal and emotional abuse; sexual violence, including rape, coercion and harassment, and bullying, including cyberbullying. Like other forms of school-related violence, school-related homophobic and transphobic violence can occur in classrooms, playgrounds, toilets and changing rooms, around schools, on the way to and from school, and online.

Europe, even though some ministers from these regions decided to support the *Call for Action by Ministers*.

Content and objectives of the Call for Action by Ministers

Governments that affirmed the Call for Action by Ministers recognize that any form of discrimination and violence in educational settings, including bullying, is an obstacle to the right to education. They also acknowledge that there is no inclusive and equitable quality education if learners experience discrimination or violence because of their actual or perceived sexual orientation and gender identity/expression; and that, therefore, this form of discrimination and violence prevents the achievement of the Sustainable Development Goal 4 that calls for "ensuring inclusive and equitable quality education for all" in the 2030 Agenda for Sustainable Development, agreed on by UN Member States in 2015.

The Call for Action by Ministers describes a series of concrete steps to improve and scale up the implementation of comprehensive education sector responses to discrimination and violence based on sexual orientation and gender identity/expression at country level. These steps are based on evidence of existing gaps and challenges, as well as promising policies and practices, which are presented in the report launched by UNESCO during the ministerial meeting 'Out in the open: education sector responses to violence based on sexual orientation and gender identity/expression'.

Process for developing the Call for Action by Ministers

The text of the Call for Action by Ministers was drafted by a small group of government represenatives from six countries (Costa Rica, Japan, the Netherlands, Swaziland, Sweden, and the USA) representing five regions: Africa, Asia-Pacific, Europe, Latin America and North America. The group was chaired by the Minister of Education, Culture and Science of the Netherlands.[155] Ministers were provided with the 'Out in the open' report, before it was officially launched at the ministerial meeting.

Text of the Call for Action by Ministers for an inclusive and equitable education for all learners in an environment free from discrimination and violence

1. Preamble

    We, Ministers and their designated representatives of Albania, Andorra, Argentina, Austria, Belgium, Bolivia (Plurinational State of), Cabo Verde, Canada, Chile, Colombia, Costa Rica, Czech Republic, Denmark, El Salvador, Fiji, Finland, France, Germany, Greece, Guatemala, Honduras, Israel, Italy, Japan, Madagascar, Malta, Mauritius, Mexico, Moldova, Montenegro, Mozambique, The Netherlands, Nicaragua, Norway, Panama, Peru, Philippines, Romania, South Africa, Spain, Sweden, Switzerland, United States of America and Uruguay:[156]

    1.1 Recall the right to education enshrined in the Universal Declaration of Human Rights (1948) and the UNESCO Convention against Discrimination in Education (1960); as well as the rights of the child to non-discrimination and to be protected against any form of physical or mental violence, injury or abuse, as set out in the Convention on the Rights of the Child (1989);

    1.2 Welcome the UNESCO report 'Out in the open: education sector responses to violence based on sexual orientation and gender identity/expression';

    1.3 Reaffirm our commitment to the 2030 Agenda for Sustainable Development which contains goals on ensuring inclusive and equitable quality education and promoting lifelong learning opportunities for all (SDG4), and specific targets relating to 'ensuring that all learners acquire the knowledge and skills needed to promote sustainable development, including, among others, through education for sustainable development and sustainable lifestyles, human rights, gender equality, promotion of a culture of peace and non-violence, global citizenship and appreciation of cultural diversity and of culture's contribution to sustainable development (target 4.7) and 'building and upgrading education facilities that are child-, disability- and gender-sensitive and provide safe, non-violent, inclusive and effective learning environments for all' (target 4.a);

    1.4 Recognize that any form of discrimination and/or violence including bullying in educational settings are an obstacle to the enjoyment of the right to education and to equal access to educational opportunities of learners, and that no country can achieve inclusive and equitable quality education or equal access to educational opportunities, if any learners are discriminated against or experience violence because of their actual or perceived sexual orientation and gender identity/expression;

1.5 Confirm our responsibility to promote human development, including education and health, as well as to implement effective strategies to educate all children and young persons, and protect them from any form of discrimination and violence; through the harmonious development of their potential and capabilities, valuing and respecting their differences and similarities, as well as ensuring the full exercise of fundamental rights of all individuals and communities.

2. Whereas advances have been made in countries around the world to fulfil the above-mentioned commitments and responsibilities, there are still significant challenges:

2.1 Evidence from Africa, Asia, Europe, Latin America and the Caribbean, North America and the Pacific consistently shows that learners who are perceived not to conform to gender norms or stereotypes i) report a much higher prevalence of violence compared to others, and ii) are more likely to experience such violence in school than at home or in their community;

2.2 The available data across regions also reveal that violence based on sexual orientation and gender identity/expression occurring in educational settings, has significant negative impacts on learners' current and long-term education, health and well-being; and therefore is a serious concern.

3. We acknowledge:

3.1 The promising policies and practices from a number of countries across the world, which demonstrate that effective education sector responses to school-related violence require a comprehensive approach that both promotes inclusion, diversity and prevents and addresses violence in a broader sense and situated context. Such an approach includes all of the following elements: effective national and school policies, relevant and appropriate curricula and learning materials, training and support for staff, support for learners and families, strategic partnerships, systematic data-gathering and monitoring of violence, prompt and effective responses to acts of school-related violence, and evaluation of responses. It involves all relevant stakeholders and is implemented at national or sub-national levels;

3.2 The significant gaps in our existing responses to violence based on sexual orientation and gender identity/expression in educational settings, as only some countries have most elements of a comprehensive education sector response in place to tackle this type of violence.

4. Based on the above considerations, we will work towards developing and implementing comprehensive responses to prevent and address discrimination and violence in all educational settings in our countries. Specifically, we commit to reinforcing our efforts to prevent and address violence including that based on sexual orientation and gender identity/expression, within the broad framework of a comprehensive education sector response to school-related violence including bullying, and while taking into account the specificities of different legal and socio-cultural contexts, ensuring the cooperation between countries to share best practices.

4.1 Monitoring systematically the prevalence of violence in educational settings, including violence based on sexual orientation and gender identity/expression, through data-gathering mechanisms and other methods;

4.2 Establishing comprehensive policies at the appropriate level (national, subnational, school) to prevent and address violence in educational settings, including violence based on sexual orientation and gender identity/expression;

4.3 Providing learners with access to age-appropriate, non-judgmental, human rights-based and accurate information on harmful gender stereotypes and issues relating to gender non-conforming behaviours, including as appropriate through inclusive curricula, learning materials and learning outcomes, information campaigns, research and partnerships with civil society and the wider school community;

4.4 Providing training and/or support to teachers and other educational and school staff to prevent and address violence in educational settings, including violence based on sexual orientation and gender identity/expression;

4.5 Taking other actions to ensure inclusive and safe school environments for all learners and provide support for those affected by discrimination and/or violence, including discrimination and/or violence based on sexual orientation and gender identity/expression, as well as their families.

4.6 Evaluating the efficiency, effectiveness and impact of education sector responses to violence, including violence based on sexual orientation and gender identity/expression;

5. We invite all countries to join in our efforts.

A draft of the Call for Action by Ministers was circulated to governments invited to the ministerial meeting prior to the meeting to solicit feedback and additional input, and further discussions were held with government representatives during the meeting itself in order to finalize the document. It was adopted by 26 countries and presented to all participants on 18 May 2016.

Lessons Learnt

The Call for Action by Ministers is based on the most up-to-date evidence on education sector responses to violence based on sexual orientation and gender identity/expression

Ministers drafted and affirmed the *Call for Action* after being presented with solid evidence on the high prevalence of violence based on sexual orientation and gender identity/expression across the world, its negative educational and health impacts, gaps in education sector responses to this form of violence, and in promising policies and interventions to prevent and address it. This evidence is summarized in the UNESCO 'Out in the open' report.

For developing the UNESCO report, data on school-related violence including gender-based violence, and violence based on sexual orientation and gender identity/expression in particular, were collected from 94 countries and territories and analyzed through different processes. An extensive literature review was carried out of over 500 different resources. A rapid assessment instrument designed for the review to collect more systematic data on education sector responses was filled in by key informants from 12 countries, and interviews were conducted with 53 key informants. UNESCO generated new evidence in regions and countries where little or no data were available, for example in Thailand and in Southern Africa. A multi-country study carried out in Botswana, Lesotho, Namibia and Swaziland on school-related gender-based violence explored, for the first time in those countries, violence targeting learners perceived as not conforming to gender norms. UNESCO also organized regional consultations in Asia-Pacific and Latin America and the Caribbean, whose findings were compiled in regional reports.[157]

Evidence on the scope and impact of violence based on sexual orientation and gender identity/expression in schools

A significant proportion of LGBT students experience violence based on sexual orientation and gender identity/expression in schools. This is shown consistently by data from Africa, Asia, Europe, Latin America and the Caribbean, North America and the Pacific, with the proportion affected ranging from 16% in Nepal to 85% in the United States. LGBT students are also more likely to experience such violence at school than at home or in the community.

LGBT students report a higher prevalence of violence at school than their non-LGBT peers. In New Zealand, for example, lesbian, gay and bisexual students were three times more likely to be bullied than their heterosexual peers and in Norway 15%-48% of lesbian, gay and bisexual students reported being bullied compared with 7% of heterosexual students.

Students who are not LGBT but are perceived not to conform to gender norms are also targets. In Thailand, for example, 24% of heterosexual students experienced violence because their gender expression was perceived as non-conforming and, in Canada, 33% of male students experienced verbal violence related to their actual or perceived sexual orientation including those who did not identify as gay or bisexual.

School-related homophobic and transphobic violence affects students' education, employment prospects and well-being. Students targeted are more likely to feel unsafe in school, miss classes or drop out. For example, in the United States, 70% of LGBT students felt unsafe at school, in Thailand, 31% of students teased or bullied for being or being perceived to be LGBT reported absence from school in the past month and, in Argentina, 45% of transgender students dropped out of school. As a result, students who experience homophobic and transphobic violence may achieve poorer academic results than their peers. LGBT students reported lower academic attainment in Australia, China, Denmark, El Salvador, Italy and Poland. Homophobic and transphobic violence also has adverse effects on mental health including increased risk of anxiety, fear, stress, loneliness, loss of confidence, low self-esteem, self-harm, depression and suicide, which also adversely affect learning.

Evidence on gaps in existing education sector responses to violence based on sexual orientation and gender identity/expression in schools

The review commissioned by UNESCO also reveals that, although the education sector has a responsibility to provide safe and inclusive learning environment for all students, few countries have all of the elements of a comprehensive education sector response in place.

The UNESCO 'Out in the open' report describes a comprehensive response as encompassing all of the following elements: effective education and school policies, inclusive curricula and training materials, training and support for staff, safe school environments that provide support for students and families, accurate information, strategic partnerships with the school community and civil society, monitoring of violence and evaluation of responses. It also includes both preventing and responding to violence, involves all relevant stakeholders and is implemented at national and sub-national levels. In the *Call for Action by Ministers,* commitments made by governments to strengthen their response refer specifically to each one of the elements of the comprehensive approach.

The Call for Action by Ministers is the outcome of a step-by-step inclusive awareness raising and mobilization process

The affirmation of the *Call for Action by Ministers* during the international ministerial meeting is the outcome of a number of activities carried out by UNESCO since 2011 to raise awareness of policy-makers of the seriousness of the prevalence of homophobic and transphobic violence worldwide, and its negative impacts.

In 2011, UNESCO convened an international expert consultation on homophobic bullying in educational institutions, which was the first consultation on this topic ever organized under the auspices of the UN. The findings were presented in the publication Good Policy and Practice in HIV and Health Education – Booklet 8: Education Sector Responses to Homophobic Bullying,[158] launched in Paris on the International Day Against Homophobia/Transphobia (IDAHOT) 2012. On the same day, UNESCO and the IDAHOT Committee published a lesson plan for teachers and educators to discuss homophobia and transphobia in the classroom.[159]

Since 2013 UNESCO has also supported activities at regional and country levels in Asia-Pacific, Latin America and the Caribbean, and Southern Africa.

In Asia-Pacific and Latin America and the Caribbean, the regional consultations organized by UNESCO brought together a broad range of stakeholders from 22 countries. These consultations were the first opportunity in each region to analyze the situation from a regional perspective, and to share best policies and practices from countries attending the consultations. Besides allowing the collection of useful data that were used for the global review commissioned by UNESCO, the consultations helped foster collaboration between civil society organizations within each region, and between civil society and governments at national level in an approach that aimed to be inclusive. In Latin America NGOs from seven countries launched a regional project to collect robust data on the scope and nature of homophobic and transphobic violence in educational settings, with support from the US-based NGO GLSEN. Following the regional consultation in Asia-Pacific, Technical Working Groups comprising representatives from government, civil society organizations, and academia were set up in China, Indonesia, the Philippines and Thailand to improve implementation of education sector responses to homophobic and transphobic violence. One important objective of these regional activities was to demonstrate that: homophobic and transphobic violence is not a phenomenon that affects only countries in the Global North; and that best policies and practices can be found in many regions,

In the four Southern African countries where UNESCO supported a study looking at violence targeting students perceived as gender non-conforming, researchers were requested to work in close collaboration with governmental authorities including ministries of education. Ministries were involved in the study design and in the analysis of the data, including through national consultative meetings at the beginning and the end of the study. The research process was a way to sensitize them to the importance of the topic, ensure better understanding and ownership of research methods and data, and mobilize policy-makers for follow-up to the study. The study also helped de-mystify the notion that issues related to sexual orientation and gender identity are 'not African'.

The inclusive process used by UNESCO, involving different regions and stakeholders, is reflected in the regional diversity of countries that support the *Call for Action by*

Ministers. It was also reflected in the large percentage of representatives from civil society who attended the ministerial meeting in May 2016 and shared their experience, recognizing that civil society organizations and particularly LGBT organizations have shown leadership and have a strong expertise in preventing and addressing homophobic and transphobic violence in and through education.

The Call for Action by Ministers is firmly linked to the rights of the child including the right to education

Since UNESCO started to support Member States in strengthening their education sector responses to violence based on sexual orientation and gender identity/expression, it has always used as the main rationale the fact that homophobic and transphobic violence in educational institutions threatens the right to education of many children and young people and is a barrier to achieving Education for All. The right to education has three dimensions: access to education on the basis of equality of opportunity and without discrimination on any grounds; quality education so that any child can fulfill his or her potential, realize opportunities for employment and develop life skills on the basis of a broad, relevant and inclusive curriculum; and respect within the learning environment - equal respect for every child, including respect for identity and integrity, and freedom from all forms of violence in a safe and healthy learning environment.

UNESCO's work on the right to education of all children and young people, including those who are LGBT or perceived as gender nonconforming, is supported by various international Declarations, Conventions and other international agreements such as the Universal Declaration of Human Rights (1948); UNESCO's Convention against Discrimination in Education (1960); the Convention on the Rights of the Child (1989); and more recently the 2030 Agenda for Sustainable Development (2015), which contains Goal 4 on 'ensuring inclusive and equitable quality education for all'.

The vast majority of UN Member States have ratified most above mentioned Agendas, Conventions and Declarations. Therefore the achievement of the right to education should be a priority for all Governments. It is also easy to understand that discrimination and violence, whatever the grounds they are based on, represent an obstacle to accessing quality education.

The affirmation of the Call for Action by Ministers is the result of a culturally-sensitive approach

As already noted, issues related to sexual orientation and gender identity/expression are very sensitive in many contexts, particularly in relation to education. For this reason UNESCO has used a culturally-sensitive approach in the activities it has conducted to support its Member States in strengthening their education sector responses to homophobic and transphobic violence.

Using a culturally-sensitive approach does not mean that nothing should be done in settings where discussing sexual orientation and gender identity/expression, or homophobia and transphobia, is challenging because it is taboo or even forbidden. It means that entry points and terminology that are used should resonate within the local cultural context.

The right to education for all children and young people is a universal entry point, as is the need to provide safe learning environments free of stigma, discrimination and violence. including gender-based violence. Homophobic and transphobic violence is a form of school-related gender-based violence. Therefore in some contexts a useful way to introduce it is by explaining that the same harmful gender norms and stereotypes that affect girls in schools, also affect boys perceived as 'effeminate' and girls perceived as 'masculine'.

The use of culturally-sensitive terminology is also key to involving all stakeholders in the discussions and policy dialogues related to education sector responses to homophobic and transphobic violence. For example, in the multi-country study supported by UNESCO in Southern Africa, all stakeholders agreed to use the following terms, particularly with students and teachers: 'diversity-related violence' that targets students who are 'perceived as different in terms of their gender, such as boys who look or act like girls and girls who look or act like boys'. This made possible data collection even in countries where homosexuality is illegal, and where therefore it was impossible to use the terms 'homosexuality' or even 'sexual orientation' during the research.

The *Call for Action by Ministers* acknowledges that it is important to 'take into account the specificities of different legal and socio-cultural contexts', which is probably why some countries were able to support it. This is only a recognition that there is not a one-size-fits-all approach and that specific entry points and different terminologies can be used.

The role of civil society has been instrumental in the whole process leading to the development of the Call for Action by Ministers and will be key for implementation and accountability of governments

Since UNESCO started its work to strengthen education sector responses to homophobic and transphobic violence, strong partnerships have been established with civil society including LGBT organizations at global, regional and national levels, recognizing their early leadership in this area and their expertise. They have gathered strategic information on the scope of violence based on sexual orientation and gender identity/expression, and have implemented innovative interventions in many countries. Those data and promising practices contributed to the evidence presented to policy-makers in the 'Out in the open' report and during the ministerial meeting.

The strong presence of representatives from civil society during the ministerial meeting will help advocacy efforts in countries that have not yet affirmed the *Call for Action by Ministers*. Civil society will also hold goverments accountable that have supported the *Call for Action*, ensuring better implementation of the commitments made to address homophobic and transphobic violence in schools.

Conclusion

All forms of discrimination and violence in schools are an obstacle to the fundamental right to quality education of children and young people and thus must be prevented and addressed. Homophobic and transphobic violence is a complex and sensitive issue to address for governments in many countries. Political will and support to address it can be mobilized through evidence-based and culturally sensitive advocacy that engages all key stakeholders as part of wider efforts to prevent school-related violence including gender-based violence.

Endnotes

[151] The meeting was the culmination of a three-year project implemented by UNESCO with financial support from the Ministry of Education, Culture and Science of the Kingdom of the Netherlands 'Education and Respect for All: *Preventing and Addressing Homophobic and Transphobic Bullying in Educational Institutions*'; and more broadly of UNESCO's activities to prevent and address school-related gender-based violence, funded by the Kingdom of Norway.

[152] Referred to as the 'Out in the open' report in this article. Available online:
- Full report in English: http://unesdoc.unesco.org/images/0024/002447/244756e.pdf;
- Summary report in English: http://unesdoc.unesco.org/images/0024/002446/244652e.pdf
- Summary report in French: http://unesdoc.unesco.org/images/0024/002446/244652f.pdf
- Summary report in Spanish: http://www.unesco.org/new/fileadmin/MULTIMEDIA/FIELD/Santiago/pdf/Abierta-mente.pdf.

[153] Current figure as of 29 July 2016.

[154] Students who are intersex may also be the subject of violence, although there is currently not enough available scientific data on this.

[155] The drafting group is composed of:
- Jet Bussemaker, Minister of Education, Culture and Science, the Netherlands
- Gustav Fridolin, Minister of Education and Research, Sweden
- Catherine E. Lhamon, Assistant Secretary, United States Department of Education – Office for Civil Rights
- Kihei Maekawa, Deputy Minister of Education, Culture, Sports, Science and Technology, Japan
- Sonia Mora Escalante, Minister of Education, Costa Rica
- Phineas Langa Magagula, Minister of Education and Training, Swaziland

[156] http://en.unesco.org/sites/default/files/call_for action_2016_08_05-en.pdf. Additional countries have supported the Call for Action by Ministers since the article was finalized.

[157] The two regional reports are:
- UNESCO (2015). *From insult to inclusion: Asia Pacific report on school bullying, violence and discrimination on the basis of sexual orientation and gender identity.* http://unesdoc.unesco.org/images/0023/002354/235414e.pdf
- UNESCO (2015). *La violencia homofóbica y transfóbica en el ámbito escolar: hacia centros educativos inclusivos y seguros en América Latina.* http://unesdoc.unesco.org/images/0024/002448/244840S.pdf

[158] Available at: http://unesdoc.unesco.org/images/0021/002164/216493e.pdf

[159] Available at: http://www.unesco.org/new/fileadmin/MULTIMEDIA/HQ/ED/pdf/IDAHO%20Lesson%20plan.pdf

Boy attends a therapy session in Lower Crossroads, South Africa
© UNICEF/UNI45251/Pirozzi

8. The role of pediatricians in bullying prevention and in addressing emergent and increasing forms of violence against children

Bernard Gerbaka, Fares BouMitri and Carla Haber

Introduction

School violence has been the focus of attention in recent years, partly due to the intense media coverage following events such as school shootings and suicides. One of the issues that has been catapulted into and remained in the spotlight is bullying, which has been tied to these major events in both the media and the academic literature. Bullying is far too often seen as an inevitable part of youth culture. But the consequences of bullying can be serious and may reverberate throughout the lifespan: affecting not only children who are bullied and children who bully, but also their families and friends.

Public health and safety professionals can and should play a major role in preventing bullying and its consequences by bringing their specialized skills and knowledge to creating the solution. Bullying has become such an important issue that it was included in the American Academy of Pediatrics (AAP) 2009 revision of its policy in regard to the role of the pediatrician in preventing youth violence. The revised policy reflects the evolving epidemiology of intentional injury, identifies emerging issues in pediatric violence and affirms the basic tenets of the original policy. One of the problems addressed by the new policy is bullying, a common form of violence that can have significant consequences for both victim and perpetrator.

AAP and LPS Policy on Youth Violence

With reference to a survey conducted in the late 1990s, the revised AAP policy statement "Role of the Pediatrician in Youth Violence Prevention" notes that violence-related injury is a substantial problem routinely encountered by pediatricians.[160] However, many pediatricians feel ill-prepared to screen for and manage any type of violence other than child abuse. Awareness of youth violence has increased since the original policy was published in 1999; however, periodic AAP surveys show a need for youth violence training and support for pediatricians. Several programmes are under way to address this need, including the programme Connected Kids: Safe, Strong, Secure.

Launched in 2005, Connected Kids: Safe, Strong, Secure gives pediatric healthcare providers a comprehensive, age-specific method to integrate violence prevention into primary care and the community. An asset-based approach to anticipatory guidance helps families raise resilient children from birth to age 21 years. The programme consists of a clinical guide, parent and patient information brochures and training materials. The clinical guide includes several worksheets and tools that help connect families to valuable community resources and reinforce important messages.[161]

An issue of emerging concern identified in the AAP policy is the association of bullying with subsequent assaultive behaviours, including high-profile school shootings. Other concerns are the association of bullying with weapon carrying; the psychological consequences of bullying (such as depression and suicidal thoughts); and the relationship between bullying and somatic conditions, disease morbidity and the development of long-term behavioural problems.

Bullying

Bullying is a form of violent behaviour that can lead to serious problems for both victim and bully. The child who is bullied is at risk for behavioural problems, physical health problems and suicidal thoughts. This should be cause for alarm given that bullying is prevalent and affects up to half of all children and adolescents worldwide.

The AAP policy defines bullying as a form of aggression in which one or more children repeatedly and intentionally intimidate, harass or physically harm a victim who cannot defend herself or himself. Others note that bullying invokes an imbalance of physical and psychological power between the persons involved. Attacks are unprovoked, systematic and purposely harmful toward the same child. Regardless of the definition, the key factors in bullying are the imbalance of power and the repeated pattern of abuse, as well as the critical point that bullying is not a developmental norm.

Bullying behaviour

Bullying behaviour is purposeful and is aimed at gaining control over another child. Bullying usually encompasses direct behaviours, such as taunting, threatening, hitting, kicking and stealing. However, bullying can also be indirect (a form known as relational aggression) and include racial slurs or the spreading of cruel rumours that cause the victim to be socially isolated by intentional exclusion. Boys tend to prefer direct methods and girls, indirect methods.

Bullying behaviours differ in severity and form. Bullying behaviours range in severity from mild (pushing, spitting and spreading rumours) to moderate (stealing lunch money, making intimidating phone calls and using racial slurs) to severe (inflicting bodily harm, threatening with a weapon and spreading malicious rumours). Forms include verbal, physical, and emotional intimidation, as well as racist and sexual bullying.

Cyberbulling

Cyberbullying is bullying that takes place using electronic technology. Electronic technology includes devices and equipment such as cell phones, computers and tablets as well as communication tools including media sites, text messages, chat and websites[162]. Over the last three years there has been an 87 % increase in the number of Childline's counselling sessions about online bullying.[163]

Bullying: the players

The players in a bullying situation include bullies and their supporters, victims and bystanders, some of whom may silently or actively support the bully or, occasionally, the victim.

Bullies: the perpetrators

Children and youth who often bully their peers are more likely than others to get into frequent fights, be injured in a fight, vandalize or steal property, drink alcohol, smoke, be truant from school, drop out of school and carry a weapon.[164] They behave in an active, outgoing, aggressive manner, using brute force or open harassment, rejecting rules and rebelling to make themselves feel superior and secure. Other bullies behave in a more subtle, reserved manner, trying not to be recognized as tormentors. Both types have the same underlying characteristics: interest in their own pleasure, desire for power over others, willingness to manipulate others to get what they want and the inability to see things from another's perspective.

The patterns of behaviour exhibited by bullies can also affect their future lives and the lives of those with whom they come into contact. Evidence indicates that children who bully often do not "outgrow" this behaviour, but carry it into their adult personal, family and work relationships—if there is no intervention. Research has shown that students (particularly boys) who bully others are especially likely to engage in other delinquent behaviours such as vandalism, shoplifting, truancy and frequent drug use.[165] A study has found that this behaviour pattern often continues into young adulthood. About 35%-40% of former bullies had three or more officially registered crime convictions by age 24, while this was true of only 10% of boys who were not bullies.[166]

Bullies find it difficult to solve problems without violence, and most have low levels of anxiety and strong self-esteem. Contrary to popular belief, little evidence supports the idea that bullies victimize because of poor self-esteem. Research shows that bullies tend to be characterized by unusually low or average levels of anxiety and insecurity, and their self-image is also about average or even relatively positive.

Children bully for a variety of reasons. Some bully to deal with difficult situations at home; some have been victims of abuse themselves. Bullies may have previously been rejected by their peers because they showed high rates of conflict, aggression and immature play and were unable to see things from the perspective of another child.

Bullied: the victims

Passive victims tend to be insecure, reacting submissively and anxiously to situations. Many of these children are physically smaller, cautious, sensitive and quiet. They tend to have a negative view of themselves, seeing themselves as failures and feeling lonely, stupid, ashamed and unattractive. However, the extent to which physical, mental or speech difficulties, glasses, skin color, weight, hygiene, posture and dress play a role in victim selection is not known.

Provocative victims tend to be quick-tempered and try to fight back if they feel insulted or attacked. Children who tend to be restless and irritable and who tease and provoke others can also become victims. Some experts suspect that some children with attention-deficit/hyperactivity disorder (ADHD) fit into this category. Other vulnerable populations are children with learning disorders, children with physical disabilities and children who are experiencing a family crisis or who are actually neglected. In general, it appears that the children who already have much to cope with in terms of physical, emotional or social disadvantage also become victims of bullies.

Bullies may target children whose characteristics deviate from the norm in size, appearance and way of thinking. However, they most often prey upon children who are shy, anxious or insecure and who lack social graces and friends. These victims tend to be close to their parents, who may be overprotective. Usually physically weaker and emotionally vulnerable, victims become easy targets who do not fight back.

Other players and bystanders

Little has been researched in regard to other players in the bullying equation. Using a sample of 462 Italian early adolescents (mean age, 13.4 years; SD = 9 months), Pozzoli and Gini[167] found that problem-solving coping strategies and perceived peer normative pressure for intervention were positively associated with active help toward a bullied peer and negatively related to passivity. They also found that distancing strategies were positively associated with passive bystanding, whereas they were negatively associated with teacher-reported defending behaviour. Self-reported defending behaviour was positively associated with personal responsibility for intervention, but only under conditions of low perceived peer pressure.

Bullying not only involves the person who bullies and the person being bullied, but it also involves the students who witness the bullying. Bystanders are those who watch bullying happen or hear about it. And depending on how bystanders respond, they can either contribute to the problem or the solution. According to the Eyes on Bullying Project, there are two types of bystanders. Hurtful bystanders are those that may instigate the bullying, laugh at the victim or cheer for the bully, or join in on the bullying once it has begun. Hurtful bystanders also include those people who passively watch the bullying and do nothing about it. Passive bystanders "provide the audience a bully craves and the silent acceptance that allows bullies to continue their hurtful behaviour".[168] Helpful bystanders are those that directly intervene while the bullying is happening by defending the victim or discouraging the bully. Helpful bystanders also include those who get help or gather support for the victim from other peers.[169]

Consequences of bullying

There is no one single cause of bullying among children. Rather, individual, family, peer, school and community factors can place a child or youth at risk for bullying his or her peers. However, there are common characteristics. Children who bully tend to be aggressive, quick to anger and impulsive; they lack empathy, have a need to dominate others and have trouble following rules.[170] Victims can experience low self-esteem, depression and anxiety, all of which may carry into adulthood. Their academic progress may be impaired, and they may find themselves isolated because their peers fear losing status or becoming victims themselves. Female victims may later find themselves in abusive relationships. Some victims even commit suicide out of sheer desperation, believing that no one will help them. A recent, frightening trend is the number of victims who commit murder because they were chronically bullied. Retaliation shootings have been executed by youths who feel inferior or mistreated. The young perpetrators of these crimes were constant targets of teasing and bullying.

Bullies may develop conduct disorders and delinquent behaviours during adolescence, as well as serious antisocial and criminal behaviour in adulthood.[171] Most bullies remain bullies throughout their lives. They typically drop out of school, have trouble holding jobs, and fail at maintaining positive close relationships. One study demonstrated that as many as 60% of bullies in grades 6 to 9 had their first criminal conviction by age 24, compared with 10% of controls who were neither bullies nor victims as children.

Roles of healthcare professionals in violence prevention[172]

Like most violent acts, bullying can have devastating consequences. Therefore, in concert with the AAP policy,[173] healthcare providers must act as leaders in violence prevention, detection and intervention in their roles as clinician, advocate, educator and researcher.

One of the goals of the U.S. Department of Health and Human Services is to "promote the economic and social well-being of individuals, families and communities". This includes protecting the safety and fostering the well-being of children and youth, encouraging the development of strong, healthy and supportive communities and addressing the needs, strengths and abilities of vulnerable populations.[174]

Furthermore, Healthy People 2020 has included the direct objective, "reduce bullying among adolescents" (IVP-35). In addition, several other objectives under injury and violence prevention and adolescent health are linked to bullying prevention. These include: "reduce physical fighting among adolescents" (IVP-34): "reduce weapon carrying by adolescents on school property" (IVP-36), and; "increase the proportion of adolescents whose parents consider them to be safe at school" (AH-8).[175]

Public health departments have expertise and the ability to make a difference in preventing bullying because of their knowledge working with a broad range of people, including different state and local agencies, community groups, and families and youth themselves. As a field, public health deals with complex issues that require multipronged, sustained interventions/strategies and public health understands the need to adapt strategies over time. It also appreciates the need to select and implement evidence-informed/promising practices and supports policy change that promotes a healthy and safe climate.

Public health programmes can use the following five strategies to help prevent bullying:

Assess relevant state law and policies related to bullying:

- Analyze current state and identify roles in relation to training, reporting systems, education, media, and state and community response systems.

- Assess/examine laws and policies and integrate into prevention (teen dating, school health and after-school programmes, primary care, school climate, etc.)

- Determine systems and programmes that enforce laws and policies.

- Work with Ministries of Education and Health (Schools Health Programmes) to disseminate information about practice and policies.

- Help coordinate and mobilize partners to support prevention laws and policies.

- Promote a public health approach.

- Help determine organizations and advocates for prevention.

Develop, implement, and evaluate interventions:

- Integrate bullying prevention into medical and health curricula, including children with special health care needs, school health and safety, school-based health clinics, primary care visits, adolescent health and community–based child and adolescent programmes.

- Work with other stakeholders within the medical community to include bullying prevention as part of anticipatory guidance.

- Provide health and human service providers, including medical providers, with resources necessary for appropriate responses for the victim, bystander and bully when bullying is identified.

- Work with Child Death Review (CDR) teams to assure bullying is considered when reviewing child and adolescent deaths and to identify prevention strategies.

- Develop and conduct public education campaigns that teach families/parents, community and children/adolescents about bullying prevention, and what their role is in prevention.

- Identify good practices.

Collect, analyze, and disseminate data:

- Work with epidemiologists to develop strategies for the surveillance of bullying. Encourage them to provide input on surveys or data collection, which can help schools understand the causes and consequences of bullying and inform prevention strategies.

- Work with Ministry of Education, school health and safety professionals, and community providers to improve data collection.

- Help coordinate data sources and promote sharing.
- Understand current Ministry of Health involvement and determine its future role in prevention.

Provide training and technical assistance to public health and other professionals:

- Provide training and technical assistance for public health professionals.
- Work with policy makers, families and NGOs to spread education about bullying prevention.
- Train public health nurses, school health nurses, medical practitioners and pediatric health providers to identify bullying and respond using appropriate interventions.
- Provide technical assistance and training to community providers including teachers, human service providers and sports/recreation programmes on recognizing and intervening using promising practices.
- Encourage schools of nursing, social work, medicine and education to include bullying identification, intervention and prevention in their curricula.

Facilitate collaborations between relevant organizations and professionals:[176]

- Participate in advisory committees related to bullying prevention.
- Partner with schools to promote social environment change, to understand the role of the bystander, to encourage staff to serve as role models and to get youth involved in prevention (mentors, suggest policy changes, active bystanders, report).
- Develop and maintain a relationship with mental health, child care and after-school programmes. Create partnerships with private companies (health insurance, etc).
- Co-sponsor trainings and education for communities.
- Work with public and municipal health to develop comprehensive plans.
- Work with Lebanese and Mediterranean and Arab pediatric societies, as well as American Academy of Pediatrics, etc.

- Facilitate training and education in pediatric events.
- Partner in school policies.

For the clinician

Clinicians should develop a comprehensive approach for anticipatory guidance, screening and counselling during routine health maintenance visits; and provide appropriate and timely treatment or referral for violence-related problems.

As clinicians, healthcare professionals can intervene with victims and bullies on all three levels of prevention:

Primary prevention. Violence prevention is a key role for child care providers, and raising resilient children is a key aspect of violence prevention. Providers should institute a plan that encourages resiliency at each wellness visit. Healthcare providers can also assist parents in raising nonviolent children:[177]

- Explain the difference between normal and abnormal
- Encourage parents to provide plenty of love and attention
- Foster positive self-esteem
- Encourage parents to talk with their children, not at them
- Emphasize the importance of parental supervision
- Aid parents in setting limits
- Teach responsibility
- Help parents teach problem-solving and decision-making skills
- Assist parents with helping their children minimize and manage stress
- Foster anger and conflict management
- Teach tolerance
- Enforce family values
- Minimize the effects of peer pressure
- Instruct parents to monitor their children's media use
- Help parents keep their children away from drugs

- Keep children away from guns and other weapons
- Empower parents to be responsible role models
- Urge parents to get involved

Secondary prevention. Healthcare providers should screen for bullying and victimization during school-age and adolescent wellness visits. Providers should also screen children who present with school phobia, mood or behavioural problems, or somatic symptoms (trouble sleeping, headaches, enuresis and stomachaches). Of note, providers should screen children and adolescents for depression and suicidal thoughts.

When asking a child about school, monitor the child's demeanor to determine whether he or she behaves in a shy or withdrawn manner, especially when discussing peer relationships and activities. Ask children about their route to and from school, because victims who are bullied during these times may be fearful of walking to and from school or riding the bus. Subtle signs, as well as obvious ones, may be present; however, realize that these signs can indicate other disorders, such as depression and substance abuse, which should be ruled out.

Possible signs of victimization include the following:[178]

- Depression and/or suicidal ideation
- Anxiety
- Moodiness or sullenness and withdrawal from family interaction
- Loss of interest in school work
- Aggression and bullying their own siblings or other children
- Unexplained bruises or injuries
- Arrival at home with torn clothes
- Disappearance of personal belongings, asking for extra money or allowance for school lunch or supplies, stealing money
- Waiting until home to use the bathroom (afraid to use school bathrooms) or enuresis
- Crying during sleep or nightmares
- Stomach-aches or mysterious illnesses invented to avoid going to school or outright refusal to go to school
- Drastic changes in sleep or eating patterns
- Desire to carry a weapon, such as a knife or gun, for protection
- Unwillingness to discuss the situation at school or making improbable excuses for the aforementioned signs.

Encourage children and their parents to verbalize their feelings about the bullying. Victims and their parents need reassurance that the healthcare provider can help them find effective ways to respond to bullying and reduce the likelihood of being bullied in the future.

Children are less likely to be bullied in a peer group. Victims with poor social skills and few friends might benefit from practicing social skills. Structured groups and activities, such as scouting, boys and girls clubs, sports, martial arts and after-school activities, help children develop these skills under adult supervision. Drama clubs teach children how to act in a manner that does not show what they feel, a skill that can be useful when being bullied.

In addition, healthcare providers can foster healthy self-esteem and teach problem-solving skills and they can help children to be assertive rather than submissive. Parents can make an appointment with their child's teacher, principal, or counsellor to discuss the problem and to ask about the school's anti-bullying policy. School personnel should take the problem seriously and investigate incidents of bullying.[179]

Detecting bullies is more difficult than detecting victims because bullies are adept at hiding their mistreatment of others. Parents may have no idea that their child is bullying another child until a teacher or another parent confronts them about it. Some parents of bullies may have noticed that their child has little concern for others, is aggressive or manipulative, abuses animals, or possesses unexplained items or money. Bullies may act cocky, arrogant, and self-assured, and they may have difficulty accepting authority. When asked about bullying, they are apt to be condescending about responding to questions. Because most bullies lack empathy, they tend to appear pleased or amused when asked how they feel about other children getting hurt. Bullies may also exhibit some of the same signs as victims, especially depression and anxiety, and they may have substance abuse problems.

Intervening with bullies can be difficult because both the parent and child may be reluctant to admit to bullying. However, healthcare providers should advise parents that their child's behaviours will have negative consequences for their child's future and must be addressed.

Like victims, bullies benefit from learning appropriate social skills. Bullies should be encouraged to participate in small-group activities, preferably with older children as role models, so that they can engage in cooperative tasks. Adult supervision is warranted during these groups, and bullies should receive positive reinforcement each time they engage in prosocial or caring behaviours, which enables them to learn more positive ways of gaining attention and affection.

Healthcare providers can work with the parents to help them learn ways to demonstrate caring and affection toward their children, as well as how to apply more consistent and appropriate disciplinary measures. Parents should be encouraged to become more involved with community activities and with other parents. If the child demonstrates significant bullying behaviour or signs of a conduct disorder, referral to a mental health professional is appropriate.

Tertiary prevention. If a child displays the consequences of bullying, referral to a mental health professional is warranted. If resources are scarce, be creative and consider alternatives, such as developing an alliance with a university psychiatric nursing, psychology, social work, or counselling programme, or investigate telepsychiatry services.

For the advocates

As advocates, healthcare providers can follow the AAP's suggestions and advocate for publicly supported community-based behaviour services, the protection of children from firearm exposure, bullying awareness programmes, responsible media programming, the role of health professionals as public health messengers and the incorporation of youth violence prevention data (i.e. screening prompts) into electronic health records.

For the educators

As educators, healthcare providers can take the lead in educating parents and other professionals about bullying.[180] But first, we must better educate ourselves. Child mental health problems, particularly violence, can no longer take a back seat to physiologic disorders and disease in medical education. The mental and emotional health of children must be an integral part of every basic healthcare curriculum, not just offered as an elective course. We need to view community health and wellness as the foundation for healthcare and a healthy childhood as the foundation for a healthy adulthood. This paradigm can also help alleviate the growing issue of insufficient clinical placements for pediatric students. Most children in need of help are not lying in hospital beds.

Clinicians who are already in practice can learn about violence prevention through formal continuing medical education or professional development programmes, take elective courses, or do rotation work in medical school or postgraduate training. Becoming educated about how we can help families includes being aware of community resources for children and adolescents who are perpetrators or victims of violence.

For the researchers

As researchers, healthcare providers can conduct studies and implement evidence-based practice projects.[181] Clinicians can participate in practice-based research on the prevention of youth violence, contribute data to existing injury surveillance systems and advocate for legislatively mandated, municipally supported active local injury surveillance systems. However, we also need to increase our focus on interdisciplinary violence research so that we can create more effective evidence-based methods to prevent, identify, and manage, youth violence, including bullying.

Conclusion

Bullying is violence and violence is a health problem that opens the door to a host of other health problems.[182] Healthcare providers must make violence prevention, identification and intervention a priority if they are to improve the quality of life for children and for their future as adults.[183]

Endnotes

[160] American Academmcy of Pediatrics (2009). Role of the Pediatrician in Youth Violence Prevention. *Pediatrics* 124(1) 393-402.

[161] American Academy of Pediatrics (2006). *Connected Kids: Safe, Strong, Secure Clinical Guide.* Spivak, H, Sege, R, Flanigan, E, Licenziato, V (Eds). Elk Grove Village, IL: American Academy of Pediatrics.

[162] David-Ferdon, C, Hertz, MF (2007). Electronic media, violence, and adolescents: An emerging public health problem. *Journal of Adolescent Health.* Dec, 41(6 Suppl 1):S1-5.

[163] Ibid.

[164] Nansel, TR, Overpeck, M, Pilla, RS, Ruan, WJ, Simons-Morton, B & Scheidt, P (2001). Bullying Behaviors Among US Youth: Prevalence and Association With Psychosocial Adjustment. *JAMA: The Journal of the American Medical Association* 285(16):2094-2100.

[165] Olweus, D (1993). *Bullying at School: What we know and what we can do.* Cambridge, MA: Blackwell Publishers, Inc.

[166] Olweus, D, Limber, S & Mihalic, SF (1999). *Blueprints for Violence Prevention, Book Nine: Bullying Prevention Programme.* Boulder, CO: Center for the Study and Prevention of Violence.

[167] Pozzoli, T & Gina, G (2010). Active defending and passive bystander behavior in bullying: the role of personal characteristics and perceived peer pressure. *Journal of Abnormal Psychology* Aug. 38(6): 815-27.

[168] Adler, M, Katz, A, Minotti, J, Slaby, R and Storey, K (2008). *Eyes on Bullying, What Can You Do?* Available at www.eyesonbullying.org/pdfs/toolkit.pdf

[169] Ibid.

[170] Health Resources and Services Administration (2011). US Dept of Health and Human Services.

[171] Roth, D, Coles, ME, & Heimburg, RG (2000). The relationship between memories of childhood teasing and anxiety and depression in adulthood. *Journal of Anxiety Disorders* 16 (2002): 149-164.

[172] Muscari, ME. PhD, CPNP, APRN-BC, CFNS.

[173] American Academy of Pediatrics (2009). Op. cit. Abstract.

[174] US Dept Health and Human Services. Accessed 2011.

[175] https://www.healthypeople.gov/ Accessed 2011.

[176] US Department of Health and Human Services. *Healthy People.* http://www.healthypeople.gov. Accessed January 25, 2011.

[177] Muscari M. (2002) *Not My Kid: 21 Steps to Raising a Nonviolent Child.* Scranton, Pa: University of Scranton Press.

[178] Sampson, R (2009). *Bullying in school.* US Department of Justice Office of Community Oriented Policing Services. Problem-Oriented Guides for Police Problem-Specific Guides Series No. 12. Available at: http://www.cops.usdoj.gov/files/RIC/Publications/e07063414-guide.pdf Accessed July 15, 2009; Muscari, M (2002). Sticks and stones: the NP's role with bullies and victims. *Journal of Pediatric Health Care* 16:22-28. Abstract; American Medical Association (2002). *Proceedings from the Educational Forum on Adolescent Health Youth Bullying, May 3.* Available at: www.ama-assn.org/ama1/pub/upload/mm/39/youthbullying.pdf Accessed July 10, 2009; Garrity, C, Baris, M (1996). Bullies and victims: a guide for pediatricians. *Contemporary Pediatrics* 13:90-115.

[179] Muscari, M. (2002). Op. cit.; American Medical Association (2002). Op. cit.; Garrity, C, Baris, M. (1996). Op. cit.

[180] Children's Safety Network, Topic Page on Bullying Prevention: (http://www.childrenssafetynetwork.org/topics/showtopic.asp?pkTopicID=15) CSN offers publications, webinars, presentations and examples of what states are doing to combat bullying.

[181] Cyberbullying Research Center. Research. http://www.cyberbullying.us/research.php. Accessed January 26, 2011.

[182] http://www.antibullyingpro.com/blog/2015/4/7/facts-on-bullying#sthash.jS9HFqLJ.dpuf

[183] National Violence Prevention Youth Resource Center (http://www.safeyouth.org/). Provides information and links to resources on bullying and violence prevention for parents, teenagers, schools, and afterschool programmes.

Children read books in class
© UNICEF/UNI9411/Pirozzi

Chapter III. School Interventions

9. Five key components in a global strategy against bullying

Dan Olweus and Susan Limber

Introduction

The current article presents five key components from the Olweus Bullying Prevention Program (OBPP) that in our view could play a central role in a global strategy against bullying. The reason for recommending this compact version of the OBPP, and not the complete programme, is that use of the full programme would require more resources in terms of time and money than many schools, communities, or countries can or would like to use. Although the particular combination of the components presented here has not been carefully evaluated in empirical research, all of these components have been evaluated with quite positive results in the context of the full programme (more on that below). Although there are good grounds for assuming that systematic work on the basis of these components will have considerable positive effects, it will be important to design empirical studies to check the validity of this assumption.

In order to successfully realize practical intervention work based on these components and strategies, a minimum requirement is that there should exist a Handbook that provides much more detail about the various strategies and measures than can be given in this short article. This article is based on portions of the two handbooks that have been a cornerstone in the implementation of the complete OBPP - a Teacher Guide and a Schoolwide Guide.[184] With some editing and updating, these guides can easily be combined into a single handbook. In the following, we assume that there exists such a Handbook and we will refer to the contents of that Handbook as the Program. In addition, since such an intervention project is designed to transfer basic knowledge contained in the Program to the staff of a school or other unit, it is also very important that there are available at least a small number of professionals with special training and implementation competence (similar to today's Certified Trainers/Consultants in the OBPP). Such professionals can assist in the training of needed professionals and serve as consultants and supporters for schools who need assistance in the implementation process.

It is important to realize that what is presented here represents a theoretically coherent and coordinated programme with a clear implementation plan. That is something very different than a summary of research findings on bullying and possible intervention strategies, for example. There seem to be very few schools that can on their own select and integrate various pieces from such overviews into coordinated and effective intervention efforts.

Component #1: Define and Measure Bullying

In order to understand and change a problem or phenomenon, it is very important that the phenomenon is well defined and circumscribed. The definition of bullying that has been used for many years and been largely accepted by both researchers and practitioners reads as follows: "A person is being bullied when he or she is exposed, repeatedly and over time, to negative actions on the part of one or more other persons, and he or she has difficulty defending himself or herself".[185] Expressed in more everyday language, one might say: "Bullying is when someone repeatedly and on purpose says or does mean and hurtful things to another person who has a hard time defending himself or herself". To reduce uncertainty, we often add: "It is also bullying when a student is teased repeatedly in a negative and hurtful way".

There are three components to this definition: a) it concerns purposeful behaviour involving unwanted negative actions; b) it typically implies a pattern of behaviour repeated over time; and c) it involves an imbalance of power or strength. It is important to understand that bullying is about *an abusive relationship* occurring in a context such as a classroom, a school, a sports club, a neighborhood etc. The targeted student can be assumed to have at least some superficial knowledge of the perpetrator(s). The fact that bullying is about abusive relationships ties bullying closely to the UN Convention on the Rights of the

Child, which requires states to protect children "from all forms of physical or mental violence, injury or abuse…" (Article 19).

The above definition was formulated already in the 1980's[186] and this definition has been largely adopted by the U.S. Centers for Disease Control (CDC) in their report about a "universal" definition of bullying.[187]

With a clear definition of the phenomenon of interest, it is possible to develop instruments to measure or estimate the phenomenon with some degree of accuracy. With regard to the OBPP, it started with the development of a questionnaire to be used in a nationwide campaign against bullying in Norway in 1983. The Olweus Bullying Questionnaire (OBQ) was expanded and revised in 1996[188] and has after that only undergone very minor changes. Gradually, a lot of information about the reliability (precision) and validity (adequacy, value) of the Questionnaire has been gathered which by and large confirms the usefulness of the instrument developed.[189] The full questionnaire and a selection of the two global questions (about being bullied and bullying others) have been used in a number of international studies, including the repeated surveys of the Health Behaviour of School Children (HBSC) study involving more than 40 countries at present.[190]

The OBQ as used in the OBPP takes about 30-40 minutes to complete for most students in the relevant grades (grade 3 and higher). If one wants a shorter version, a selection of the most important items of the Questionnaire would provide information about the prevalence (the percentage) of bullied and bullying students in the school, split by gender and grade (age), and about the prevalence of the different forms of bullying (direct physical, direct verbal, indirect/relational, and electronic/cyberbullying). In addition, a short version should include a question about where bullying occurs, in order to identify "hot spots" in the school, and one or two questions about students' perceptions of the level of anti-bullying activities on the part of their classroom/main teacher and other adults at school. Such a shortened version of the Questionnaire would only take 15-20 minutes to administer. If desirable, other questions of relevance could be added.

The information contained in such a survey, and presented to the school in a printed report with user-friendly graphs, is an indispensable tool in the school's anti-bullying work. First, the school leadership and staff will in this way get a reasonably realistic picture of the level and "architecture" of the bully/victim problems in their own school. The associated heightened awareness of the school situation usually leads to increased engagement and a willingness to initiate efforts for the benefit of the students. In addition, the survey information is of great value for the school leadership and staff in planning and designing the practical implementation of the Program.

A repeated survey with the same questionnaire one year later will help the leadership and staff monitor and assess their degree of success/lack of success. For example: Are there any noteworthy and meaningful changes compared to the results from the first survey?; What have we succeeded with?; and what do we need to work harder on? Although results for an individual school must be interpreted cautiously, the Questionnaire provides very useful feedback information to the school.

Component #2: Establish a Bullying Prevention Coordinating Committee (BPCC)

In order to get the key elements of the global strategy adequately implemented in a school, it is critically important to establish a Bullying Prevention Coordinating Committee (BPCC). An overarching task of the Committee is to create a shared focus on the goal of reducing and preventing bully/victim problem, and to make all human resources at the school coordinate their efforts to reach that goal. Additional tasks of the BPCC include:

- administer the questionnaire and evaluate and disseminate the results

- provide training and programme information to all teachers and other staff

- ensure that introduction and use of the various programme components are coordinated and proceed as planned

- represent the programme to caretakers/parents, the community, and the media.

A bullying prevention committee typically consists of 8-14 persons and should include the lead administrator of the school building (principal or assistant principal). Other members are typically a teacher from each grade level, a mental health professional (as applicable), a member of the non-teaching staff, and one or two parents. Where appropriate, one or two student representatives may also serve on the committee (typically middle, junior, or high school grades). One of the members who has a good knowledge of the school and is a person with a strong dedication to anti-bullying, working along the lines described in the Program, is selected to be a Program (on-site) Coordinator. The Coordinator will have special responsibility for various practical and organizational tasks associated with implementation of the Program and often serves as chair of the committee. The members of this committee receive special training, develop a concrete plan for implementing the Program in the school and meet regularly throughout the school year to ensure effective and coordinated implementation.

Since the BPCC is responsible for adequate implementation of the Program in the school it is very important that all members of the committee acquire a good knowledge of the programme and its strategies and measures used to address bullying. It is possible in principle that the committee with use of the Program Handbook and some online Program modules could achieve this on their own. However, to do so with some success would probably require more dedication and organizational effort than most ordinary schools can provide.

Use of a trainer with good knowledge of and experience with the Program (with certification as a Program trainer/consultant) will in most cases be a simpler and more effective solution. In the full Program, we have usually recommended a full two-day training of the BPCC. However, with development of some pre-implementation online modules and/or organization of a couple of structured committee meetings prior to Program start, a one-day training of the committee would probably suffice. After the training, the trainer should provide at least one year of in-person or telephone consultation to the school's on-site coordinator to help ensure fidelity to the model and to problem-solve as needed. This contact over the whole implementation period with a trainer with good knowledge of the Program is likely to greatly facilitate the implementation process.

An important task for the BPCC is to introduce the Program to all other school personnel, including administrators, teachers, bus drivers, custodians, cafeteria workers, lunchroom and playground supervisors, and after-school programme providers. This is typically done in a full-day session (or two half-day blocks) led by members of the committee (often the on-site coordinator with the assistance of the trainer).

The Handbook contains structured agendas for both the BPCC and the all-staff trainings.

Component #3: Revise the School's Supervisory System

An important task for the BPCC is to review and refine the school's supervisory system, so that bullying is less likely to happen. Administration of the Bullying Questionnaire will help identify "hot spots" in the school where bullying episodes tend to occur more often than in other places.

Typically, hot spots for bullying are areas where adult-student ratios are poor, where there are many students assembled at the same time and areas staffed by personnel who are perceived by the students to have less authority. Such locations include the playground, the athletic fields, locker rooms, the lunch rooms (if available) and buses.

Areas where students are out of direct view can also be hot spots such as restrooms, hallways that have no classrooms and places out of view on the school groups. It is also worth noting that a considerable number of students report that they are bullied in their classrooms (with teacher present or absent). Although attention may be focused primarily on hot spots, it is important to realize that bullying may occur in all areas of the school.

Research has suggested that there are less bullying problems when there more adults out to supervise the students.[191] But it is not possible to recommend a specific number of supervising adults (per 100 students, for example) during recess/break periods, since there are many school-specific factors to consider, including the size and layout of the school grounds and how breaks are organized. The goal is to have an adequate number of adults among the students so that there is good supervision of what the students are doing. Since much bullying occurs during break periods, the likelihood of discovering bullying (and other negative behaviour) must be high.

However, a good supervisory system is not just a matter of having enough supervising staff. The attitudes and behaviours of the supervising adults are of utmost importance. A staff member who does not intervene in a possible bullying situation communicates to the students that bullying is okay and will not lead to any consequences for the perpetrators. It also serves to reduce bystander empathy for students who are bullied and decreases the likelihood that they will respond to assist and follow school rule number 2 (see below).

In contrast, when supervising adults do intervene firmly and consistently, this sends an important signal to the bullying student or students and possible bystanders: "We don't accept bullying in our school and such behaviour will be stopped and/or negative consequences will be given". Such intervention also shows that adults care about, support, and protect students who are bullied which will help them feel safer from future bullying episodes.

It is important that the school's supervisory system is co-ordinated so that all staff consistently react to bullying and take similar actions when faced with negative behaviour. In addition, the BPCC may want to develop a log or other system for systematic exchange of information about possible bullying episodes. In this way, students at risk of bullying or being bullied or left out might be identified and the situation sensitively addressed before a fully developed bullying problem has arisen.

Component #4: Introduce School Rules against Bullying and Hold Class Meetings

An important way to address bullying problems is to introduce a few anti-bullying school rules and to apply positive and negative consequences to reinforce these rules. In the OBPP there are four such rules:

1. We will not bully other students.

2. We will try to help students who are bullied.

3. We will try to include students who are left out.

4. If we know that somebody is being bullied, we will tell an adult at school and an adult at home.

These rules cover both direct and indirect forms of bullying, including social isolation and intentional exclusion from the peer group. They are rules for the entire school and for each classroom and are often posted in all classrooms. The rules have been carefully developed to effectively address different aspects of bullying. For this reason, they should not be replaced or modified, except for possible minor word changes in rules 2-4.

With every classroom in the school following the same rules, they are easier to enforce and students know more clearly what behaviour is expected. This common set of rules sends a signal to students, parents, and others that the school has a unified and coordinated policy against bullying.

Even though the school very likely has a code of conduct or discipline policy, this should not replace the four anti-bullying rules. At the same time, these rules provide specific guidelines for bullying and will be an important supplement to the school's discipline policy.

For the rules against bullying to be effective–that is, to change student behaviour and norms–they should be clear and have consequences when they are followed or broken. As is well-documented by research, when individuals receive positive consequences for their behaviour, they are more likely to behave in the same way in similar situations in the future. Accordingly, it is important that teachers provide abundant positive reinforcement when students follow the rules.

Unfortunately, positive reinforcement (and ignoring) is usually not enough to get aggressive students to change their behaviour. In many situations it necessary to use negative consequences as well. Use of negative consequences is particularly relevant in relation to violations of the main rule: "We will not bully other students". When some form of negative consequence is considered, it is important to remember that: such a consequence should be somewhat disagreeable or uncomfortable but not involve revenge, adult overreaction, or hostility; be appropriate for the student's age, gender, and personality; and be logically related to the negative behaviour of the student, if possible. One way to achieve this may be to engage the students in discussions about suitable consequences for rule-breaking behaviour in class meetings

It is very important that the students get a clear understanding of what the various rules actually mean and how they play out in their daily school lives. A good way of making the rules concrete is to hold regular (weekly) classroom meetings with the students. These meetings usually last for 20-40 minutes, depending on the students' age. In a classroom meeting, the teacher is more of a facilitator than teacher and it is a great advantage if the meetings have a different structure and character than the ordinary teaching set-up. Students usually sit in a circle or half circle ("having circle time") and the teacher may engage the students in role plays and similar, "non-traditional" methods to have them practice, and evaluate, different ways of reacting in simulated bullying situations (The Handbook will have many useful examples to work from).

Among other things, class meetings are designed to:

- teach students what bullying is, the meaning of the four anti-bullying rules, and different ways of reacting when bullying occurs
- help students learn more about themselves and their feelings and reactions and those of their peers
- build a sense of community and belonging and to develop a set of norms about bullying (and other important issues)
- help the teacher learn more about the relationships among the classmates and their power struggles, and, more generally, what goes on in the group – the "inner life" of the class.

Component #5: Address Bullying on the Individual Level

Before briefly describing how individual bullying problems can be handled, it should be emphasized that implementation of some of the school and class-wide preventive measures discussed above can reduce the likelihood of bullying and the need for individual interventions. For example, the introduction of school rules against bullying followed by class discussions and the development of an effective supervisory system may contribute to the detection of emerging bullying problems.

However, these group-level effects are often not enough, and it is necessary to develop a set of clear strategies for dealing with suspected or identified cases of bullying problems.[192]

In a situation where a teacher or staff member suspects that one of his or her students is being bullied but s/he is not certain, there are several ways to obtain more information, such as talking with colleagues, increasing observation, speaking informally with the student, contacting the parents of the student who is potentially bullied, or administering a simple sociometric survey (for example, asking students to nominate three classmates they would like to collaborate with on a project).

If a staff member becomes aware of a likely bullying problem, a first step is to arrange one or more meetings with the student who has been reported to be bullied, and his or her parent(s). These meetings could be held with the student only (away from the other students) and then with the parent(s), or the student and parent could meet together with the teacher. The purpose of these meetings is to get very detailed information about the situation, offer support, and provide assurance about the commitment of the school staff to stopping the bullying.

Once enough detailed information has been gathered, the staff member will need to directly meet with the bullying student or students. This should be done as quickly as possible after having identified the student(s) involved or suspected. It may be helpful to have another member of the school staff included in such meetings. Doing so sends a clear message that this is a situation that is taken seriously.

If more than one student is involved in the bullying, the teacher should not talk with the students together as a group but have individual talks with each of them in quick succession so they have little opportunity to share what was discussed. It is often the case that one student has played a "leader" role in the bullying, and it is a good idea to talk to that student first, whenever possible.

At this meeting, the teacher should confront the bullying students with the information about their roles in the bullying, set possible consequences, and make it very clear: "We don't accept bullying in our school, and we will see to it that it stops".

Separate follow-up meetings should be held with the involved students within one or two weeks to assess whether the bullying has stopped. Additional meetings may be held, as needed, to find out if the positive results have been maintained, or if additional support and interventions are required.

Briefly about the OBPP

The OBPP is a research-based, whole-school comprehensive approach that includes school-wide, classroom, individual components. The Program is focused on both short-term and long-term change that will create a safe and positive school environment. The overarching goals of the OBPP are to reduce existing bullying problems among students, prevent new bullying problems, and achieve better peer relations.[193] These goals are pursued by restructuring the school environment to reduce opportunities and rewards for bullying behaviour and to build a sense of community.

The OBPP is built on four basic principles. Adults at school should: (a) show warmth and positive interest in students, (b) set firm limits to unacceptable behaviour, (c) use consistent positive consequences to acknowledge and reinforce appropriate behaviour and non-physical, non-hostile consequences when rules are broken, and (d) function as authorities and positive role models.[194] These principles have been translated into interventions at the school, classroom and individual levels.[195]

To date, seven large-scale evaluations of the OBPP have been carried out in Norway, involving more than 30,000 students from more than 300 schools.[196] Findings have revealed consistently positive Program effects among students in grades 4-7, typically with reductions in bullying problems in the 35-50% range after eight months of intervention.[197] Although positive findings have also been obtained with students in grades 8-10, results have been less consistent and it has taken longer to achieve as strong effects as with younger students.[198] In possibly the first study of long-term effects of an anti-bullying programme, Olweus followed students from 14 schools in Oslo (with approximately 3,000 students at each assessment) and observed reductions in self-reports of victimization of 40% and self-reported bullying of 51% over a period of five years.[199]

The OBPP has been introduced on a large-scale basis and with positive results (unpublished) in several countries outside Norway: Iceland, Sweden, Lithuania, and the U.S. In the U.S. more than 800 schools have implemented the Program and an evaluation of the OBPP (with quite positive results) involving 210 Pennsylvania schools followed over two years has also been undertaken.[200]

The OBPP has also been positively evaluated in various meta-analyses. In the most comprehensive meta-analysis conducted so far comprising all anti-bullying programmes in the world (at that time), the authors concluded that the OBPP could "be the basis of future programs"[201] and "programs inspired by the work of Dan Olweus worked best".[202]

Endnotes

[184] The current article is, with permission from Hazelden Publishing, to a considerable degree based on texts in Olweus, D, & Limber, SP (2007). *Olweus Bullying Prevention Program: Teacher guide.* Center City, MN: Hazelden: and Olweus, D, Limber, SP, Flerx, V, Mullin, N, Riese, J, & Snyder, M (2007). *Olweus Bullying Prevention Program: Schoolwide guide.* Center City, MN: Hazelden.

[185] Olweus, D (1993). *Bullying at school: What we know and what we can do.* New York: Blackwell.; Olweus, D (2013). School bullying: Development and some important challenges. *Annual Review of Clinical Psychology,* 9, 751-780.; Olweus, D, Limber, SP, Flerx, V, Mullin, N, Riese, J, & Snyder, M (2007). *Olweus Bullying Prevention Program: Schoolwide guide.* Center City, MN: Hazelden.

[186] Olweus, D (1993). Op. cit.

[187] Gladden, RM, Vivolo-Kantor, AM, Hamburger, ME, & Lumpkin, CD (2014). *Bullying surveillance among youths: Uniform definitions for public health and recommended data elements, version 1.0.* Atlanta, GA: National Center for Injury Prevention and Control, Centers for Disease Control and Prevention and U.S. Department of Education.

[188] Olweus, D (1996). Op. cit.; Olweus, D. (2007). *Olweus bullying questionnaire.* Center City, MN: Hazelden.

[189] Olweus, D & Limber, SP (2010a). The Olweus Bullying Prevention Program: Implementation and Evaluation Over Two Decades. In SR Jimerson, SM Swearer, & DL Espelage (Eds), *Handbook of bullying in schools: An international perspective* (pp. 377-401). New York: Routledge. Olweus, D, & Limber, SP (2010b). Bullying in school: Evaluation and dissemination of the Olweus Bullying Prevention Program. *American Journal of Orthopsychiatry,* 80, 124-134.; Olweus, D (2013). Op. cit.; Solberg, ME, & Olweus, D (2003). Prevalence estimation of school bullying with the Olweus Bully/Victim Questionnaire. *Aggressive behavior,* 29, 239-268.

[190] Craig, W, Harel-Fisch, Y, Fogel-Grinvald, H, Dostaler, S, Hetland, J, Simons-Morton, B, *et al.* (2009). A cross-national profile of bullying and victimization among adolescents in 40 countries. *International Journal of Public Health,* 54, 216-224.

[191] Olweus, D (1993). Op. cit.

[192] The Handbook gives detailed information about how this can be done.

[193] Olweus, D (1993). Op. cit.; Olweus, D & Limber, SP (2010a). Op. cit.; Olweus, D & Limber, SP (2010b). Op. cit

[194] Olweus, D. (1993). Op. cit.; Olweus et al. (2007). Op. cit.

[195] Olweus, D (1993). Op. cit.; Olweus and Limber (2010a,b). Op. cit.

[196] Olweus, D (2005). A useful evaluation design, and effects of the Olweus Bullying Prevention Program. *Psychology, Crime & Law,* 11, 389-402.; Olweus and Limber (2010a,b). Op. cit.

[197] Olweus and Limber (2010a,b). Op. cit.

[198] Ibid.

[199] Ibid.

[200] Limber, SP, Olweus, D, Wang, W,& Breivik, K (2016). Evaluation of the Olweus Bullying Prevention Program: *A Large Scale Study of U.S. Students in Grades 3-11.* Manuscript to be submitted.

[201] Ttofi, M., & Farrington, D. (2009). What works in preventing bullying: Effective elements of programs. *Journal of Aggression, Conflict and Peace Research,* 1(1), 13-24.

[202] Ttofi, MM, & Farrington, DP (2011). Effectiveness of school-based programs to reduce bullying: A systematic and meta-analytic review. *Journal of Experimental Criminology,* 7(1), 27-56.; More information about the OBPP can be found at www.HazeldenBettyFord.org/olweus or www.clemson.edu/olweus.

Masha, 17, helps a girl complete a questionnaire, Ukraine
© UNICEF/UNI43398/Pirozzi

10. Making large-scale, sustainable change: experiences with the KiVa anti-bullying programme

Sanna Herkama and Christina Salmivalli

Introduction

In 2006, the Finnish Government decided to support the development of an evidence-based bullying prevention programme and its large-scale implementation across schools in Finland. At that time, no-one could foresee that the KiVa anti-bullying programme would eventually be implemented by 90% of Finland's basic education schools, that it would have remarkable effects on the prevalence of bullying problems, and would be evaluated and implemented in numerous countries outside of Finland. Studies indicate that KiVa is effective in decreasing bullying and victimization, but evidence also shows that the programme is scalable and sustainable. In the present chapter, we will introduce the background and the theoretical base of the KiVa programme.[203] Also the main findings of the evaluation studies conducted so far and the content of the KiVa anti-bullying programme are presented. Furthermore, we will contemplate the key elements of implementing and sustaining a large scale intervention programme over the long run.

Legislative changes leading to the development of a national anti-bullying programme in Finland

The development of the KiVa anti-bullying programme in Finland is an example of how strength of will and commitment on the part of politicians, policy makers, researchers, and school staff can make a difference, influencing the well-being of numerous children and adolescents across an entire country. The development of the KiVa programme was originally an answer to the demand to reduce bullying since changes in legislation seemed not to be enough. For decades, a safe school environment and students' wellbeing have been given attention in the public discourse and policy making in Finland. For instance, the Finnish Basic Education Act has stated since 1999 that each and every student has the right to safe school environment. But even though the law was further amended in 2003 to include a clearer statement that the education provider "shall draw up a plan in connection with curriculum design, for safeguarding pupils against violence, bullying, and harassment, execute the plan, and supervise adherence to it and its implementation"[204] there was no apparent reduction in the prevalence of bullying. For example, the School Health Promotion Study conducted regularly by the National Institute for Health and Welfare indicated that the prevalence of victimized students had remained approximately the same in Finnish middle schools (grades 8 and 9, which are included in the study) since the late 1990s.

Other large-scale international surveys also indicated the need to take further action. The results obtained from OECD's (Organization for Economic Cooperation and Development) PISA (Programme of International Student Assessment) study and the World Health Organization's HBSC (Health Behaviour in School Aged Children) study in 2006 were controversial; although Finnish students did perform academically very well (PISA), their well-being at school was low (HBSC). It became clear that the legislative changes alone were not enough; something more was needed in order to deliver change nationwide.

This was the moment when the Ministry of Education and Culture in Finland decided to allocate resources to a more systematic and long-lasting anti-bullying work nationwide. A contract was made with the University of Turku to develop and evaluate a new intervention programme aimed at preventing and reducing bullying and minimizing its negative consequences. This led in turn to the creation of the KiVa anti-bullying programme at the University of Turku, by the Department of Psychology and the Centre for Learning Research.

Mechanism of change: school bullying as group phenomenon

The expert team responsible for the development of the KiVa anti-bullying programme had studied bullying for a long time, focusing especially on the peer group dynamics related to bullying and the implications for prevention/intervention work. This approach became the theoretical backbone of the programme. A theoretical base, supported by empirical evidence, provides a solid starting point for building a strong programme, the working mechanisms of which can also be tested in evaluation studies.

The participant role approach to bullying[205] captures the essence of the social architecture of bullying. The role of peer bystanders is the core of the KiVa programme. The basic idea is to make bullying behaviour less rewarding for the perpetrator by changing bystander responses. If the students bullying others are not rewarded for their behaviour they are less likely to bully others in the future. Peers may sustain or decrease the behaviour of bullies by either supporting the bully or by giving neither attention nor approval for his or her behaviour. Influencing the bystanders is likely to be easier than trying the influence the perpetrators directly; they may have deepseated cognitions regarding the use of aggression and their behaviour is often socially rewarded and thus functional.

Numerous studies provide support for KiVa's theoretical base. They confirm the notion that bystanders' behaviour plays a crucial role in bullying. For instance, the more the classmates tend to reinforce the bully's behaviour, the higher the frequency of bullying in a classroom.[206] In contrast, high levels of defending behaviour (peers providing support for victimized peers and showing that they do not approve of bullying) is associated with less frequent bullying behaviour. Evaluation studies have shown that in KiVa schools (as compared with control schools) only one year after the implementation of KiVa there was less victimization, bullying, and reinforcing of the bully, but more empathy towards victimized peers and more capacity to support and defend them.[207] In other words, the KiVa programme brings about changes in emotions, cognitions, as well as actual behaviours of children and young people.

Interestingly, the theoretical model of KiVa is further supported when mediating mechanisms of the programme are investigated. More precisely, the decrease of bullying in KiVa schools is mediated through changes in students' attitudes toward bullying and their perceptions of classmates' tendency to reinforce the bullies or defend the victims.[208] In addition, changes in students' perception of their teachers' anti-bullying attitudes (students in KiVa schools start perceiving that their teachers are clearly against bullying) lead to a reduction in bullying behaviour. In practice, these results reflect the importance of communicating one's anti-bullying attitudes, stating out loud that bullying is not tolerated – and this should be done by children and young people themselves, as well as their teachers.

Evaluating the effectiveness of the KiVa anti-bullying programme

The evaluation studies conducted during the randomized controlled trial (RCT) in 2007–2009 indicate that the KiVa anti-bullying programme is effective in reducing bullying and victimization. During the first stage of the RCT in 2007–2008 more than 8,000 students (grades 4–6 of elementary school) participated in the data collection. After only nine months of implementing KiVa, the prevalence of self-reported victims and bullies were found to have decreased by 30%-40% and 17%-33%, respectively in KiVa schools compared to control schools.[209] The second stage took place in 2008–2009 with nearly 7,000 students from grades 1–3 and over 16,000 middle school students (grades 7–9) participating in the data collection. The effects were found to be moderate in lower grades but more inconsistent in middle school.[210]

As could be expected, the effectiveness of the programme during the nationwide rollout (2009–2010) was overall somewhat weaker than observed during the RCT. The number of self-reported victims and bullies decreased by 15% and 14%, respectively.[211] But it should be noted that this is a significant proportion of students. If the decrease were generalized to the population of around 500,000 students participating in basic education in Finland such an effect would correspond to a reduction of approximately 12,500 victims and 7,500 bullies during one school year.

A positive trend has been maintained since the broad rollout in 2009. More schools have started implementing KiVa and their progress has been monitored by annual student and staff online surveys. Approximately 1500 schools, with around 200,000 students, have participated in this data collection. The surveys offer information about the prevalence of victimization and bullying across years. Self-reported victimization and bullying have decreased considerably in six years being 17.2% at the baseline and 12.6% after six years of implementation (see Figure 1).

Figure 1.
Reduction in being bullied or bullying others (at least 2 to 3 times a month in the last couple of months) in 2009–2015 in Finnish schools (Ns = 634–2,126) implementing the Kiva anti-bullying programme (grades 1–9).

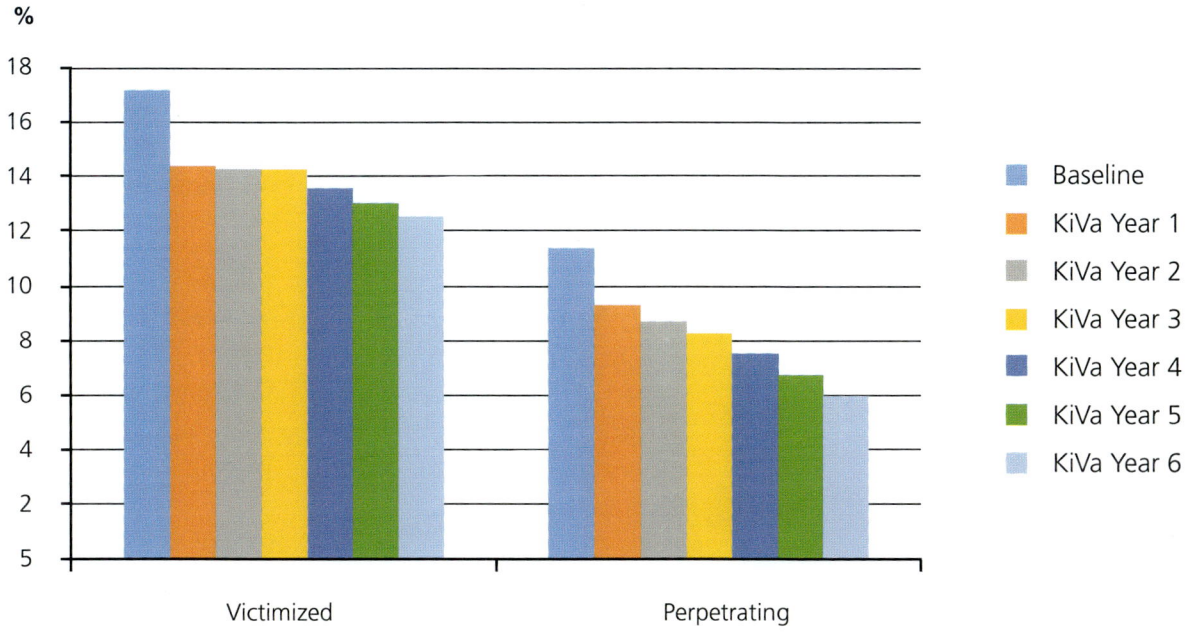

The proportion of student perpetrators has decreased from 11.4% to 5.9% respectively. As all schools involved in this data collection are implementing KiVa, we cannot tell whether a similar trend has taken place in other schools as well: we are currently in the process of combining our data with those from other nationwide surveys.

From time to time, the question is posed as to whether general anti-bullying practices, such as KiVa, are effective in reducing all forms of bullying. This question is particularly raised in regard to cyberbullying. The evaluation studies of KiVa indicate that systematic anti-bullying strategies can be effective in reducing all forms of bullying, including cyberbullying. The KiVa programme has been found to reduce cyberbullying and cyber-victimization in elementary schools and to some extent in middle schools.[212] Furthermore, the studies indicate that various forms of bullying are interrelated. If a student is being bullied in one way he or she is typically targeted by several other forms of negative behaviour and this can also happen online.[213] In general, the KiVa anti-bullying programme takes the view that bullying and cyberbullying are not separate phenomena. Cyberbullying is understood as a type of bullying which needs to be given special attention but which can be reduced by targeting the mechanisms behind bullying in general.

The KiVa programme was primarily designed to target bullying and victimization not to improve the school climate or feelings of general safety. But as might have been expected, reduced bullying was also connected to a decline in anxiety, the more positive perception of peers[214] as well as to increased enjoyment of school, improved perceptions of the classroom and school climates, and increased academic motivation.[215] In practice these findings imply that well-planned and executed anti-bullying practices will not only reduce bullying but also improve the child's overall school experience.

The KiVa anti-bullying programme: concrete and systematic tools

In order to achieve consistently successful implementation an intervention programme needs to be systematic and solid. If the programme offers answers to questions like "Who should do the preventive work?", "Who is in charge of solving the acute cases of bullying?" and "What should be done in practice and when?" it is more likely to be successfully implemented at the school. An effective intervention programme at its best offers clear and detailed guidelines for the whole school community to prevent bullying and to effectively tackle all cases.

In practice, the KiVa anti-bullying programme consists of universal and indicated actions (see Table 1). Universal actions focus on preventing bullying by creating an anti-bullying culture. Schools may communicate and show in many ways that they are a KiVa school. They may organize Back-To-School nights for parents, meetings for staff, and a KiVa kick-off at the beginning of each school year for students. The idea is to disseminate widely the basic idea of a school without bullying. Furthermore, there are highly visible vests for teachers to wear while supervising at recess time and posters to signal that the school implements KiVa and that bullying is therefore not tolerated.

Table 1.
Universal and indicated actions included the KiVa anti-bullying programme.

Universal actions	Indicated or specific actions
Staff meeting	Tackling the cases coming to attention
Kick-off	
Parents' newsletter, guide, and Back-to-School night	Series of discussions with the victim and the perpetrator/s effectuated by KiVa teams
Visible symbols, such as posters, vests	Classroom teacher offers support
KiVa student lessons and themes	A few high-status classmates are invited to offer support for the victim
Online KiVa games	
Annual online survey for both students and staff	Parents are informed

An essential part of the preventive work includes student lessons (primary school) and the presentation of themes (middle school). The lessons and themes, delivered during regular school hours, include topics related to social-emotional skills and group dynamics generally, as well as issues related to bullying specifically. For instance, issues such as recognizing bullying, understanding the role of bystanders in the bullying process, safe strategies to support the victim, and the consequences of bullying are addressed. The manuals are concrete with the goal for each lesson being described along with detailed descriptions of various teaching methods and activities (e.g. group discussion, videos, learning-by-doing). In addition, there are three age-specific virtual learning environments available online for the schools implementing KiVa. These online games provide additional material to the student lessons, along with exercises to rehearse the topics covered during the lessons.

Indicated actions are put into operation when cases of bullying are being brought up. Each school implementing KiVa is advised to nominate staff members to be part of KiVa team responsible for handling such cases. They are provided with detailed instructions and training regarding the procedure. There is empirical evidence that the approach is highly efficient. Victimized children who had participated in the discussions reported two weeks after the discussion that the bullying had stopped (78%) or at least decreased (20%).[216]

In addition, student and staff surveys are organized annually for KiVa schools. These schools receive automatically generated feedback on both surveys. This allows schools firstly to follow the trends of the prevalence of bullying and victimization at their own school. Secondly, the student survey offers the possibility of comparing the results to the national trend. Thirdly, the surveys indicate what has been done in an attempt to tackle bullying during the year and what has been achieved. This is a simple and concrete way to evaluate the input compared to the achievements accomplished at the school level.

The KiVa anti-bullying programme promoting whole school approach

The KiVa anti-bullying programme is designed as a whole school programme. Even the logo of the programme reflects the idea that the entire school community is holding hands together and standing up for the same purpose, to stop bullying. KiVa is an acronym, which stands for Kiusaamista Vastaan, against bullying. In the KiVa programme the school community is interpreted broadly and everyone has their own role in tackling bullying. Because the programme is based on the idea that bullying is a group phenomenon every student is seen as part of, not only the problem, but also the solution. Therefore, it is also the students' responsibility to put an end to bullying. Teachers, on the other hand, are at the heart of raising awareness, providing students with the confidence and the strategies to respond constructively to bullying. Parents have the important role of supporting the implementation of the KiVa programme and extending KiVa and its core principles to everyday life at home. Each school implementing the programme has a KiVa team responsible for tackling the acute cases of bullying and ensuring that every student has a safe school environment. This requires some negotiating over who will be included in the KiVa team and over how the KiVa team functions in practice (e.g. which cases to appoint to the KiVa team, where and when the KiVa team meets).

The whole school approach means also an effective launch of the programme from the very beginning. If the basic aim is to create a school without bullying it is essential that every member of the community is included and knows this from the beginning. Furthermore, KiVa should not be a short-term project but rather it should become part of the school's everyday practices. Anti-bullying work is not something that comes and goes: rather the idea underpinning KiVa is to create a school culture where bullying is not tolerated. In practice, we have noticed that taking this task seriously requires considerable resources and effort. Quite typically a school starting on the KiVa anti-bullying programme faces the questions of what the programme is actually about and how can it be implemented. Once these questions are negotiated and the answers are clear the school can implement KiVa successfully. Taken together, the KiVa programme requires that the whole school stands up to bullying. It is designed to become an integral part of the school's everyday life.

The KiVa anti-bullying programme in the long run – supporting implementation

At the moment approximately 90% of the 2400 schools offering basic education in Finland are registered KiVa programme users. Some of them have already implemented KiVa over seven years. The question arises as to how the programme can be effectively sustained over time. An anti-bullying programme can only be efficient if it is implemented properly. This notion holds for the KiVa programme as well. For example, the number and quality of lessons that teachers deliver is associated with the magnitude of change in student-reported victimization.[217] More precisely, the more time teachers used to prepare the KiVa lessons and the higher the proportion of tasks they delivered during the lessons, the larger the reductions in victimization.

Some aspects of implementation have remained strong and others have declined during the roll-out of KiVa in Finland. There are two negative trends connected to KiVa lessons to be noted. Firstly, the implementation of student lessons decreases during each school year. That is, many teachers begin with active lesson delivery, but this falls short towards the middle and especially the end of each school year. Secondly, the overall level of lesson delivery decreases across the years. In 2009–2010, for example, an average of 78% of the KiVa lessons were delivered by teachers, but in 2014–2015 this proportion was only 64%.

In regard to indicated actions there are a few notable trends. Firstly, the number of cases handled by KiVa teams has slightly decreased across the years (from 7.5 to 6.2 cases per year). Importantly, findings based on annual surveys show that the proportion of students who have been in a KiVa team discussion and found it effective, has increased over the years. Furthermore, the follow-up meetings organized a few weeks after the KiVa team discussions and the documentation of the bullying cases have both become more common. These both play an important role in tackling emerging cases. The follow-up meetings in which the KiVa team members meet again with the students who had been involved in bullying are perhaps the most central factor contributing to the efficiency of the indicated actions. Documenting cases of bullying, on the other hand, makes is possible to understand the overall situation of bullying in the school. All of these trends indicate that the programme is heading in the right direction.

The KiVa programme has been found to be effective in reducing victimization and bullying but it is only effective if it is consistently and thoroughly implemented. If the importance of anti-bullying practices were widely recognized on the part of the staff of all schools and municipalities a lot more could be done in future. In practice, for example, a head teacher holds a key role in creating space for high-quality anti-bullying work. Our experiences with the KiVa programme indicate that the level of implementation seems to be higher in schools where the head teacher's support for and commitment to anti-bullying is high.[218]

Conclusion

The KiVa anti-bullying programme is an example where theory and an evidence-based approach, combined with systematic and sustainable implementation nationwide, can deliver desirable social outcomes. These elements are at the heart of the success of the approach. At the moment the core question arising is how to guarantee sustainable and effective implementation in the long run. Teachers hold a central role in implementing a high quality programme. The students change but the teachers and other staff are there to stay. They need occasional motivation boosts and support for their extremely valuable work. KiVa newsletters, quality recommendations regarding high-quality programme implementation, a nationally visible campaign, biennial KiVa days, and the provision of training and support for schools, are of vital importance in keeping up the KiVa spirit in schools. Sharing best practices and experiences seem to be extremely important for teachers.

To conclude, reducing school bullying is not a hopeless task but it certainly is not easy. A realistic aim for a prevention programme such as KiVa is to reduce the prevalence of bullying in the long term and to ensure the sustainability of its carefully designed practices.

Endnotes

[203] See for more detailed description of the program: Salmivalli, C, Poskiparta, E, Ahtola, A, & Haataja, A (2013). The Implementation and effectiveness of the KiVa antibullying program in Finland. *European Psychologist, 18,* 79–88; Herkama, S, Saarento, S, & Salmivalli, C (in press). *The KiVa antibullying program: Lessons learned and future directions.*

[204] See http://www.finlex.fi/en/

[205] Salmivalli, C, Lagerspetz, KM.J, Björkqvist, K, Österman, K, & Kaukiainen, A (1996). Bullying as a group process: Participant roles and their relations to social status within the group. *Aggressive Behavior, 22,* 1–15.

[206] Salmivalli, C, Voeten, M, & Poskiparta, E (2011). Bystanders matter: Associations between reinforcing, defending, and the frequency of bullying in classrooms. *Journal of Clinical Child and Adolescent Psychology, 40,* 668–676.

[207] Kärnä, A, Voeten, M, Little, TD, Poskiparta, E, Kaljonen, A & Salmivalli, C (2011). A large-scale evaluation of the KiVa antibullying program: Grades 4–6. *Child Development, 82,* 311–330.

[208] Saarento, S, Boulton, AJ, & Salmivalli, C (2015). Reducing bullying and victimization: Student- and classroom-level mechanisms of change. *Journal of Abnormal Child Psychology, 43,* 61–76.

[209] Kärnä, A, Voeten, M, Little, TD, Poskiparta, E, Kaljonen, A & Salmivalli, C (2011). Op. cit.

[210] Kärnä, A, Voeten, M, Little, TD, Alanen, E, Poskiparta, E & Salmivalli, C (2013). Effectiveness of the KiVa antibullying program: Grades 1–3 and 7–9. *Journal of Educational Psychology, 105,* 535–551.

[211] Kärnä, A, Voeten, M, Little, TD, Poskiparta, E, Alanen, E & Salmivalli, C (2011). Going to scale: A nonrandomized nationwide trial of the KiVa antibullying program for Grades 1–9. *Journal of Consulting and Clinical Psychology, 79,* 796–805.

[212] Williford, A, Elledge, LC, Boulton, AJ, DePaolis, KJ, Little, TD & Salmivalli, C (2013). Effects of the KiVa antibullying program on cyberbullying and cybervictimization frequency among Finnish youth. *Journal of Clinical Child & Adolescent Psychology, 42,* 820–833.

[213] Salmivalli, C, Kärnä, A, & Poskiparta, E (2011). Counteracting bullying in Finland: The KiVa program and its effects on different forms of being bullied. *International Journal of Behavioral Development, 35,* 405–411.

[214] Williford, A, Boulton, A, Noland, B, Little, TD, Kärnä, A, & Salmivalli, C (2012). Effects of the KiVa anti-bullying program on adolescents' depression, anxiety, and perception of peers. *Journal of abnormal child psychology, 40,* 289–300.

[215] Salmivalli, C, Garandeau, CF & Veenstra, R (2012). KiVa antibullying program: Implications for school adjustment. In AM Ryan & GW Ladd (Eds.), *Peer relationships and adjustment at school* (pp. 279–305). Charlotte, NC: Information Age.

[216] Garandeau, CF, Poskiparta, E, & Salmivalli, C (2014). Tackling acute cases of school bullying in the KiVa anti-bullying program: A comparison of two approaches. *Journal of Abnormal Child Psychology, 42,* 981–991.

[217] Haataja, A, Voeten, M, Boulton, AJ, Ahtola, A, Poskiparta, E & Salmivalli, C (2014). The KiVa antibullying curriculum and outcome: Does fidelity matter? *Journal of School Psychology,* 52, 479–493.

[218] Ahtola, A, Haataja, A, Kärnä, A, Poskiparta, E & Salmivalli, C (2013). Implementation of anti-bullying lessons in primary classrooms: How important is head teachers support? *Educational Research,* 55, 376–392.

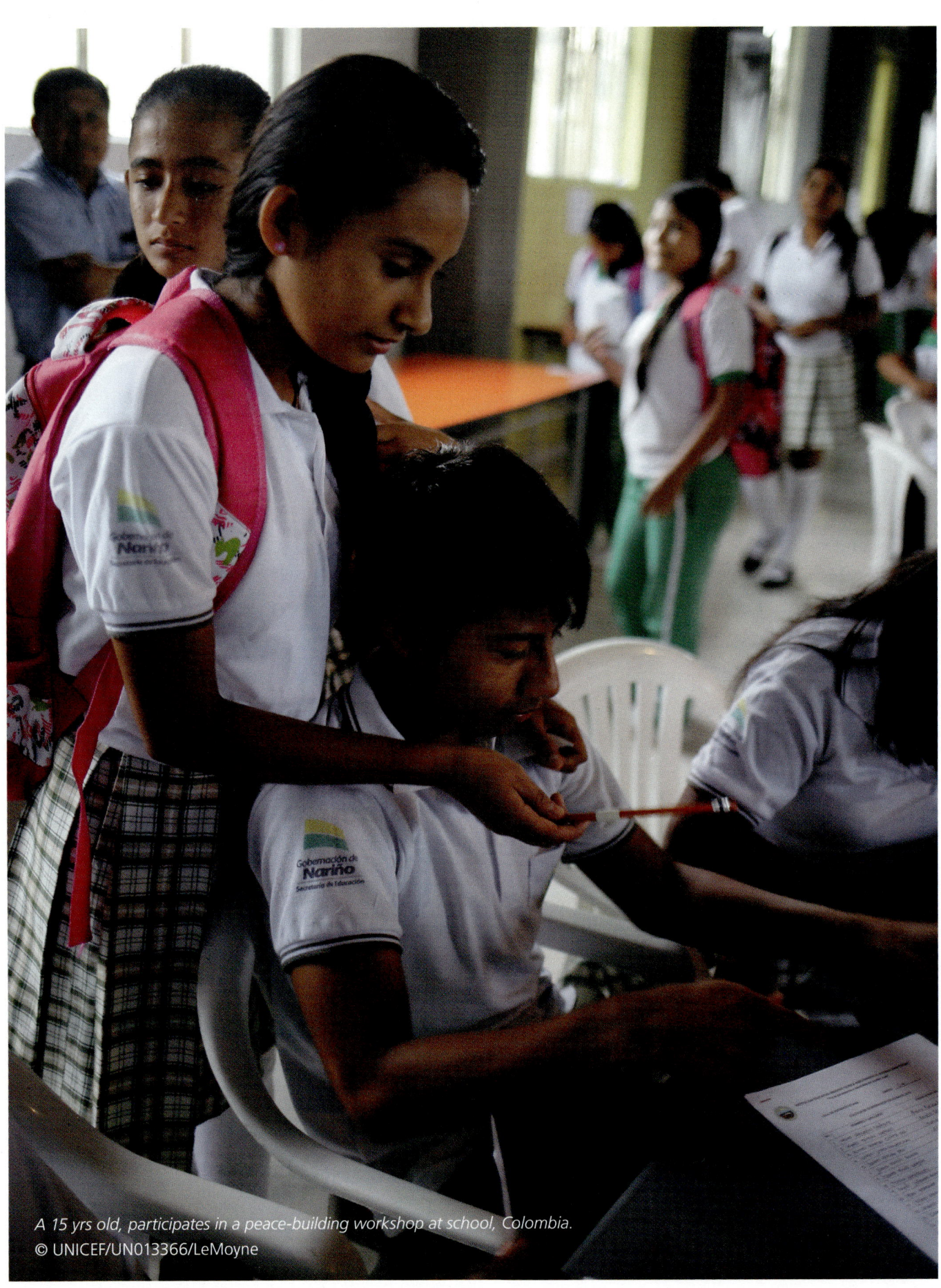

A 15 yrs old, participates in a peace-building workshop at school, Colombia.
© UNICEF/UN013366/LeMoyne

11. Bullying from a gender-based violence perspective
Julie Hanson Swanson and Katharina Anton-Erxleben

Introduction

Gender-based violence in and around educational settings is a global phenomenon. Worldwide, 246 million young boys and girls experience violence at or on their way to school every year. This paper provides the rationale for grounding bullying within a gendered framework of school-related gender-based violence (SRGBV). It examines the cost of bullying to governments in low and middle-income countries and its impact on student well-being and academic performance. A conceptual framework and toolkit for measuring SRGBV is also discussed.

What is School-Related Gender-Based Violence?

School-related gender-based violence is physical, sexual or psychological violence or abuse that is based on gendered stereotypes or that targets students on the basis of their sex, sexuality or gender identities. School-related gender-based violence reinforces gender roles and perpetuates gender inequalities. It includes rape, unwanted sexual touching, unwanted sexual comments, corporal punishment, and bullying. Violence can take place in formal and non-formal schools, on school grounds, going to and from school, in school dormitories, in cyberspace or through mobile phone technology. School-related gender-based violence may be perpetrated by teachers, students, or community members. Both girls and boys can be victims, as well as perpetrators.

Why is it Important to Conceptualize Bullying as Gendered?

Gender is a social construct that refers to relations between and among men and women and boys and girls, based on their relative roles in the home, school, community and society. Gender norms dictate what types of behaviours are generally considered acceptable, appropriate, or desirable for women, men, boys and girls. These are usually centred on conceptions of femininity and masculinity. As a social construct, gender norms and roles vary across cultures, are dynamic and can change over time. School violence is gendered as it is inextricably linked with power and social dynamics, gender inequalities, sexuality, and gender identity[219]. Conceptualizing school violence as profoundly gendered provides a coherent framework for analysis, informs prevention interventions, and explicitly identifies girls and boys as both potential victims and perpetrators.

In places where gender inequality is the norm, boys often learn to express their masculinity through dominant and aggressive behaviour, and girls often learn to be passive, submissive, and accepting of violence directed against them. When boys are socialized to dominate others verbally or physically to prove their masculinity, they internalize a mindset that can lead to bullying and other forms of gender-based violence. Boys who do not fit into conventional notions of masculinity may be emotionally or physically abused, as are girls who do not fit into conventional notions of femininity. When teachers and other school personnel respond to incidents of violence by saying, "Boys will be boys", "Girls ask for it,", or "Girls need to act like girls" then these statements reinforce the belief that specific forms of violence are an unchallenged way of life and are, therefore, acceptable. These entrenched gender norms and beliefs are self-reinforcing and serve to perpetuate violence in schools and elsewhere.

The gendered differences in bullying experienced by boys and girls are not always recognized. Boys and girls are bullied at similar rates,[220] but boys are more often perpetrators than girls[221], and the type of bullying that girls and boys experience is different: girls more often experience psychological bullying[222] such as gossip and name calling and boys more often experience physical bullying.[223] Conformity with heterosexual gender norms also affects who gets bullied[224] and homophobic bullying (i.e., bullying related to perceived or real non-heterosexual gender identities) especially often crosses the line into sexual harassment.[225]

As part of any bullying intervention at the school level, programmes need to challenge gender stereotypes that foster inequitable power relationships between boys and girls. This includes challenging gender norms that pressure boys into violent, aggressive behaviours that harm themselves and others and norms that pressure girls to not assert themselves and increase their risk of being victims. Children need the tools to express themselves assertively rather than aggressively and to respond to conflict in non-violent ways. Schools also need to be safe spaces to protect children who do not conform to societal norms of masculinity and femininity from being bullied.

What are the Costs to Bullying?

Emotional/Physical Costs. The negative effects of bullying are well-documented and often severe. Children who are victims of bullying are more likely to experience emotional and mental health problems.[226] The most common mental health issues that have been associated with bullying are depression and thoughts of suicide.[227] A cross-cultural study[228] found that more than 30% of bullied students reported feelings of sadness and more than 20% had thoughts of suicide. Psychological problems appear to be worse for sexual minorities who are bullied than for other students.[229] Children who are the victims of non-sexual, school-related violence are also much more likely to participate in risky behaviours, including using drugs, smoking cigarettes, drinking alcohol, and having unsafe sex.[230]

In addition, physical symptoms have been associated with the experience of bullying. Across countries, Nansel and colleagues found that both victims and perpetrators of bullying experienced health problems at a higher rate than those who were not involved in bullying.[231] Other studies also confirmed these effects, with health problems differentially worse for girls than for boys.[232] Health problems such as headaches, stomach aches, and having trouble sleeping are common.[233] In one study, more than 70% of bullied students reported having insomnia.[234] Because bullying and the threat of bullying usually exist across time, sustained changes in educational, mental, and physical outcomes can be detected.[235]

Academic Costs. Few studies in any part of the world have examined the cost of bullying on students' educational achievement. RTI International was commissioned by USAID to conduct a literature review of the available evidence on school violence and learning, with particular, but not sole, reference to developing countries. The Literature Review on the Intersection of Safe Learning Environments and Educational Achievement found support for a relationship between school violence and learning.[236] For example, the Progress in International Reading Literacy Study (PIRLS) and the Trends in International Mathematics and Science Study (TIMSS), two of the very few large-scale studies that provide internationally comparable data on a variety of education indicators, show a systematic correlation between bullying and other measures of

Figure 1.
Frequency of student reporting of weekly bullying

Note: Data provided by IEA's PIRLS and TIMSS 2011. In total, 36,602 students are in the bar graph. By country, Botswana includes 13,795, Ghana 7,323, and South Africa, 15,848 students

school safety and discipline with lower test scores both in developed and developing countries.[237]

While these correlational studies do not imply a causal effect and cannot separate effects of school safety, discipline, and bullying from other characteristics of these schools, such as lack of resources and lack of trained teachers among others, a follow-up study conducted a "deeper dive" into existing 2011 PIRLS and TIMMS data. USAID commissioned the study, The Relationship Between School-Related Gender-Based Violence and Student Performance in Botswana, Ghana, and South Africa, with the Center on Conflict and Development at Texas A&M University to identify and quantify a causal effect of bullying on academic performance and identify other demographic and economic covariates that influence academic performance. By using different statistical techniques the study was able to move beyond merely showing a correlation and supports an interpretation in which bullying has a causal effect on achievement.

The study revealed that bullying is extremely pervasive in Botswana, Ghana, and South Africa, with approximately 80% of the surveyed students bullied monthly and almost 50% bullied weekly, and that bullying was one of the key drivers of lower academic performance (Figure 1).[238] For example, in Botswana, students who experience bullying score lower than those who are not bullied by between 14 and 32 points on the international science, math and reading tests, which corresponds to a 4% decrease in reading scores to an 8% decrease in science test scores. In Ghana, students who experience bullying perform worse by approximately 17 and 23 points corresponding to a five to 7% decrease. In South Africa, students who are bullied score 25 points less than those who are not bullied, corresponding to a 6% decrease in reading scores. Figure 2 shows the decrease in performance attributed to bullying in Botswana. Some of the other factors studied also had an effect on students' performance, such as parents' education or teachers' experience, which are often thought of as strong determinants of students' ability to succeed in school. However, bullying seems to outweigh all of these factors.

Interestingly, there are gender differential impacts of bullying on academic performance that are substantial but differ among countries: in Botswana, female students who experienced bullying score 28 points less on average than those who are not bullied; while their bullied male peers suffer by 21 points— an approximate average difference of 7 points. In South Africa the reverse is true, with male students who experienced bullying scoring 27

Figure 2.
Effects of weekly bullying in Botswana on academic performance, PSM estimate

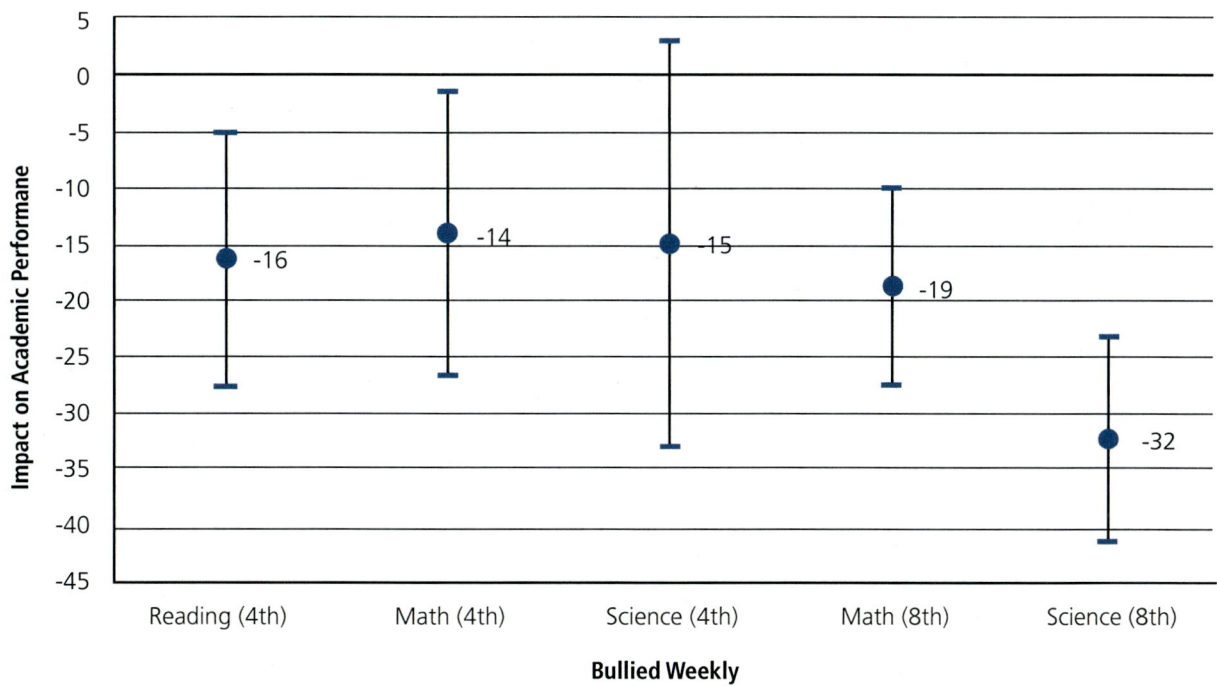

Note: Data provided by IEA's PIRLS and TIMSS 2011. Reading score is only available for 4th graders. However, the other subjects contain both 4th and 8th graders.

points less on average than those who are not bullied as compared to 19 points for bullied female students. In Ghana there was a not a significant difference between boys and girls.

Financial Costs. A recent analysis of TIMSS, PIRLS, prePIRLS, and the Programme for International Student Assessment (PISA) data shows that bullying, low school safety, and lack of discipline can be associated with the loss of one primary grade of schooling, which translates to a yearly cost of around US$17 billion to low and middle-income countries — as compared to US$13 billion, which is the total yearly amount spent on overseas assistance grants for education interventions.[239] Although US$17 billion is a significant sum, it is nonetheless a conservative estimate because: a) it is limited to children who stay in school and are tested; b) it does not include indirect costs, such as diverting teacher and principal attention to the problem, requiring additional teachers or law enforcement resources or additional time for ministry of education officials for dealing with cases of severe maltreatment; and c) this estimate does not include the cost of any type of violence prevention programming.

Why Generate Data on Bullying within an SRGBV Measurement Framework?

The current evidence base on the emotional, physical, academic, and financial costs of bullying is important but insufficient. The Literature Review on the Intersection of Safe Learning Environments and Educational Achievement concluded that "the complex interplay of school violence and disruption, academic achievement, and prevention approaches is not well understood".[240] This is especially true of developing countries because to date, relevant research in developed countries has far outweighed that in developing countries. Regions other than sub-Saharan Africa are especially under-represented. The analyses of TIMSS and PIRLS data make an important case, but leave many questions unanswered. For example, in their current form, PIRLS and TIMSS cannot provide insights about the diverse experiences of individual students arising from their social identities. Furthermore, they are somewhat limited in what aspects of bullying and school safety more broadly they provide information on, and are silent on other forms of SRGBV, such as corporal punishment and sexual violence. While much of the research on bullying has been conducted in developed countries, other types of violence have often been studied in Africa, resulting in a large gap of knowledge about SRGBV in other regions.

Generally, studies on SRGBV have used different measurement instruments and indicator definitions. In short, research on the linkages between school safety, violence, educational achievement, and costs, is sparse and patchy, making reliable comparisons among locations or analyses of trends difficult.

School-related gender-based violence is still relatively new as a development field and a globally recognized framework with standardized definitions, indicators, and evaluation methodologies does not yet exist. Given that SRGBV cuts across such diverse areas as corporal punishment, sexual violence and bullying, pulling the strands together to make a cohesive whole that could generate comprehensive, internationally comparable data would make an important contribution to raising awareness and influencing policy and funding decisions.

To fill this gap, USAID is developing a conceptual framework and measurement instrument that will capture the most common forms of SRGBV and provide guidance on conducting rigorous SRGBV research, monitoring and evaluation. This toolkit is being developed in partnership with the Global Partners' Working Group to End SRGBV, which is co-hosted by the United Nations Girls' Education Initiative (UNGEI) and the United Nations Educational, Scientific, and Cultural Organization (UNESCO). For this Conceptual Framework and Toolkit for Measuring School-Related Gender-Based Violence, the various forms of SRGBV were categorized into three broad groups: bullying and other non-sexual forms of intimidation; corporal punishment; and sexual violence (See Figure 3).

As the lack of standardized definitions has been identified as a gap in researching all forms of SRGBV, "bullying", as well as the other types of SRGBV, has been defined within the framework as comprehensively as possible by drawing on a broad body of literature. Bullying is characterized as a non-sexual form of violence that includes a range of psychological and physical acts of intimidation, which may be detrimental to the academic, social, emotional, and physical development of the children and young people who experience it.[241] Bullying can also take on sexual forms; therefore, it is not always easy to distinguish it from sexual harassment. However, in this conceptual measurement framework, acts of physical and psychological intimidation that are primarily of a sexual nature are defined as "sexual harassment" and are considered to be a form of sexual violence to keep the multiple dimensions of the measurement framework separate.

Figure 3.
Conceptual Framework for Measuring SRGBV

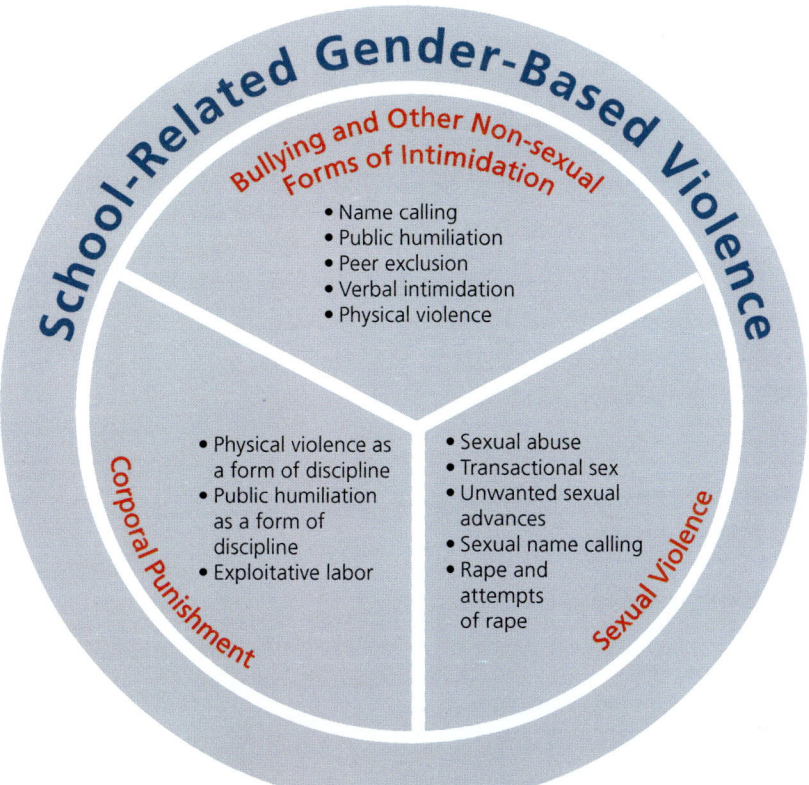

The category of bullying and non-sexual forms of intimidation in the measurement framework include physical bullying (e.g., pulling on someone's clothes or hair, grabbing a bag), verbal bullying (e.g., name calling, public humiliation or teasing), and implicit bullying (sometimes referred to as relational bullying).[242] Implicit bullying includes the following: excluding a peer from social circles on the playground or in the cafeteria, spreading rumours, or telling fellow peers "not to be his or her friend." Petty theft that is marked by intimidation is also a form of bullying, particularly if it is repetitive.[243]

Children from around the world also experience other acts of intimidation, including threats or acts of non-sexual physical assault experienced while students travel to and from school and in school by teachers and peers, as well as excessive, unrelenting use of profanity.[244] With the advent of smartphones and the social media, acts of intimidation and threats are being perpetrated through SMS (text) messages and on social media. "Cyberbullying" has been defined as "aggressive, intentional acts carried out by groups or individuals using electronic forms of contact, repeatedly and over time, against victims who cannot easily defend themselves".[245]

The two most defining characteristics of bullying and other non-sexual forms of intimidation are the intention to harm, either physically or psychologically, and the power differential that exists between the perpetrator and the victim. The power differential that exists between the perpetrator and the victim make specific populations more vulnerable to intimidation and bullying. These populations include students who are younger than the perpetrator; students who are perceived as not portraying strong heterosexual identities; children from poor families; children of ethnic, religious, or racial minorities; children with disabilities and orphaned children.[246]

A New Conceptual Framework for Measuring SRGBV

The Conceptual Framework for Measuring SRGBV is supported by a toolkit that consists of a suite of survey instruments that can be used in applied research, during routine monitoring, and during impact evaluations of SRGBV prevention and response programmes. The instruments were developed for: 1) students aged 8 to 18 years (broken down to 8-12, 13-15, and 16-18 age groups); 2) teachers and other school personnel; and 3) parents and other

> **Box 1: Definition and Types of Bullying**
>
> Bullying is defined as any non-sexual form of intimidation that is perpetrated with intention to harm, either physically or psychologically. Although the prevalence of bullying has been shown to be similar for girls and boys, the experience of bullying is different for girls and boys. Girls are more likely than boys to be the victim of psychological bullying, such as gossip and name calling, whereas boys may experience more physical victimization. The act of bullying is grounded in the power differential that exists between the perpetrator and the victim. Acts of physical bullying range from severe acts of physical violence such as beatings to less harsh acts of violence such as pulling at someone's clothes or hair or grabbing students' belongings. Acts of psychological bullying include name calling, public humiliation, and other forms of teasing, excluding sexual harassment. Intentional exclusion of a peer from social circles (sometimes referred to as "relational bullying") and theft are also forms of bullying as is intimidating students via text messaging or on social media sites, referred to as cyberbullying. Bullying and other non-sexual forms of intimidation can be perpetrated by peers, teachers, other school staff, and persons encountered on the way to and from school.[247]

caregivers at the primary or secondary school level. They were informed by a recent literature review on how SRGBV is defined and studied and draw from existing questionnaires and surveys focusing on different aspects of SRGBV (e.g., bullying, sexual harassment, corporal punishment).[248]

The surveys focus on the one hand on generating quantitative data on the nature and extent of the various forms of SRGBV discussed above, including bullying, but also probe attitudes and beliefs about gender equality, gender norms, and the power relations that produce and perpetuate SRGBV, which is crucial to understanding bullying and other forms of SRGBV in the context of gender dynamics more broadly. The surveys also collect background information about the school climate and student demographics to better understand potential risk factors.

The modules that compose each of the three survey sets are as follows:

SRGBV Scenarios. The SRGBV measurement toolkit provides a set of SRGBV scenarios (i.e., stories to serve as an "icebreaker") and associated interview guidelines from which users can select additional or replacement icebreakers to be used with the Survey of Experiences of SRGBV: Students or as an additional or alternative tool to collect information about students' experiences of SRGBV. This is based on research that demonstrates that during direct interviews, gradually moving from less threatening conversations to the more difficult ones such as victimization or perpetration of violence is advisable. Play or icebreaking sessions are commonly used as an entry into more substantive individual or group discussions.[249] Stories, pictures, video clips, and puppets have all been used as stimuli to seed conversation about violence against children.[250]

Survey of experiences with SRGBV. The student survey includes questions regarding a student's experience with bullying and sexual violence as both a victim and perpetrator and with corporal punishment as a victim. The teacher survey is designed to collect two types of information from teachers and other school personnel. The first series of questions collects information about their knowledge of sexual violence that is perpetrated against students by other teachers or school personnel. The second series of questions collects information from teachers and other school personnel about their perceptions of the levels of specific acts of SRGBV, including different acts of bullying, corporal punishment, and sexual violence.

Survey of Teacher Disciplinary Practices. During this survey, teachers listen to statements read by the researcher that describe different disciplinary practices and different strategies for encouraging students in their behaviour and schoolwork.

Surveys of Attitudes and Beliefs. One of the most common strategies of SRGBV prevention interventions is to transform the attitudes and beliefs that have served to produce and perpetuate gendered violence in and around schools. The Surveys of Attitudes and Beliefs are designed to collect information from students, teachers and other school personnel, and parents or caregivers regarding their attitudes and beliefs about gender equality, gender norms, and the prevailing power relations that exist in the school, community and home.

Surveys of Perceptions of School Climate. The instruments include measures of respondents' perceptions of school climate along the following dimensions: students' sense of belonging in the school, acceptance of diversity, and inclusion; child protective practices and structures; discipline and fairness; student–student relationships; student–teacher relationships; and teacher–staff relationships. The purpose of the surveys is to obtain perspectives from students, teachers and other school personnel, and parents or caregivers about how positive the school environment is.

Survey of Student Demographics and Socio-Economic Wealth. Students who live in poverty, orphans, and those with disabilities are among those at high risk for being targets of all forms of SRGBV. This survey is designed to provide the user with an opportunity to characterize the student respondents and investigate these risk factors in the local context.

Together, the survey instruments are envisioned to give a comprehensive picture of the prevalence, dynamics, and gender dimensions of SRGBV. It enables research to link different forms of violence, including bullying, to underlying attitudes and beliefs, norms, and power relations, and will help fill some of the gaps in our understanding of school violence. Some of the instruments are currently being piloted by the Literacy Achievement and Retention Activity (LARA) in Uganda, a USAID-funded programme implemented by RTI International aiming to improve reading skills and retention in primary grades through better reading instruction and reduction of SRGBV.

Conclusion

Bullying has a significant cost on education systems, and students' well-being and academic achievement across developing countries. Bullying can be associated with the loss of one primary grade of schooling, which translates to a yearly cost of around US$17 billion to low and middle-income countries. Students who are bullied have experienced an 8% decrease in science test scores and a 6% decrease in reading scores on global achievement tests. The implication for policymakers and donors is that if forms of SRGBV such as bullying are allowed to continue unchecked in schools, this will reduce test scores and the potential of education investments cannot be fully achieved.

Bullying is merely one aspect of gender-based violence that impacts on the daily lives of girls and boys worldwide. Bullying, corporal punishment and sexual violence, collectively known as school-related gender-based violence, must be addressed within a gender framework, which will best serve to prevent SRGBV and sustain this transformation in the long run.

Endnotes

[219] Leach, F et al. (Eds) (2006). *Combating gender violence in and around schools.* Stoke on Trent, Trentham Books.

[220] Due, P et al. (2005). Bullying and Symptoms among School-Aged Children: International Comparative Cross Sectional Study in 28 Countries. *European Journal of Public Health,* 15(2).

[221] Hussein, MH (2010). The Peer Interaction in Primary School Questionnaire: Testing for Measurement Equivalence and Latent Mean Differences in Bullying between Gender in Egypt, Saudi Arabia and the USA. *Social Psychology of Education,* 13(1).

[222] Carrera-Fernandez, M et al. (2013). Bullying Among Spanish Secondary Education Students: The Role of Gender Traits, Sexism, and Homophobia. *Journal of Interpersonal Violence,* 28(14).

[223] Roman, M et al. (2011). Latin America: School Bullying and Academic Achievement. *Cepal Review,* 104.

[224] Drury, K et al. (2013). Victimization and Gender Identity in Single-sex and Mixed-sex Schools: Examining Contextual Variations in Pressure to Conform to Gender Norms. *Sex Roles,* 69(7-8); Gruber, J et al. (2008). Comparing the Impact of Bullying and Sexual Harassment Victimization on the Mental and Physical Health of Adolescents. *Sex Roles,* 59(1/2); Navarro, R et al. (2011). Bullying-victimization Problems and Aggressive Tendencies in Spanish Secondary Schools Students: The Role of Gender Stereotypical Traits. *Social Psychology of Education,* 14(4); Toomey, RB et al. (2010). Gender-nonconforming Lesbian, Gay, Bisexual, and Transgender Youth: School Victimization and Young Adult Psychosocial Adjustment. *Developmental Psychology,* 46(6).

[225] Bisika, T et al. (2009). Gender-Violence and Education in Malawi: A Study of Violence Against Girls as an Obstruction to Universal Primary School Education. *Journal of Gender Studies* 18(3); Espelage, D et al. (2012). Bullying Perpetration and Subsequent Sexual Violence Perpetration among Middle School Students. *Journal of Adolescent Health,* 50(1).

[226] Nansel, TR et al. (2004). Cross-national consistency in the relationship between bullying behaviors and psychosocial adjustment. *Archives of Pediatrics & Adolescent Medicine* 158(8):730–736.

[227] Ncontsa, V et al. (2013). The nature, causes and effects of school violence in South African high schools. *South African Journal of Education* 33(3). 15 pages; Kim, YS et al. (2005). School bullying and suicidal risk in Korean middle school students. *Pediatrics* 115(2):357–363.

[228] Fleming, LC et al. (2009). Bullying among middle-school students in low and middle-income countries. *Health Promotion International* 25(1):73–84.

[229] Toomey, R et al. (2013). Gender-nonconforming lesbian, gay, bisexual, and transgender youth: School victimization and young adult psychosocial adjustment. *Psychology of Sexual Orientation and Gender Diversity* 1(S):71–80.

[230] Fleming, LC et al. (2009). Op. cit.

[231] Nansel, TR et al. (2004). Op. cit.

[232] Yen, CF et al. (2013). Association between types of involvement in school bullying and different dimensions of anxiety symptoms and the moderating effects of age and gender in Taiwanese adolescents. *Child Abuse & Neglect* 37(4):263–272.

[233] Gruber, J et al. (2008). Op. cit.

[234] Fleming, LC et al. (2009). Op. cit.

[235] RTI International. (2016). *Literature Review on School-Related Gender-Based Violence: How it is Defined and Studied.* Washington, DC, US Agency for International Development.

[236] RTI International. (2013). *Literature Review on the Intersection of Safe Learning Environments and Educational Achievement.* Washington, DC, U.S. Agency for International Development.

[237] Mullis, IVS et al. (2012a). *TIMSS 2011 International Results in Mathematics.* TIMSS and PIRLS International Study Center, Boston College, Chestnut Hill, MA; Mullis, IVS et al. (2012b). *Progress in International Reading Study (PIRLS) 2011 International Results in Reading.* TIMSS and PIRLS International Study Center, Boston College, Chestnut Hill, MA.

[238] Kibriya et al. (2016). *The Effects of School-Related Gender-Based Violence on Academic Performance: Evidence from Botswana, Ghana, and South Africa.* College Station, Texas, Center on Conflict and Development, Texas A&M University.

[239] RTI, International. (2015). *Fact Sheet: What is the Cost of School-Related Gender-Based Violence?* Washington, DC, U.S. Agency for International Development.

[240] Cornell, DG et al. (2010). Why do school order and safety matter? *Educational Researcher* 39: 7-15.

[241] Fleming, LC et al. (2009). Op. cit.:73–84; Gruber, J et al. (2008). Op. cit.; Kibriya et al. (2016). Op. cit.; Nansel, TR et al. (2004). Op. cit.; Roman, M et al. (2011). Op. cit.; RTI International. (2013). Op. cit.

[242] Olweus, D et al. (2010). Bullying in school: Evaluation and dissemination of the Olweus Bullying Prevention Program. *American Journal of Orthopsychiatry* 80(1):124–134.

[243] Ncontsa, V et al. (2013). Op. cit.; Roman, M et al. (2011). Op. cit.

[244] Bisika, T et al. (2009). Op. cit.; Roman, M et al. (2011). Op. cit.; Parkes, J et al. (2011). *Stop Violence Against Girls in School: A Cross-Country Analysis of Baseline Research from Ghana, Kenya and Mozambique.* Johannesburg, South Africa: ActionAid International. Available at http://www.actionaidusa.org/sites/files/actionaid/svags__a_cross_country_analysis_of_baseline_research_from_ghana_kenya_and_mozambique.pdf

[245] Burton, P et al. (2009). Inescapable violence: *Cyber bullying and electronic violence against young people in South Africa.* Centre for Justice and Crime Prevention, CJCP Issue Paper, No. 8. Available at http://cyberbullying.ezipezi.com/downloads/IssuePaper8-InescapableViolence-CyberAggression.pdf

[246] Bisika, T et al. (2009). Op. cit.; Parkes, J et al. (2011). Op. cit; Ringrose, J et al. (2010). Normative cruelties and gender deviants: The performative effects of bully discourses for girls and boys in school. *British Educational Research Journal* 36(4):573–596.

[247] Olweus, D (1993). *Bullying at School: What We Know and What We Can Do.* Malden, MA, Blackwell Publishing.

[248] RTI International. (2016). Op. cit.

[249] Kacker, L et al. (2007). *Study on Child Abuse: India 2007.* New Delhi, India, India Ministry of Women and Child Development.

[250] Ennew, J *et al.* (2004). *Resource Handbook: How to Research the Physical and Emotional Punishment of Children.* Bangkok, Thailand, International Save the Children Alliance; Kacker, L *et al.* (2007). Op. cit.; Bonati, G (2006). *Monitoring and Evaluation with Children: A Short Guide.* Lome, Togo, Plan Togo; Save the Children. (2004). *So You Want to Involve Children in Research? A Toolkit Supporting Children's Meaningful and Ethical Participation in Research Relating to Violence Against Children.* Stockholm, Sweden, Save the Children.

Laura and Ludmila are two of 13 children participating in a photography workshop, Russian Federation.
© UNICEF/UNI42372/Pirozzi

12. Tailoring different bullying prevention approaches to a national context

Ersilia Menesini and Annalaura Nocentini

Introduction

Research into aggressive behaviour and particularly into bullying has increased significantly over the last 30 years. One of the reasons for this is a rise in concern for the protection of human rights in general, including in particular the right of children not to be victimized.[251] There has also been an increase in the understanding of the pervasive long-term effects that such victimization has on children. Bullying compromises several of the rights outlined in the United Nations Convention on the Rights of the Child including the right to education.[252]

The prevalence of the phenomenon of bullying across the world and its serious short-term and long-term psychological consequences has prompted researchers to consider and evaluate intervention models. Recent meta-analyses have highlighted a wide variety of results, with some interventions shown to be highly effective while others have had little impact.[253] There are several possible explanations for this, one of which is that interventions can be less than effective when based on inadequate research and theories.[25] Another aspect often overlooked in evaluations is that interventions can have different impacts on different population sub-groups.[255]

Interventions aimed at targeting the whole school, in a holistic approach, seem to be the most effective. Research shows that these produce an average decrease in bullying of 20%-23% and a decrease in victimization of 17%-20%, though the effects seem to vary across the different programmes.[256] However, whole-school programmes are often complex since they aim at targeting individual students, teachers, school staff, as well as parents and all classrooms. They also include different components targeted at the different groups: students, teachers and parents. Although some components might work better than others if used independently, it appears likely that they are most effective when used together.

Anti-bullying intervention in Italy: evidence of effectiveness

Bullying problems in Italy are particularly relevant today. A recent international survey conducted by the World Health Organization, Health Behaviour in School-aged Children, showed an increasing rate of bullying in children in Italy aged 11 from 2010 to 2014.[257] These increases ranged from 20.7% to 25.7% for males and from 9.2% to 17.3% for females. However, in terms of interventions to address the bullying problems in Italy, these have mostly been unsystematic, only carried-out at class-level, and rarely evaluated in terms of efficacy.[258] Thus, there is a clear and urgent need in Italy for interventions that are both evidence-based and more systematically implemented.

In order to fill the gap in evidence-based interventions in Italy our research group at the University of Florence decided to work in two parallel directions: 1) To consider how to adapt the Finnish KiVa anti-bullying programme to the Italian culture and situation[259] and; 2) To develop and evaluate an innovative Italian prevention programme for adolescents - *The Notrap! Program*.[260]

Adapting an already existing evidence-based intervention such as KiVa has several benefits, considering the long process needed to meet the standards of evidence. However, replicating the evaluation studies of evidence-based interventions involves challenges such as: balancing fidelity to the original programme with adaptation; tailoring the intervention to meet the cultural needs of the new context and participants; and adjusting organizational structures to accommodate the specific requirements of the programme. On the other hand, working with "home grown" programmes makes it possible to meet the specific demands of differing cultural and organizational structures and address the specific needs and characteristics of the local target population.

Starting from these considerations, we decided to: 1) adapt and evaluate an imported evidence-based intervention for a bullying prevention with younger children, given the lack of such an intervention in Italy for this developmental stage; and 2) develop and evaluate "home grown" anti-bullying programmes for adolescents, drawing on the experiences of the research group with older children. The evaluation of both these programmes showed them to be effective in Italy.

The KiVa anti-bullying programme in Italy was evaluated through a randomized control trial of 2,042 students in grades 4 and 6. Multilevel models showed that KiVa reduced bullying and victimization and increased pro-victim attitudes and empathy toward the victim in grade 4, with effect sizes from .24 to .40. In grade 6, KiVa reduced bullying, victimization and pro-bullying attitudes: the effects were smaller as compared to grade 4, yet still significant. For the evaluation of *The NoTrap! Program*, developed in Italy, two quasi-experimental trials involving adolescents attending their first year at different high schools were conducted. In Trial 1, results showed that target variables were stable for the control group but decreased significantly over time for the experimental group. Results were also stable at the follow-up, six months later. In Trial 2, results consistently indicated that there was a decrease in bullying and cyberbullying over time (pre- and post-test) in the experimental group but not in the control group and that this decrease was similar for boys and girls.

Although these two programmes are active in some Italian schools, they have not been implemented widely nor consistently across the country. In fact, despite the Italian Ministry of Education being engaged in the prevention of bullying since 2007, no national initiatives have been undertaken to combat the problem. Schools have been encouraged to work on prevention but they have not been provided with either specific programmes or toolkits. In April 2015 new guidelines were presented by the Ministry to schools in Italy. In these guidelines specific attention is devoted to cyberbullying and online risks to students. Specifically, each school, networking with other schools, and drawing on existing human and financial resources, is called upon to put in place the necessary preventive actions as well as specific training modules to prevent the effect of bullying on children and students. In the area of ICT, the Ministry of Education is coordinating the Safer Internet Centre Italy (a portal with online and face to face actions supported by the EU) in efforts to provide schools with toolkits and materials to monitor and address bullying and cyberbullying.[261]

Future Directions: from universal prevention to indicated interventions

Although we know that prevention and a whole-school approach are the most promising ways to address bullying[262] we agree with the Italian Ministry of Education on the necessity to work immediately towards a minimum standard protocol to address bullying incidents in school contexts. But in this field, there are few studies on the effectiveness of indicated interventions that confront bullying.[263]

To provide an insight into how this might be done, we can refer to the classifications used often in health and preventive interventions: primary, secondary and tertiary preventions; and also to the most recent classifications that distinguish between universal, selected, and indicated preventions.

Primary prevention against bullying aims to teach children and teenagers positive ways to interact with classmates and to enable them to understand the harmful consequences of taking part in certain conduct. Secondary prevention or indicated interventions (as classified by the American Institute of Medicine) is undertaken in response to particular bullying incidents: it may provide interventions with either the victim or the bully. The goal at this stage is to manage the case, giving support to the victim or mediating future conflicts. Finally, the tertiary prevention approach consists in the treatment and rehabilitation of young people involved in the problem: in particular, it addresses monitoring of the phenomena, counselling facilities, therapeutic interventions for victims, addressing complaints and undertaking any significant actions needed to deal with bullies.

The distinction between universal, selected and indicated has been introduced by the American Institute of Medicine to better define the term primary prevention in relation to different subgroups of population. Universal prevention, in fact, includes strategies that are delivered to broad populations without consideration of individual differences in risk behaviour. Indicated prevention, on the other hand, designs interventions to address certain risk conditions. Specifically, indicated populations are identified on the basis of individual risk factors or initiation behaviours. An example of an indicated group with respect to bullying would be those students, either bullies or victims, who are involved in the problem.

Universal prevention of bullying is of fundamental importance in order to create a culture and an ethic of anti-bullying in the school. It needs to be understood as a rule that shows mutual respect among all students and adults. But prevention does not always work the same way with all students and in all contexts: even in schools where there is a good universal prevention programme, it is still possible to find bullying or cyberbullying incidents. The school cannot expect to ignore these and hope that such situations will be resolved by themselves without any specific intervention. Such emergencies must be addressed by the schools and managed in order to: 1) stop/alleviate the suffering of the victim; 2) enhance awareness in the bullies or in the cyberbullies about the impact of what they have done; 3) show all the other students that bullying is not accepted in the school and that these incidents will not be allowed to happen without intervention; and 4) show parents of the victims, and more generally the parents of all students at the school, that the school knows how to handle such cases.

Although in Italy there are some interventions for primary prevention of bullying in specific schools, there is no national programme or distribution of developed toolkits against bullying and there is no uniform approach to the problem. Levels of awareness of the problems of bullying and the interventions available to address it also vary widely in different areas and schools around the country. Therefore it is critical that the government and researchers work together in order to provide schools with a minimum standard of intervention to address and confront the problem.

This is why we decided, in collaboration with the Ministry of Education, to work on an experimental project to address bullying incidents in school settings with the aim of providing a standardized and evaluated protocol to intervene in such situations.

From a literature review there are several methods and strategies to respond to bullying[264]. The different methods are not alternatives to prevention, but rather can be integrated or used in relation to the specific characteristics of the problem. These methods can be grouped into six main categories:

1. The traditional disciplinary approach
2. The approach to enhance the social skills of the victim
3. The mediation approach
4. The restorative approach
5. The method of group support
6. The shared concern method

Below, we examine the benefits and risks for each method.

The traditional disciplinary approach

This approach involves the use of direct sanctions against the bullies. It can be used in schools where there are regulations about the acceptability of particular behaviour and explanations of the consequences of the violation of these rules. Usually the consequences involve a penalty for the responsible student. This approach sends a clear message to all students about the unacceptability of certain behaviour and shows the bully that he or she will be punished for the incident. For the use of this approach to be effective, there must be a clear definition and communication of standards of behaviour and of their consequences in the school. Furthermore, there must be class discussions on the rules of conduct and of the criteria for justifying the use of sanctions. With this approach the entire school community and parents need to be aware of the existence and systematic application of this system. Disciplinary action must be accompanied by counselling activities with the students, and when possible with parents, explaining why decisions were taken.

The use of sanctions has limitations including that it does not necessarily result in a change in attitudes and behaviours: the older kids are less prone to be influenced by the fear of sanctions and the sanction can be perceived as a "vindictive action" and reinforce the negative identity of the bully. The scientific literature has shown that this method is not more effective than other non-punitive strategies. Recent studies suggest that the effectiveness of disciplinary practices is dependent on context, such as school stage (primary/secondary), the chronicity of bullying and the type of disciplinary practice.

The approach to enhance the social skills of the victim

This approach tends to help the victim to deal with the bullying situation effectively through promoting some of his/her personal and social skills. The possible application of this is through assertiveness training for the victims: increasing their capacity to learn how to make friends, and empowering them to use emotional intelligence in an interpersonal context.

This approach cannot be used in cases of physical bullying, or when there is a significant imbalance of power between the bully and the victim. Some children may not be able to develop such abilities, and the method might be too expensive for the schools in terms of resources. Finally, a major limitation of this approach is that it only considers one side of the problem. So in general the suggestion is to use this method in conjunction with others.

The mediation approach

This approach involves inviting students who are in conflict, such as bullies and victims, to take part in a discussion with a mediator who aims to help them find a solution to the conflict. Mediators can be both adults and students.[265] Through mediation it is easier to get to a constructive resolution of the problem, to explore the dynamics of the conflict and to clarify mutual responsibilities. It is easier to reach a good compromise for both sides, to process sustainable solutions and to adopt the most promising ones. If the process is well-conducted, the two parts can reach an intermediate solution, without blaming anyone for what happened.

The major limitation of this method is that both sides need to be motivated to find a joint solution to the conflict. It is also difficult to carry out if there is a marked disparity of power between the bully and the victim because this imbalance can surface during the mediation process.

The restorative approach

This strategy seeks to "repair problematic relationships" such as those between the bully and the victim; it asks the bully to empathize with the suffering of the victim and the victim to forgive what has happened.

The remedial practices focus on repairing the damage done to the victim in an attempt to save the relationship, rather than punishing the bully. The process involves all stakeholders and anyone else who might be affected. This method may be conducted in different ways, for example with only the involved students rather than with the whole class. The 'Community Conference' includes third parties such as friends, families and other people involved, such as the police. For example restorative practices for less severe cases are conducted through a remedial dialogue between different students (e.g. an informal chat in the hallway), or in a meeting in a small group of students (e.g. circle time). More serious levels instead include class meetings (e.g. group problem-solving) or community meetings with students, parents and teachers.

When used properly by trained personnel, the restorative approach can produce excellent results, especially if it is shared by the school community. It turns out to be particularly effective when the bully is brought to a genuine sense of remorse.

The method of group support

This method was originally defined as the "no blame approach". It provides that bullies meet other students who support the victim: the purpose of the meeting is to make the bully empathize with the suffering of the victim, to feel remorse and make him/her act in a constructive and positive way towards the victim. This approach places a strong emphasis on the role of the group in resolving the problem. Together with individual interviews with the victim and the bully this process is designed to empower the so-called silent majority, those bystanders who see the problem but do not do anything to stop the bullying and help the victim. Since it is a non-punitive approach, it is more likely to encourage victims to speak about the incident and to persuade bullies to empathize with the victim. This happens particularly when other students are seen to support the victims. Such an approach also helps the bully to commit himself or herself to act in a constructive manner towards the victim.

Differently to both the restorative approach and the shared concern method, the bullies and the victims do not meet together and therefore they cannot find a joint solution to the problem. This method has however proven to be most effective when there are many peers who can support the victim.

The shared concern method (or Pikas method)

This is a non-punitive method used with groups of students suspected to have taken part in bullying others. The approach facilitates the emergence of a solution to the problem of the bully and the victim through a series of talks among the parties involved. Using a non-accusatory approach in individual interviews, bullies are brought to understand the impact on the victim and they are more likely to engage in constructive action. The second step in this approach includes a meeting between the bully and the victim to plan together an agreed solution.

This method can be applied even in severe cases of bullying, and is particularly suited to cases of group bullying. Time needs to be spent on the interviews during the process and also on the follow-up monitoring of the situation.

These six methods can be re-classified into four main groups: 1) disciplinary approaches, 2) approaches focused on the victim, 3) approaches centred on mediation, and 4) humanistic approaches (restorative approach, group support approach, shared concern method).

The first two approaches act only on one side of the problem: by means of applying a punishment to the bully and by building the victim's capacity to respond, respectively. The approach centred on mediation instead acts with both sides, bully and victim, focusing on the future and on solving the problem. In the humanistic approaches the method highlights the desire to understand both the bully and the victim as individuals. This demands an ability to listen and to establish a genuine two-way communication, to make changes not only in behaviour, but also in attitudes, cognitions and feelings. In these last approaches the contribution of the group is fundamental as a source of support for the victim and as a mechanism of group change.

These different approaches to dealing with bullying can respond to the wide range of motivations that drive the behaviour, and they each have a particular area of application for the specific characteristics of the particular bullying incident.

Potentially each of the methods may be effective in specific situations; for that reason we think that schools cannot choose the best method to use before knowing the specificities of the phenomenon within their own institutions. We recommend therefore that the school and the teachers become involved in understanding the different methods and in working out which one is best suited to the particular manifestation of the problem in their own institutions.

The Italian model of indicative actions in case of emergency

Taking into consideration the above, the Italian project for indicated populations and contexts aims to test and standardize a protocol procedure to address bullying and victimization when it comes to the attention of the school. This protocol will see the active collaboration of various partners including schools, society, community health services, law enforcement, and for the most serious cases, the intervention of a task force made up of experts at the national level.

In particular, the protocol is expected to involve the following steps:

- Initial phase of the project requiring the drafting of a protocol of collaboration between schools and local institutions (social and health services, police, non profit organizations) for possible interventions.

- In parallel to this phase, a team of teachers would be trained together with local organizations involved in the cooperation protocol.

- The next stage would see the launch of an awareness-building campaign about the school project aimed at parents, teachers and children. Each school would define this presentation of the school's involvement in the project.

- In emergency situations, the expert team established at the school would provide a first screening of the case of bullying (case assessment). Depending on the severity and type, the case would be handled by a specialized team established within the school or sent to local services.

- At the first stage the school team would handle the case using one or more of the methods discussed above. In parallel to the intervention with the direct protagonists in the case, the team would also use strategies involving a wider groups of students to strengthen the capacity of the wider class group to avoid similar incidents.

- As a last resort, where all previous interventions have proven ineffective, the intervention of a national task force composed of professionals identified by the Ministry of Education would be sought. The intervention of the national task force can contemplate actions on two levels: 1) individual interventions involving victim and potential aggressors, and 2) community level interventions, including with teachers and parents. The goal of these actions at a national level is to respond to bullying that has not been addressed at the school level and stimulate a community recovery process that addresses the problem.

Conclusion

This project will be implemented first, in 2017, on a small scale in Tuscany, in Italy, and will then go on to be evaluated. The general aim of the project is to standardize a protocol that can be used by schools to deal with the problems of bullying and to address their feelings of powerlessness in the face of bullying and violence. Schools need such a protocol in order to establish systems that will enable them to deal with bullying and respond to the incidents that happen in their own institutions. The protocol will support their efforts to relieve the suffering of the victims and stop the bullying behaviour.

Furthermore these protocols can help schools to manage the relationships with the families of victims and of the bullies and also with other community agencies involved in addressing the problem. Finally these protocols need to be incorporated systematically into school policies and integrated within the school regulations, thus becoming an integral part of the functioning of the school. Such a whole-school adoption of anti-bullying procedures is essential to address the problem in a long-lasting and sustainable way.

Endnotes

[251] Greene, MB (2006). Bullying in schools: A plea for measure of human rights. *Journal of Social Issues* 62(1): 63–79.

[252] United Nations Convention on the Rights of the Child, 1989.

[253] Evans, CBR, Fraser, MW, Cotter, KL (2014). The effectiveness of school-based bullying prevention programs: A systematic review. *Aggression and Violent Behavior* 19(5): 532-544; Ferguson, CJ, San Miguel, C, Kilburn, JC, Sanchez P (2007). The effectiveness of school-based anti-bullying programs: A meta-analytic review. *Criminal Justice Review* 32: 401 – 414.

[254] Ttofi, MM & Farrington, DP (2011). Effectiveness of schoolbased programs to reduce bullying: a systematic and metaanalytic review. *Journal of Experimental Criminology* 7: 27–56.

[255] Pluess, M & Belsky, J (2013). Vantage Sensitivity: Individual Differences in Response to Positive Experiences. *Psychological Bulletin* 139(4): 901-916.

[256] Ttofi, MM & Farrington, DP (2011). Op. cit.

[257] World Health Organization (WHO) (2009-2014). *Health behaviour in school-aged children.* WHO. See http://www.hbsc.org/

[258] Menesini, E & Nocentini A (2015). Il bullismo a scuola. Come prevenirlo, come intervenire. *Collana Psicologia e Scuola.* Firenze: Giunti Scuola & Giunti O.S

[259] Nocentini, A & Menesini, E (2016). *KiVa AntiBullying program in Italy: Evidence of Effectiveness in a Randomized Control Trial,* Prevention Science.

[260] Palladino, BE, Nocentini, A & Menesini, E (2016). Evidence-based intervention against bullying and cyberbullying: evaluation of the Noncadiamointrappola! program through two independent trials. *Aggressive Behaviour* 42: 194-206

[261] See http://www.generazioniconnesse.it/

[262] Ttofi, MM & Farrington, DP (2011). Op. cit.

[263] Thompson, F & Smith PK (2010). *The Use and Effectiveness of Anti-Bullying Strategies in Schools.* Research Report DFE-RR098. Italian Department of Education.

[264] Rigby, K (2014). How teachers address cases of bullying in schools: a comparison of five reactive approaches. *Educational Psychology in Practice* 30(4): 409-419

[265] Menesini, E (2003) (a cura di) *Il bullismo: le azioni efficaci della scuola.* Trento: Erickson Edizioni.

Girl counts on a large abacus in a mathematics class, Pakistan
© UNICEF/UNI40069/Zaidi

Chapter IV. Children's Exposure to Bullying: Data and Regional Trends

13. Global data on the bullying of school-aged children[266]

Dominic Richardson and Chii Fen Hiu[267]

Introduction

Bullying is a damaging and yet avoidable experience for many children across the globe. No matter how defined, the most recent major international surveys of children report average bullying rates between 29% and 46% of children in the countries they study.

Bullying is not only a key indicator of children's well-being but an important marker for comparing global social development. Evidence from the bullying literature shows that both victims and perpetrators of bullying in childhood suffer in terms of personal social development, education and health, with negative effects persisting into adulthood. When children are affected by bullying, they fail to take advantage of the development opportunities open to them in the communities and schools in which they live their lives. For parents and teachers, high rates of bullying amongst children should raise warning flags regarding child rights' failings. For policymakers in particular, this highlights the need to improve on existing child policies, and points to the potential that bullying has for incurring future social costs.

Concerns about the impact of school bullying on children's learning and development have contributed to it becoming a globally recognised challenge. Every region in the world collects information on children's experiences of bullying, and bullying items are included as standard in most comparative child health or education surveys. But despite these regional efforts, and bullying's impact across sectors, a validated global measure is not readily available because of a lack of consensus in how bullying is defined across surveys, and the differences in the ages of children studied.

Nonetheless, much can be learned using available data about bullying risks, and how it affects different children at regional and country levels. This chapter reviews the sources of data, and presents some of the findings, before summarising the main findings of a paper that develops a method to compare bullying amongst children globally, using available cross-national school-based surveys.

The findings of this chapter show that bullying is a complex phenomenon that takes multiple forms, and is experienced to widely varying degrees across the globe. Importantly, whether defined simply as teasing, being excluded, or experiencing physical violence, around one in three school-children globally report experiences of bullying at least once in the preceding couple of months[268]. Bullying is most common amongst school children in poorer countries around the globe, and though not consistently so, in most countries boys and younger children experience more bullying.

The chapter is structured as follows. Section 1 outlines some of the key reasons school-bullying needs to be addressed. Section 2 introduces the comparative sources of data available to estimate and study school-bullying globally. Section 3 presents data by survey, showing how bullying varies across regions of the world, and how these vary by gender. Section 4 briefly discusses how different survey sources might be compared to produce a global estimate of bullying risks. Section 5 concludes with a global comparison of relative bullying risk by categorising countries into low-, medium- and high-risk bullying groups.

1. The need to address bullying in schools: for children's rights, well-being and school effectiveness

Addressing bullying in schools is important for a number of reasons. First, from a child rights perspective, all adults, whether parents, teachers, school principals or policymakers, have a responsibility to ensure that children under their care are safe from violence and the risk of violence, and are facilitated in accessing their rights to be heard, to be educated and to be healthy, amongst others.[269] Action to combat bullying in schools is undoubtedly a major contributor to the realization of children's rights.

Second, with regard to child well-being, bullying in schools has been a long-standing concern for educationalists, health professionals, child advocates, researchers and policymakers alike. Bullying has been linked to a variety of negative child well-being outcomes, including poorer education results and mental health problems such as anxiety and depression symptoms, suicidal thoughts and actions, self-harm and violent behaviour, which have been found to persist into adulthood.[270] These associations have been found in both developed and developing countries.[271]

Moreover, bullying is not only a concern for the victim's well-being; research has shown that being the child that bullies is also associated with poorer child and later-life outcomes.[272] In particular, bullies have been shown to exhibit higher antisocial and risk-taking behaviour, as well as later criminal offending.[273] Importantly, being both a perpetrator of bullying as well as the victim further compounds risks for psychological and conduct problems.[274]

Bullying does not only represent a cost to the children involved, it is also a serious concern for policymakers and professionals working with children. Education constitutes the largest public investment in children in the vast majority of countries globally,[275] and is a key factor in breaking cycles of disadvantage and dependency. Due to its damaging effects on learning and behaviour (e.g. disrupted classrooms, and children being unable to concentrate on lessons due to fear[276]), bullying in schools could reduce the effectiveness of public investment in children. Beyond decreasing the cost effectiveness of education and child policies more generally, experiences of bullying may lead children to contribute less to the social and economic development of the communities and countries in which they live or incur future costs through risk-taking and criminal behaviour.

2. Comparative data sources on school-bullying: what, where and how is bullying studied

Following a search for available, comparative, and recent estimates of school-bullying across countries, six international surveys were identified. Altogether these surveys collected data in over 150 countries globally, and mostly from 11- to 15-year-olds (for detailed source information see notes to Table 1; for a global map by source, see Figure 8).

For the majority of these countries, data focussed on 12- to 13-year-olds in particular, and for the vast majority, most recent information estimates of bullying were less than a decade old.[277] The six international surveys are:

- Health Behaviour in School-aged Children (HBSC; 2001/2; 2009/10; 2013/4 – 36 countries; 11- to 15-year-olds)

- Global School-based Student Health Surveys (GSHS; 2003-2014 – 85 countries; 13- to 15-year-olds)

- Trends in Mathematics and Science Study (TIMSS; 2011 – 46 countries; 11- to 15-year-olds)

- Children's Worlds Report (2015 – 16 countries; 12-year-olds)

- Second Regional Comparative and Explanatory Study by LLECE (SERCE, 2008 – 16 countries; 6th Graders/11- to 12-year-olds)

- Third Regional Comparative and Explanatory Study by LLECE (TERCE, 2015 – 15 countries and the State of Nuevo Leon; 6th Graders/11- to 12-year-olds).

Table 1 reports the way in which bullying is defined and itemised by each survey. It compares the definitions of bullying used, as well as the timescales and frequencies that children are asked to refer to when reporting their experiences of being bullied. From the information in Table 1 it is worth noting that:

- What constitutes the experience of being bullied varies from a broad definition including experiences of being teased or being excluded, such as that used by HBSC and GSHS, to more narrow definitions around threats and physical violence, such as in TERCE.

- Frequency of bullying refers to the number of instances a child experiences being bullied over a defined period of time, which ranges from once in a month (i.e. about monthly, as in TIMSS; or a couple of months, as in HBSC) to more severe bullying rates of 2-3 times a month or more (or about weekly, as in TIMSS).

- Some of the surveys' items specifically refer to bullying in school, such as SERCE and TERCE, and HBSC; others do not. All surveys sample school-going children, in the school setting (i.e. they exclude out-of-school children).

Table 1:
How bullying data is defined and itemised by survey

Survey	Bullying definition	Frequency
Children's World	• Being left out by other students • Being hit by other students	• Bullied once in the last month • Bullied 2-3 times in the last month • Bullied more than 3 times in the last month
HBSC	"…a student is being bullied when another student, or a group of students, say or do nasty and unpleasant things to him or her. It is also bullying when a student is teased repeatedly in a way he or she does not like or when he or she is deliberately left out of things. But it is not bullying when two students of about the same strength or power argue or fight. It is also not bullying when a student is teased in a friendly and playful way."	• • Bullied once or more (a month) at school in the past couple of months • Bullied 2-3 times (a month) or more in the past couple of months
GSHS	• As HBSC	• Bullied on one or more days during past 30 days
SERCE	• Robbed • Insulted or threatened • Physically bullied	• Bullied at school during the past month
TERCE	• Teased • Threatened • Left out • Hit • Forced to do things • Afraid	• Bullied at school during the past month
TIMSS	Made fun of or called names, left out of games or activities, spread lies about, stolen from, hit or hurt and made to do things they didn't want to do by other students.	• About weekly: experiencing each of 3 of 6 behaviours "once or twice a month" (i.e. bullied 3-6 times a month) and in addition, each of the other three "a few times a year" on average • About monthly: between weekly and never • Almost never: never experiencing 3 of 6 bullying behaviours, and each of the other 3 "a few times a year" on average

Sources: Trends in Mathematics and Science Study (TIMSS, 2016), The Children's World Survey (IscWEB, 2016), Health Behaviour in School-aged Children Study (HBSC, 2016), The Global School-based Student Health Surveys (WHO/GSHS, 2016), Second Regional Comparative and Explanatory Study (SERCE) and the Third Regional Comparative and Explanatory Study (TERCE, see UNESCO, 2016).[276]

3. Comparing bullying across countries by survey

Although each comparative survey is slightly different (some define bullying more broadly, and look at different age ranges and time spans (when bullying last occurred)), they can all be used to estimate the proportion of children that have experienced some form of bullying at least once in the past months or couple of months. For this reason, the comparisons below focus on data in the surveys that ask about bullying in the past couple of months, of any kind, as defined in the survey itself. The focus is on average experiences across the age groups covered in the survey, with gender breakdowns included as available (not all surveys distinguish between girls' and boys' experiences of bullying).

The comparisons are introduced in order based on surveys with the most countries compared. Where countries report to more than one survey, they are included where the data they report is most recent. Eight countries are in more than one comparison because they were surveyed in the same year in two separate collections (e.g. Chile in 2013 for GSHS and TERCE, see also data for Colombia, Ecuador, Ghana, Lebanon, Qatar, England, and the State of Palestine).

Figure 1:
In GSHS collections, there is a ten-fold difference between countries with low and high rates of bullying

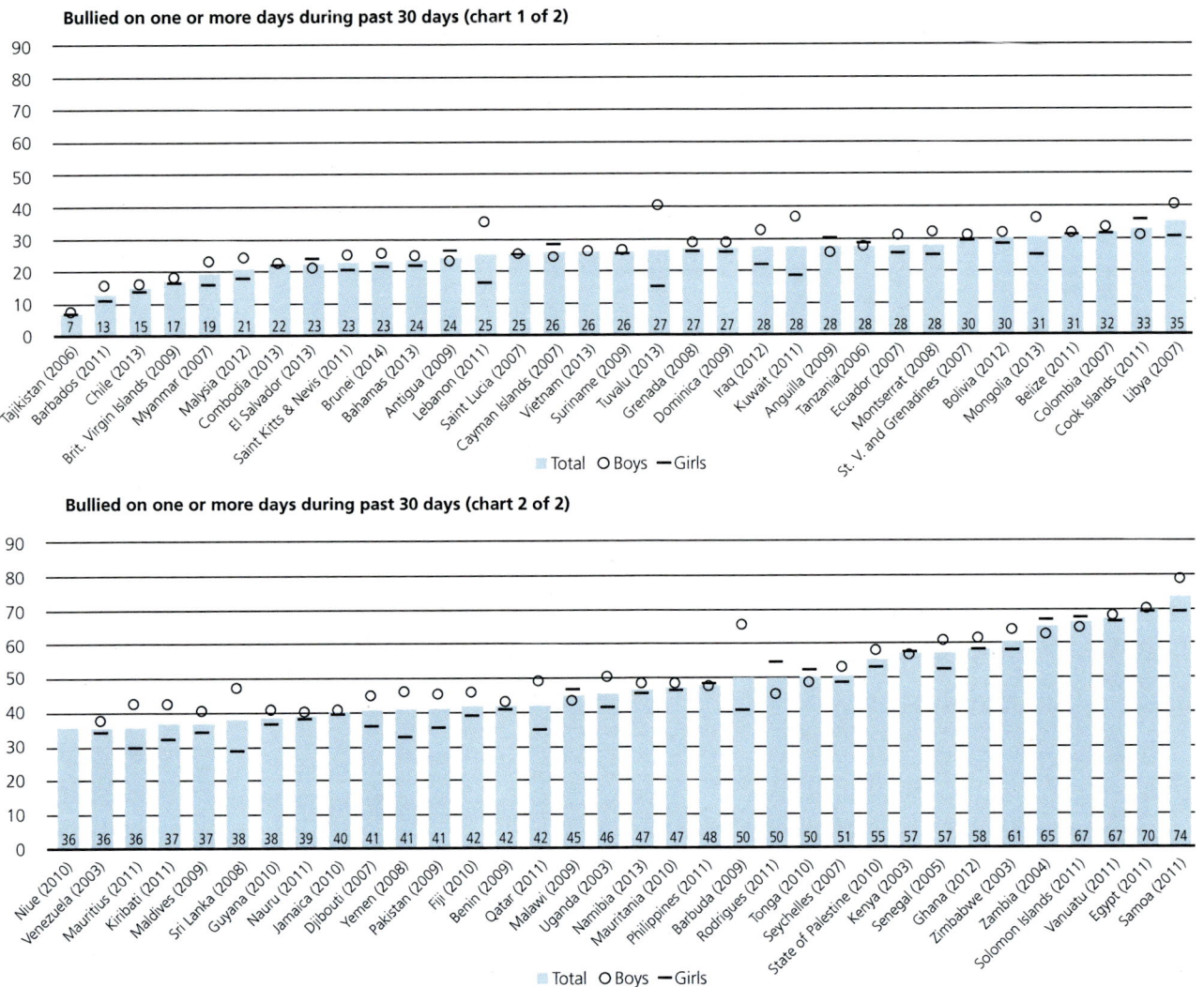

Source: Author's analysis of The Global School-based Student Health Surveys.

3.1 Findings by survey

Figure 1 reports comparisons between countries from the GSHS (The Global School-based Student Health Surveys). GSHS data accounts for 67 of the 143 countries with data (151 with double counts). The two charts in Figure 1 order countries on the basis of low to high bullying prevalence (bullied on one or more days in the past 30, bullying is defined in Table 1), with Tajikistan in 2006 reporting the lowest bullying rates at 7% and Samoa in 2011 reporting the highest rates at 74%.

Figure 1 also presents the gender breakdowns available by country. Circles represent the boys' estimates, and dashes, the girls' estimates. In 75% of cases, boys are reporting higher rates of bullying than girls in the survey data. In most cases differences are likely to be too small to be significant, but in countries such as Barbuda and Tuvalu the difference in bullying rates by sex are over 20%, and in Iraq, Kuwait, Lebanon, Mauritius, Mongolia, Sri Lanka, and Yemen, rates for boys are at least 10% higher.

For the few countries reporting higher rates of bullying amongst girls, Anguilla, Cook Islands and Zambia report the largest difference, where girls experience more bullying than boys by around 5 percentage points on average.

Although it is hard to spot any meaningful regional patterns in a comparison of 68 countries, it is notable that South Pacific Islands and African states make up the nine highest ranking bullying countries in the GSHS data. Eight of the lowest ranking 9 countries (excluding the lowest ranking country, Tajikistan) are from South East Asia or Latin America and the Caribbean region.

Figure 2.
The highest rates of bullying reported across all surveys is found in the TIMSS data for Ghana and Botswana

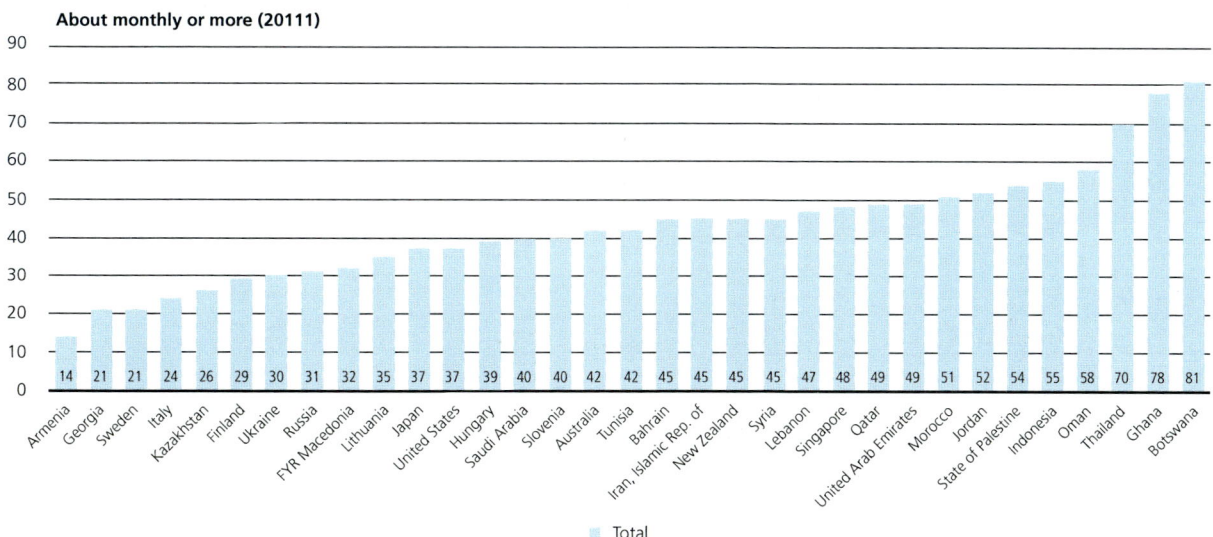

Note: Gender breakdowns are available in the TIMSS data, but not reported here. Readers should refer to the TIMSS website and available data downloads.

Source: Author's analysis of TIMSS, 2011.

The next most populated data source is the TIMSS (Trends in Mathematics and Science Study), with 33 country estimates. Figure 2 reports rates for all children, by country, experiencing being made fun of or called names, left out of games or activities, spread lies about, stolen from, hit or hurt and made to do things they didn't want to do by other students, monthly or more often. Data are from 2011.

The most notable finding compared to GSHS data, is that although the range of responses is broadly similar, both the lowest and the highest estimates are higher than that found for GSHS. In fact, in TIMSS, the highest rates of bullying are reported in Ghana and Botswana at 78% and 81% respectively.

Following the high levels reported in Ghana and Botswana – and with the exception of New Zealand – are a group of countries from either East Asia or the Middle East and North African region with above average bullying estimates. The nine lowest ranking countries, from Armenia to FYR Macedonia, are all CEE/CIS or European states.

Figure 3 reports bullying estimates taken from the Health Behaviour in School-aged Children Study (HBSC) in 2009.[279] HBSC primarily covers European and North American countries, surveys three cohorts of children at ages 11, 13 and 15, and like GSHS is designed to study health and health behaviours in school-aged populations. Perhaps due to similarities in the countries taking part in HBSC (in terms of social and economic development), the range of bullying experiences across HBSC countries is lower than in most other surveys, with the lowest rates of bullying in the Czech Republic, at 15%, being one-third of the highest reported rates in Latvia.

Compared to GSHS, the difference between the sexes' reports of bullying are small, although boys are again more likely to experience bullying: on average across HBSC countries reported here, 31% of boys reported being bullied compared to 27% of girls. The biggest differences are seen in Austria, Belgium and Portugal – all relatively high bullying countries – where estimates for bullying of boys is around 10 percentage points higher than that of girls. In only Canada and the United Kingdom is the bullying of girls more common, but the differences are small at 1.5% and 1% respectively.

The Children's World survey is the newest of all child surveys used in this paper. The Children's World survey is distinguished from other surveys as it is neither primarily a health or education study, but a self-defined 'child well-being' study focussed on children's time use, and children's self-reports and opinions of lived experiences at home and in their schools.

Figure 4 reports the rates of children, by country, who say they are being left out of things by other students in their school, or being hit by other students, at least once in the

Figure 3.
No country responding to the HBSC question reports a rate of bullying below 15%, the average rate is 43%

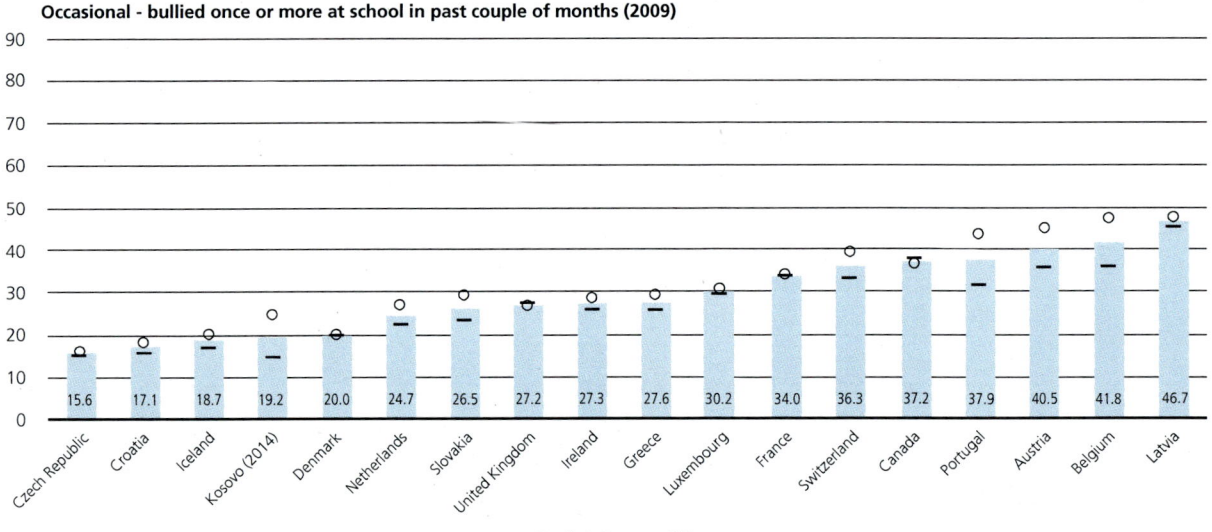

Note: Estimates are the average of the three age cohorts, 11, 13 and 15. Bullying is defined as when "…a student is being bullied when another student, or a group of students, say or do nasty and unpleasant things to him or her. It is also bullying when a student is teased repeatedly in a way he or she does not like or when he or she is deliberately left out of things. But it is not bullying when two students of about the same strength or power argue or fight. It is also not bullying when a student is teased in a friendly and playful way."

Source: Author's analysis of HBSC, 2009.

Figure 4.
Children's world data shows that over half of children on average report bullying

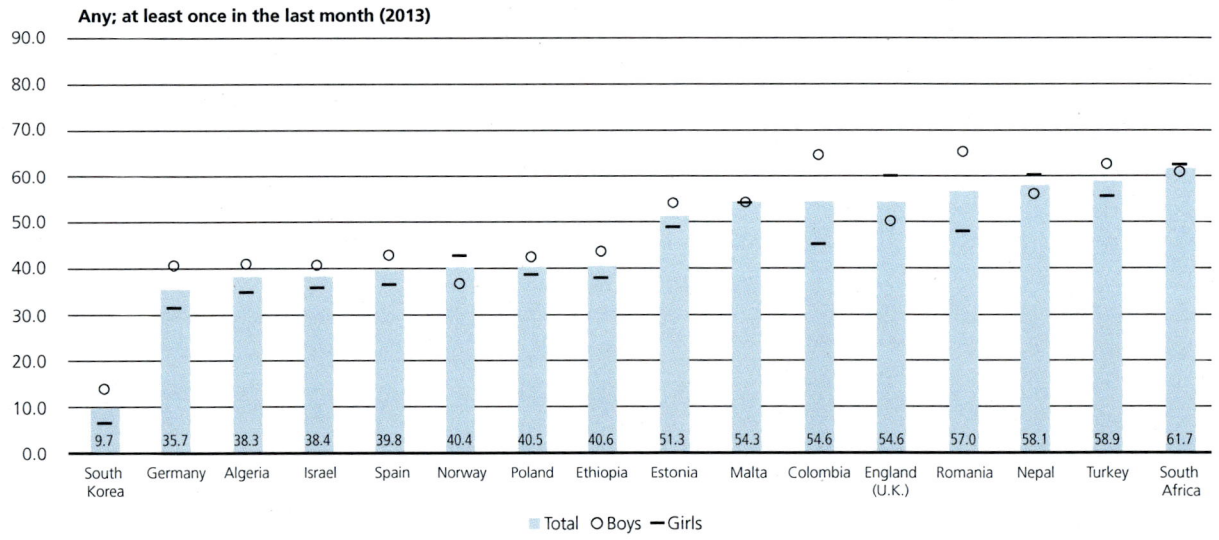

Note: Data for England is not representative of experiences of children in other parts of the United Kingdom (Northern Ireland, Scotland and Wales). At the time of publication of the last Children's World Survey report,[280] a collection for Wales was ongoing.

Source: Author's analysis of Children's World data, 2013.

last month. Data is for 2013, and for children aged 12. At a rate of just under 10%, children in South Korea report the lowest levels of bullying by a long way; in contrast almost 3 in every 5 children in South Africa report being hit or left out of things by the school peers.

The Children's World results, of all the survey data presented, produces the highest average rate of bullying in its sample of countries, at 46%. As with other surveys, rates of bullying amongst boys are higher than those for girls, by around 4% percentage points, at 48% and 44% respectively. Notably, in Romania and Colombia boys experience bullying rates nearly 20 percentage points higher than those experienced by girls. In contrast to findings elsewhere, however, of the five countries with higher bullying rates for girls, three countries (Nepal, Norway, and England) report large differences in favour of boys, whose experiences of bullying are 4, 6 and 10 percentage points lower than rates reported by girls.

The Children's World survey, like TIMSS, is a survey that samples countries at different levels of income (HBSC, TERCE and GSHS focus on regional or development settings), and for this reason provides some insight on the link between bullying and development. Unlike TIMSS however, there is no clear clustering of countries by region, and the top and bottom of the bullying range in Figure 4 includes both high-income and low- or middle-income countries.

Finally, Figure 5 compares rates of bullying among countries in the TERCE survey from 2013. TERCE is the second survey included in this chapter that has been designed to measure learning outcomes (the other is TIMSS). TERCE exclusively covers countries in the Latin America and Caribbean region, and it is probably this regional focus that explains why the estimates from this survey cover the smallest range of reported experiences of bullying (see Figure 5).

On average, 41% of children in the TERCE surveys report that they have been teased, threatened, left out, hit, forced to do things, or been afraid at school in the past month. Bullying experiences are least common in Costa Rica (31%) and most common in Dominican Republic, where almost 1 in 2 children experience bullying. Across all countries, there is little evidence of regional variation: meaning that neither the Central American, South American nor Caribbean countries cluster in the results.

By sex, results show that although boys are generally at a higher risk more often, more countries in this survey produce estimates where bullying outcomes for girls are worse. Difference by sex are small however, with the biggest gap in favour of girls found in Colombia (a five percent age-gap), and the biggest gap in favour of boys found in Uruguay (a three percent-point gap).

Figure 5.
In the Latin American and Caribbean Countries between a third and a half of children report bullying

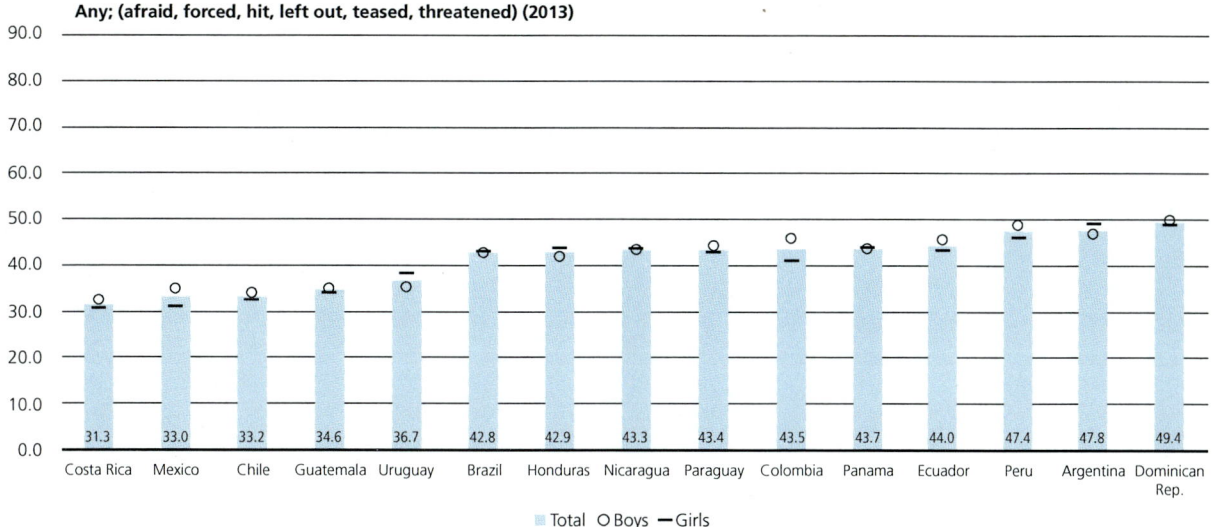

Note: SERCE data for Cuba (reporting a bullying rate of 13.2% in 2006 for children aged 11.5 on average) was the only country estimate from SERCE and so not separately charted. SERCE estimates are not included in the TERCE chart above as differences in bullying definitions mean that the raw estimates are incomparable with TERCE raw estimates. No gender breakdowns were available for SERCE data.

Source: Author's analysis of TERCE, 2013.

3.1.1 Summarising the survey results

What is clear from these comparisons is that at the age of children, where they are and how bullying data is collected is likely to affect the final raw estimates produced for each country.

This is shown when looking at the countries included in more than one survey, and how the data for the same year, asked of different children in different ways produces variable findings. For example, Chile's GSHS estimate - based on responses from older children - is 18 points lower than that reported for Chile in the TERCE comparison, Colombia's estimate for GSHS is 12 points lower than its TERCE estimate, and 23 percentage points lower than its Children's World estimate. In fact, only the State of Palestine produces near identical figures over two surveys (54% and 55% in TIMSS and GSHS respectively).

However, given the differences in the ages of children and the ways bullying is studied, the important question is not whether there are differences, but whether these differences are real (younger children generally experience more bullying, which could explain lower overall rates produced in the GSHS studies).

The following section presents a summary of a method used in Richardson and Hiu (forthcoming UNICEF Innocenti Working Paper)[281] to test the reliability of estimates across surveys and produce a global comparison of relative risk of bullying.

3.2 Can bullying rates be compared globally?

As clearly shown above, there is plenty of available information on the extent of bullying experienced by school-aged children globally. Over 150 countries are covered in six separate surveys, many of which include breakdowns by sex. Moreover, most of these surveys include information on family background that would allow for additional analysis of bullying by family wealth or poverty.[282]

But what else is shown above, and in more detail in the working paper[283], is that although these country-level estimates of bullying are comparable within each survey, these raw figures are not comparable across surveys as

---

Box 1: Children and topics missing from these surveys, and potential implications

All of the studies reviewed in this paper derived their estimates of bullying from school-based surveys. School-based surveys are selective in terms of their target population, as are all surveys, in different ways. First, school-based surveys will sample only schools, and follow up with a sampling of pupils in the school itself. Schools are generally sampled in a country proportionate to its size (large and small schools), within regions, and school types. In schools, the studies can randomly sample the pupils or the classes in the school. Commonly surveys involving assessments (such as TIMSS) will exclude schools that are not mainstream schools (e.g. schools for children with special educational needs). When certain schools are excluded from sampling, or when children out of school for various reasons, such as fear of being bullied (which can vary widely by country and age) are excluded due to collection methods, reported results are likely to underestimate the extent of bullying, which could occur also outside the school setting, as the most vulnerable children are often not represented.

School-based studies are also commonly restricted in terms of the topics they can explore when surveying children. For example, items on children's drug use and sexual health, which are part of the Health Behaviour in School-aged Children study, have been excluded by various countries.[284] Aside from behaviours that are considered taboo, sensitive questions can also include items that schools or survey coordinators feel are likely to stigmatise the child. As a result, surveys that could otherwise inform the extent of bullying experienced by children from certain sociocultural groups (foster children, migrants, LGBT children) more often than not do not provide the additional information (or sometimes necessary oversampling) for such important breakdowns to be examined.

Finally an entire topic missing from this study is cyberbullying. At present there is little comparative information on cyberbullying, an issue gaining increasing attention as the use of handheld mobile devices for communication and access to social networks is becoming more common. At present cyberbullying is only being surveyed as part of EU Kids Online, a European-based survey of children's internet use in Europe.[285]

UNICEF Office of Research is also beginning a pilot study of adolescent Internet use, including cyberbullying, in three additional countries: Philippines, Serbia and South Africa (for more information please see: http://www.unicef-irc.org/article/1194/).

average rates, and the variances of the raw data (the differences between the highest and lowest rates), are significantly different due to differences in collection methods.

What this means for a potential global comparison is that absolute figures cannot be used to determine the difference in bullying-risk between countries in different surveys, and neither can raw differences from the average experience. What potentially could be used is a measure of relative risk in categories (whether a country has a high, low or medium risk, compared to other countries using the same survey). This option of 'relative risk groups' is tested below.

4. Developing a global comparison using 'relative risk groups'

4.1 Are survey estimates reliable by country?

The first step in developing relative risk groups is to determine whether bullying estimates are reliable between surveys, or whether differences between country estimates from different surveys are consistent or random.

To undertake this test, Figure 6 below correlates results for 53 countries that answer more than one item on bullying in different surveys around the same year.[286] If countries' lower and higher estimates correlate, it suggests that differences in survey estimates are consistent (even though absolute values differ), and not random, and there is room for 'relative risk groups' to be categorised across the surveys.

Figure 6 shows that although there is some difference in the maximum and minimum estimates reported by the same country from the different studies, there is a clear correlation in the data, and a lack of notable outliers, which indicates that the studies are comparable across the group, and between maximum and minimum estimates there is a fair amount of reliability in the sample.

4.2 The process of normalising the data, and basic validation

The second step in developing a global comparison of bullying using relative risk groups is to normalise, and validate, the new 'relative risk measure' by comparing it to raw bullying estimates for evidence of survey source bias.

Normalising data is a process where raw estimates are rescaled to allow for the bullying rates in each country to be interpreted as high or low relative to other countries in the same surveys, using the same definition, in the same year,[287] on children of the same age. The normalisation process is undertaken by survey question, year, and age (or average age) to ensure that survey estimates from different collections are not combined, and to control for potential effects of variation in bullying over time and by child age. Results reported in Richardson and Hiu,[288] show that following normalisation, survey source is no longer associated with differences in country-level estimates of bullying risk.

4.3 Validating country grouping for a global comparison

The third step in developing a global comparison of bullying using relative risk groups is to calculate and to compare the raw estimate groupings to the groupings using normalised data to assess whether the group comparisons are valid, or in other words, that the categories of relative risk map meaningfully to the original data. This test is undertaken by Richardson and Hiu, using cluster analysis to categorise raw and normalised data into low, medium and high groups by surveys, before comparing countries' placement on a global, high, medium and low scale. Results of this test showed that following adjustments to cluster older data from GSHS waves and the exclusion of one estimate (for Swaziland), no unexpected

**Figure 6.
Differences in high and low estimates by country are reasonably consistent across surveys**

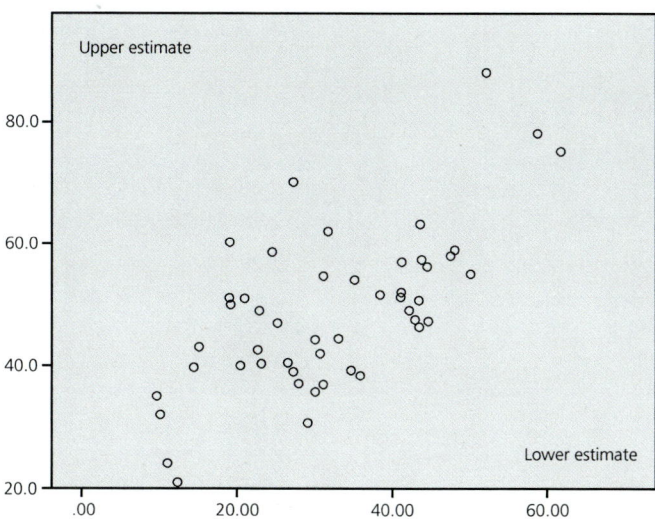

Note: Raw estimates are plotted for 53 countries. Correlation coefficient = 0.66 (p<0.001).

Source: Author's analysis of the bullying surveys.

movement between low, middle and high groups were found (i.e. countries moving from low-raw to high-normalised groups or vice versa).

5. Comparing bullying across the world: where is the risk and what does it mean?

The final section of this chapter looks at global bullying risk, reported by country and by region as reported in Richardson and Hiu[289] following the normalization, validation and standardization processes. Importantly, results in this section (in the map) are most confidently interpreted as 'the relative risk of bullying in a given country relative to countries across the world using similar methods of defining and collecting bullying data'.

5.1 Global relative bullying risk: findings by country

Figure 7 provides a global map of bullying by low, medium and high risk. The vast majority of the countries have usable data, and the map has been shaded according to the risk of bullying from light grey (low) to black (high). Gaps in the data (white areas) – where no useable bullying data is found - are most notable in Central and West Africa, South Asia, parts of Central and Eastern Europe and the CIS, and islands in the Pacific. Bullying risks in smaller countries (not visible on the maps) are presented using a separate key in Figure 7.

At a glance, the global map shows more countries with higher relative risk in the western hemisphere, and more countries with lower relative risk in the eastern hemisphere. However, this picture serves best to highlight the variation in experiences of bullying within regions (though it is worth remembering that variation will exist within countries, and between socio-economic and socio-demographic groups, and which cannot be uncovered using this analysis).

Canada, the western side of South America, Southern Africa, parts of Eastern Europe, and the MENA region, and islands in the Pacific are all places with the highest relative risk of bullying according to data from their most recent

Figure 7.
Global map of relative bullying risk

Source: Richardson and Hiu, forthcoming.[290]

Disclaimer: The boundaries and names shown and the designations used on this map do not imply official endorsement or acceptance by the United Nations.

surveys. Countries in Western Europe, the United States of America, eastern parts of South America, much of the Middle East and North Africa, Australia, Japan and Mongolia, are all countries with medium risks of bullying. Few countries in Central and South America are low bullying-risk countries, compared to many countries in Northern Europe through to South East Asia, including Russia, as well as Kazakhstan, South Korea and Thailand.

A brief conclusion

In summary, there is plenty of available data, globally, to assess bullying risks within and between countries. What is more, these bullying data are collected in children's surveys on education, health or well-being, providing numerous options to analyze potential determinants of bullying to inform the responses needed to address excessively high rates of bullying across many countries worldwide.

Moreover, despite a loss in detail in the scale, and much regional data not being comparable, it is possible to harmonise national-level data, to define and validate a measure of bullying-risk for global comparison. However, bullying-risk in the case of this comparison is relative, and good quality data that allows comparisons of true levels of bullying across all countries should be the ambition. Either through harmonization of data collections, by ages of children, years and definitions, or through the development of an entirely new survey, hope remains that good quality and actionable data on the extent and severity of bullying of all children can be collected to inform policymakers, practitioners and parents alike as they act on behalf of the best interests of children.

Figure 8.
Global map of bullying data by sources

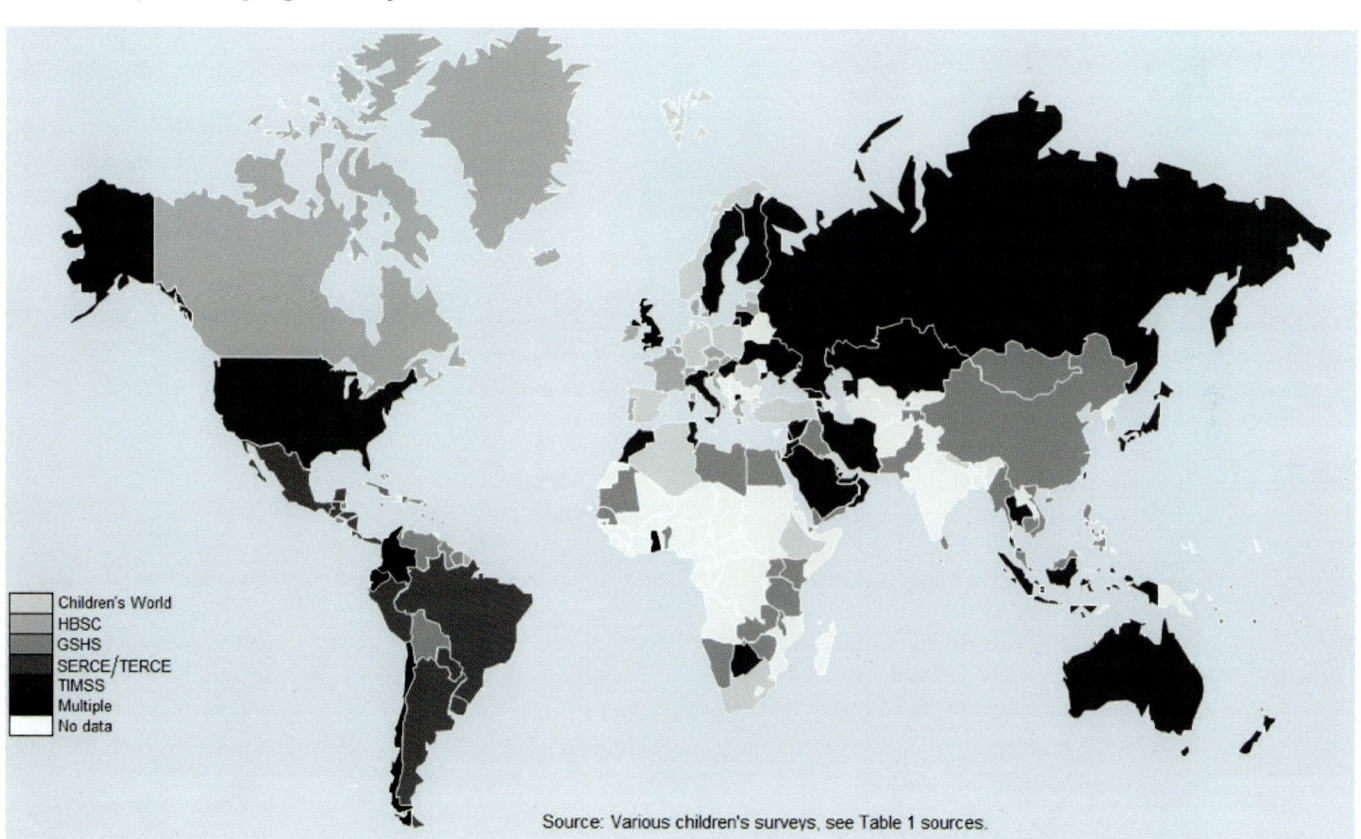

Source: Various children's surveys, see Table 1 sources.

Disclaimer: The boundaries and names shown and the designations used on this map do not imply official endorsement or acceptance by the United Nations.

Endnotes

[266] This chapter draws freely from a forthcoming Unicef Innocenti working paper 'Developing a Global Indicator on Bullying of School-aged Children', by the same authors.

[267] Dominic Richardson is with the UNICEF Office of Research, Innocenti, and Chii Fen Hiu is at Oxford University, United Kingdom

[268] The definition of bullying as the experience of any type (teased, left out of play, had lies spread about them, been threatened, hit, forced to do things, had things stolen, or made to feel afraid), at least once in a couple of months, has been selected as the most robust definition for global, national and by-region comparisons.

[269] UNCRC (1989). United Nations Convention on the Rights of the Child.

[270] See: Schwartz, D, Lansford, JE, Dodge, KA, Pettit, GS, & Bates, JE (2015). Peer victimization during middle childhood as a lead indicator of internalizing problems and diagnostic outcomes in late adolescence. *Journal of Clinical Child & Adolescent Psychology* 44(3): 393-404; Arseneault, L, Bowes, L, & Shakoor, S (2010). Bullying victimization in youths and mental health problems: 'Much ado about nothing'? *Psychological medicine* 40(05): 717-729; Rudolph, KD, Lansford, JE, Agoston, AM, Sugimura, N, Schwartz, D, Dodge, KA, & Bates, JE (2014). Peer victimization and social alienation: predicting deviant peer affiliation in middle school. *Child development,* 85(1): 124-139; Wolke, D, Copeland, WE, Angold, A, & Costello, EJ (2013). Impact of bullying in childhood on adult health, wealth, crime, and social outcomes. *Psychological science,* 24(10), 1958-1970; Copeland, WE, Wolke, D, Angold, A, & Costello, E J (2013). Adult psychiatric outcomes of bullying and being bullied by peers in childhood and adolescence. *JAMA psychiatry* 70(4): 419-426; Olweus, D (1994). Bullying at school: long-term outcomes for the victims and an effective school-based intervention program; *Aggressive behavior: Current perspectives,* pp.97-139; Rueger, SY, Malecki, CK, & Demaray, MK (2011). Stability of peer victimization in early adolescence: Effects of timing and duration. *Journal of School Psychology* 49(4): 443-464.

[271] Boyes, ME, Bowes, L, Cluver, LD, Ward, CL & Badcock, NA (2014). Bullying victimisation, internalising symptoms, and conduct problems in South African children and adolescents: a longitudinal investigation. *Journal of abnormal child psychology* 42(8): 1313-1324; Brown, DW, Riley, L, Butchart, A & Kann, L (2008). Bullying among youth from eight African countries and associations with adverse health behaviors. *Future Medicine,* 289-299.

[272] Copeland, WE, Wolke, D, Angold, ., & Costello, EJ (2013). Adult psychiatric outcomes of bullying and being bullied by peers in childhood and adolescence. *JAMA psychiatry* 70(4): 419-426.

[273] Liang, H, Flisher, AJ, & Lombard, CJ (2007). Bullying, violence, and risk behavior in South African school students. *Child abuse & neglect,* 31(2), 161-171; Ttofi, M. M., Farrington, DP, Lösel, F, & Loeber, R (2011). The predictive efficiency of school bullying versus later offending: A systematic/meta-analytic review of longitudinal studies. *Criminal Behaviour and Mental Health,* 21(2): 80-89.

[274] Haynie, DL, Nansel, T, Eitel, P, Crump, AD, Saylor, K, Yu, K & Simons-Morton, B (2001). Bullies, victims, and bully/victims: Distinct groups of at-risk youth. *The Journal of Early Adolescence,* 21(1): 29-49. Copeland, W. E., Wolke, D., Angold, A., & Costello, E. J. (2013). Adult psychiatric outcomes of bullying and being bullied by peers in childhood and adolescence. *JAMA psychiatry,* 70(4): 419-426.

[275] see OECD (2016) OECD Family database, age-spending profiles, downloaded at: http://www.oecd.org/els/family/PF1_6_Public_spending_by_age_of_children.pdf. World Bank (2016) World Bank Data, downloaded at http://data.worldbank.org/, accessed January, 2016.

[276] See Richardson, Benitez and Hiu, (2016) Strong Schools in the Latin American and Caribbean Region: UNICEF Innocenti working paper series, forthcoming.

[277] Apart from Kenya (2003; GSHS), Uganda (2003; GSHS), Zimbabwe (2003; GSHS), Zambia (2004; GSHS), Israel (2001; HBSC), Botswana (2005; GSHS), and Senegal (2005; GSHS) all data was collected within the last 10 years.

[278] HBSC (2016), Health Behaviour in School-aged Children Study, available at http://www.hbsc.org/, accessed for this paper in November 2015.; IscWEB (2016), The Children's World Survey, available at http://www.isciweb.org/, accessed for this paper in November 2015.; TIMSS (2016), Trends in Mathematics and Science Study, available at http://timssandpirls.bc.edu/, accessed for this paper in November 2015.; UNESCO (2016) Education Assessment-LLECE (TERCE and SERCE), available at http://www.unesco.org/new/en/santiago/education/education-assessment-llece/WHO/GSHS (2016) Global School-based Student Health Surveys, available at http://www.who.int/chp/gshs/en/, accessed for this paper in November 2015.

[279] At the time the bullying dataset was developed for the analysis in this report (particularly that undertaken for sections 5 and 6) HBSC has published a new wave of data for 2014/15. Interested readers should refer to the HBSC website (hbsc.org).

[280] Rees, G & Main, G (eds) (2015). *Children's views on their lives and well-being in 15 countries: An initial report on the Children's Worlds survey, 2013-14.* York, UK: Children's Worlds Project (ISCWeB)

[281] Richardson, D & Hiu, CF (2016) *'Developing a Global Indicator on Bullying of School-aged Children',* Innocenti Working Paper Series, Forthcoming.

[282] What is clear however, is that school based surveys are not yet systematically asking about children's sexual orientation, or whether they have a disability, or come from a migrant background. For these reasons, further analysis on equity and risk and school-bullying is not yet possible using these surveys. Moreover, as yet, the surveys do not include data cyber-bullying (see Box 1).

[283] Op. Cit.

[284] See Richardson, D. and N. Ali (2014), An Evaluation of International Surveys of Children. OECD SEM Working paper, No. 146.

[285] Görzig, A (2011). *Who bullies and who is bullied online?: a study of 9-16 year old internet users in 25 European countries.* EU Kids Online, London, UK. http://eprints.lse.ac.uk/39601/

286 See Richardson, D & Hiu, CF (2016) *'Developing a Global Indicator on Bullying of School-aged Children'*, Innocenti Working Paper Series, forthcoming. Data for these 53 cases are not reported in the main text of this chapter, which reports only the most recent data.
287 In the case of surveys with different years or waves, years have been aligned for comparability before normalization.
288 Richardson, D & Hiu, CF (2016) *'Developing a Global Indicator on Bullying of School-aged Children'*, Innocenti Working Paper Series, Forthcoming.
289 Ibid.
290 Ibid.

Girl with cell phone, Colombia.
© UNICEF/UN013292/LeMoyne

14. Cyberbullying: incidence, trends and consequences

Sonia Livingstone, Mariya Stoilova and Anthony Kelly[291]

Introduction: What's the problem?

It is widely believed by policy makers and the public that, as children gain more access, and make more extensive use of the internet in their everyday lives, the associated risks to children's safety and well-being are increasing commensurately.[292] Certainly the popular media convey a strong impression that it is mobile phones and the internet that now constitute a major threat to children's safety in the digital age. But perhaps these media panics are misleading, distracting attention from the continued underlying problems that children face in their daily lives?

Focusing on cyberbullying, this chapter examines the evidence for the claim that new media bring new problems. We ask whether the frequency of cyberbullying is increasing as internet use spreads among children around the world. And if so, is cyberbullying in some way replacing traditional bullying, so that peer aggression that used to be expressed physically, face-to-face, is now migrating to mobile and online platforms and being expressed via the distribution of hurtful images and messages? Or, is cyberbullying occurring independently of traditional bullying, perhaps involving different children and with different kinds of consequences? Or, as we shall argue, is something more complicated occurring as new forms of peer aggression emerge that mix traditional and cyberbullying, and with shifting boundaries between cyberbullying and other forms of online aggression?

The belief that online risks of harm to children are rising has triggered government, industry, and parental efforts designed to manage and mitigate such risks of harm. In relation to cyberbullying, the value of an evidence review that answers the above questions lies in the potential to guide cyberbullying policy and practical interventions: should efforts to address traditional bullying now switch their focus to address problems on mobile and online platforms, or should they work in parallel with new initiatives, or is an integrated approach preferable? And do the answers to these questions vary, depending on culture or country?

Aims and methods

Four methods were used to research this chapter, concentrating on the period 2010-2016, given the rapid pace of technological change: (i) a web-based search of three databases (Web of Science – including results from SciELO, Scopus, and Google Scholar) using such search terms as cyberbullying, bullying, online, internet, and longitudinal; (ii) a search through the bibliographies of existing reviews and meta-analyses of the literature on cyberbullying for relevant sources; (iii) we consulted experts in the field of cyberbullying, including their literature suggestions where relevant to the aims of the paper; (iv) we drew on the authors' extensive bibliography which already included diverse studies of children's changing relationships with digital media over time. For all sources identified, we further examined their bibliographies specifically for articles cited that focused on change over time, as these proved to be scarce.

Approximately one in three children around the world are now online, in one way or another; further, while most research thus far has been conducted in the global North, it is in the global South that most future internet users are to be found.[293] But despite the global diversity in the conditions of childhood, much of the research literature appears to imply that bullying and cyberbullying are universal phenomena – taking a similar form wherever they occur and, insofar as 'children will be children' and increasingly they have digital devices, also occurring everywhere in the world. We sought out findings from the global South to complement the extensive body of global North literature on cyberbullying but these proved to be scarce,[294] with especially little cross-national comparative research that uses constant definitions and measures.[295] It is not therefore possible, with the present state of knowledge, to develop confident conclusions and recommendations regarding many parts of the world where children have only recently gained access to the internet and mobile technology, and where associated forms of peer aggression, including cyberbullying, are yet to be researched.

Traditional bullying and cyberbullying compared

Bullying among children – broadly, the repeated physical, verbal or symbolic aggression intentionally expressed by one or more peers towards a less powerful victim – is understood in somewhat different ways in different cultures, and thus terminology and definitions vary.[296] For example, in China more emphasis is placed on social status and forms of social exclusion.[297] In the US it has been argued that bullying is a form of harassment.[298] In the UK it is strongly associated with school, but in Germany the word 'mobbing' derives from the workplace.[299] Unsurprisingly, approaches to measurement also vary, especially over whether bullying must be intentional, repeated, or related to a power imbalance among peers.[300] Estimates of incidence, again unsurprisingly, also vary, although using standardised definitions and measurement across 42 European countries, the Health Behaviour in School Children (HBSC) survey reported an average of 11% of 11-15-year-olds had been bullied at school at least two or three times in the past couple of months.[301]

The definition of cyberbullying is even more unstable, partly because it is a newer phenomenon, occurring on still-evolving technological devices and platforms.[302] While at core it concerns aggression expressed by peers through digital (online or mobile) technologies targeting a child victim,[303] some assert that the aggression need not be repeated, since cyberbullying messages are easily and widely shared, multiplying the harm by multiplying the number of bystanders and the persistent possibility of future sharing. Others have argued power imbalances operate differently, if at all, online.

While bullying has traditionally occurred in a host of places little monitored by adults (the school bus, the local park or back street, the school toilets), cyberbullying also occurs in places little monitored by adults (by text messages on a personal mobile phone, in multiplayer online games, on social networking sites – especially those that parents have not used or even heard of). But while traditional bullying depends on the co-location of perpetrator and victim, cyberbullying can occur around the clock, reaching into the victim's private and once-safe places, its messages hitting home without the perpetrator necessarily being aware of their effects, and they may circulate long after the perpetrator has forgotten about them. Importantly, the anonymity afforded by many online platforms is widely held to facilitate disinhibition and deindividuation.[304] In other words, perpetrators feel able to act aggressively online in ways they would not when face-to-face with potential victims, because the social norms that constrain them are weaker when they cannot be identified and because they cannot see the emotional effect on their victim.[305]

In terms of demography it appears that, while traditionally bullying is perpetrated more by boys and younger teenagers, cyberbullying occurs relatively equally among boys and girls[306] and across the teenage years.[307] This may reflect the stronger social norms that constrain the actions of girls and older teenagers in 'real world' physical locations, suggesting that the motivations[308] that drive cyberbullying are themselves more evenly distributed than has been evident from their manifestation in traditional bullying. It may also be that age and gender interact, since in one study girls were "more likely to report cyber-bullying [others] during early adolescence while males were more likely to be cyberbullies during later adolescence."[309]

In terms of victims, research suggests that, both offline and online, victims are more likely to come from minority ethnic or LGBT groups, to be disabled or facing mental health, emotional or familial difficulties.[310] In terms of harm, the debate rages as to whether the consequences of cyberbullying are lesser,[311] similar or worse[312] than from traditional bullying. It does appear, however, that online as offline, bullying of others places the bully also at risk of victimisation.[313]

Incidence of cyberbullying over time

While it is clear that access to and use of mobile and online technologies continues to rise among children,[314] it is much less clear that cyberbullying is rising commensurately, notwithstanding popular perceptions of rising risk of harm. Some research has charted evidence of rising cyberbullying in the early 2000s across several countries,[315] although others observe that the evidence for rising or stable incidence is mixed.[316] In the USA,[317] UK,[318] and Belgium[319] it seems the rate of cyberbullying has peaked. An influential international review concluded that:

> the rates found in our research, though cross-sectional, have not demonstrated any significant trend as increasing or decreasing over the last ten years. Furthermore, there is no cross-sectional or longitudinal research that we have reviewed which portrays such a tendency.[320]

Interestingly, there is also little evidence for an overall rise in bullying around the world. Comparing findings for 33 countries from 2001 to 2010, the HBSC survey reports "decreasing trends in bullying victimization among boys and girls across a third of participating countries; with few countries reporting increasing trends in bullying victimization."[321] This implies that, insofar as there is scattered evidence of a rise in cyberbullying, this may be due more to increased access to technology than to an increase in the underlying conditions of aggression among children.

As yet, few studies have tracked the incidence of cyberbullying even over the period of a decade. The exception is the Youth Internet Safety Survey, which measured the broader concept of 'online harassment' rather than cyberbullying specifically. This found that 6% of US 10- to 17-year-olds reported such incidents in 2000, 9% in 2005, and 11% in 2010.[322] More recent studies, albeit over shorter time periods, suggest equally modest increases. Comparing findings in 2010 and 2014 in Europe, the EU Kids Online project reported a small increase in cyberbullying (from 8% of 9- to 16-year-olds to 12%, across seven countries).[323] The Kids Online Brazil study of 9- to 17-year-olds reported a rise in cyberbullying from 9% in 2012 to 15% in 2014, especially among girls, across a period in which internet access spread among children in Brazil.[324]

Thus while these time periods are fairly short, and trends are modest, they generally point in an upwards direction. What remains unknown is whether these trends reflect increased risk in proportion to the increase in internet use. Or, do they instead reflect increased awareness and, thus, increased reporting, whether as a result of increased familiarity with the internet or because of active policy and safety initiatives. In other words, the common-sense perception of rising rates of cyberbullying may reflect growing public awareness of such risks, with more young people able to talk publicly about being cyberbullied and high levels of media attention to tragic incidents linked to cyberbullying.[325] Complicating matters, in a country such as South Korea, where internet use has been very high for some years, a five year study revealed decreasing rates of cyberbullying, albeit that cyberbullying is still more frequent than in Europe.[326]

In short, there is evidence of a slight rise in cyberbullying over recent years in some countries, but evidence of a peak in incidence in others, especially where internet use has itself possibly peaked in terms of reach. Interpreting such evidence is confounded by the likelihood that, as society comes to rely ever more on internet use, public awareness of the associated risks also rises, so that seeming growth in risk to children may be attributed to a greater willingness to report.

Explaining trends in cyberbullying is even more complex, and more research in more countries is certainly advisable before strong conclusions are reached or before the experience of any one country is used to ground policy or practice in another. Generally speaking, it does seem that cyberbullying is a new form – perhaps a reconfiguration – of traditional bullying, because many studies report a strong correlation between traditional bullying and cyberbullying.[327] Moreover, in many studies, traditional bullying remains more common than cyberbullying – for instance, in Europe, as shown by both EU Kids Online[328] and HBSC surveys,[329] and in the USA,[330] where it is noteworthy that, still, most incidents occur offline-only, or both on- and offline, while fewer incidents occur online-only.[331]

Yet, while this might lead us to conclude that traditional bullying not only remains the bigger problem but is also 'migrating' onto online and mobile platforms, in some countries there is evidence that cyberbullying is a distinct problem with its own characteristics. For example, in Turkey[332] and France[333] the relation between traditional and cyberbullying is weaker, and in some contexts (for example, in Thailand)[334] cyberbullying is becoming more common than traditional bullying. Thus it appears that offline bullying practices are, in some ways, migrating online but in other ways, peer aggression is taking new forms and finding expression in new ways online.

Indeed, given the changeable technological and social conditions under which cyberbullying occurs, and given that the criteria of intentionality, repetition[335] and power imbalance[336] are less important than for traditional bullying, it can be hard to distinguish cyberbullying from other forms of mobile and online aggression.[337] These include 'trolling', stalking, harassment, 'outing', 'sexting', 'hating', racist/hateful language and other forms of abusive comments and online actions. In consequence, delineating cyberbullying from other kinds of online aggression is not straightforward and, arguably, becoming less so. Furthermore, the very nature of the online environment is producing new ambiguities, blurring the distinctions between bully and victim[338] and even bystander,[339] for instance; or blurring the boundaries between bullying and other risks (for example, sexual harassment).[340] It even blurs the boundaries between cyberbullying and other –

perhaps innocent - forms of online 'drama'.[341] In a fluid context with changing technological affordances (in terms of visibility, privacy, persistence, and so on), defining clear demarcations among types of practice is difficult, and it is made more complex by children's own pleasure in experimenting with new and sometimes transgressive forms of communication 'under the radar' of adult scrutiny.[342]

Conclusions

Because cyberbullying is conducted at a distance, leaving no physical mark and mediated only by words and images, it seems that teachers, parents and policy-makers have been slow to recognise the potential severity of the consequences, perhaps believing the old English saying that "sticks and stone may break your bones but words will never hurt you." One lesson of cyberbullying research, however, is that words shape identities, social relations, and well-being. This lesson has been driven home by the few but notable incidents of suicide,[343] among other harms such as loss of empathy,[344] linked to (though not caused in any simple sense by)[345] cyberbullying. Yet some of the phenomena commonly labelled as cyberbullying blur into ordinary and often harmless interactions among children as they explore and experiment with the internet and mobile technology.

This chapter has reviewed why, in terms of the conditions that motivate it,[346] there are good reasons to conclude that "cyberbullying should be considered within the context of bullying rather than as a separate entity" or as a practice newly invented for the digital age.[347] Since "traditional bullying seems to carry over into cyberbullying, [but] cyberbullying does not appear to turn into bullying,"[348] it may also be that interventions found to reduce traditional bullying may also help reduce cyberbullying.[349]

On the other hand, there is also merit in exploring technology-oriented solutions to complement traditional approaches, especially for those cases or contexts where the link between traditional and cyberbullying is weaker. There is also merit in exploring technology-oriented solutions insofar as the specificities of the online environment and its contextual embedding in children's daily lives appear to complicate or reconfigure traditional bullying in new ways.[350]

Indeed, while it is unlikely that traditional bullying ever constituted a single or simple phenomenon, what is striking today is, in the words of one Australian study, the "extremely complicated combinations of traditional and cyberbullying perpetration and victimization in which the students engaged."[351] Thus it may be concluded that separate discussion of traditional bullying and cyberbullying definitions, incidence and policy misses the deeper trend, which is to recognise the increasing connections between the two. The research question, then, should not be whether cyberbullying is best explained by either the conditions that shape mobile and internet use or the conditions underlying traditional bullying and other forms of societal aggression. Rather, we should be asking when, where and how do mobile and online technologies facilitate bullying by mediating, mitigating or amplifying forms of peer aggression so as to fuse traditional and cyberbullying in both familiar and new ways.

Endnotes

291 We thank the following for their contributions to this article: Alexandre Barbosa, Cetic.br, Brazil; Fiona Brooks, Faculty of Health, University of Technology Sydney, Australia; Patrick Burton, Centre for Justice and Crime Prevention, South Africa; Marilyn Campbell, School of Cultural and Professional Learning, Queensland University of Technology, Australia; Anne Collier, The Net Safety Collaborative, USA; Sandra Cortesi, Berkman Center for Internet and Society, Harvard University, USA; Heidi Vandebosch, Department of Communication Studies, University of Antwerp, Belgium; David Finkelhor, Crimes against Children Research Center, Department of Sociology, University of New Hampshire, USA; Vivian Chen Hsueh-Hua, Nanyang Technological University, Singapore; Sun Sun Lim, Department of Communications and New Media, National University of Singapore, Singapore; Justin Patchin, Cyberbullying Research Center, University of Wisconsin-Eau Claire, USA; Peter K Smith, Unit for School and Family Studies, Department of Psychology, Goldsmiths, University of London, UK; Elisabeth Staksrud, Department of Media and Communication, University of Oslo, Norway; Nancy Willard, Embrace Civility in the Digital Age, USA; Michelle Ybarra, Center for Innovative Public Health Research, USA.

292 Sabella, RA et al. (2013). Cyberbullying myths and realities. *Computers in Human Behavior,* 29(6): 2703-2711.

293 Livingstone, S et al. (2015). *One in Three: The Task for Global Internet Governance in Addressing Children's Rights.* Global Commission on Internet Governance: Paper Series. London: CIGI and Chatham House. Available at: https://ourinternet.org/publication/one-in-three-internet-governance-and-childrens-rights/.

294 Li, Q et al. (2011). *Cyberbullying in the Global Playground: Research from International Perspectives.* Malden, MA: Wiley-Blackwell.

295 Baek, J, Bullock, LM (2014). Cyberbullying: A Cross-cultural Perspective. *Emotional and Behavioural Difficulties,* 19(2): 226-238.

296 Chester, KL et al. (2015). Cross-national Time Trends in Bullying Victimization in 33 Countries among Children Aged 11, 13 and 15 from 2002 to 2010. *The European Journal of Public Health,* 25(suppl 2): 61-64.

297 Chan, HC et al. (2015). Traditional School Bullying and Cyberbullying in Chinese Societies: Prevalence and a Review of the Whole-School Intervention Approach. *Aggression and Violent Behavior,* 23: 98-108.

298 Wright, MF (2014). Longitudinal Investigation of the Associations Between Adolescents' Popularity and Cyber Social Behaviors. *Journal of School Violence,* 13(3): 291-314.

299 Livingstone, S et al. (Eds) (2012). *Children, Risk and Safety Online: Research and Policy Challenges in Comparative Perspective.* Bristol: The Policy Press.

300 Livingstone, S, Smith, PK (2014). Annual Research Review: Harms Experienced by Child Users of Online and Mobile Technologies: the Nature, Prevalence and Management of Sexual and Aggressive Risks in the Digital Age. *Journal of Child Psychology and Psychiatry,* 55(6): 635-654.

301 Inchley, J et al. (2016) (Eds). *Growing up unequal: gender and socioeconomic differences in young people's health and well-being.* Health Behaviour in School-aged Children (HBSC) study: international report from the 2013/2014 survey. Copenhagen, WHO Regional Office for Europe (Health Policy for Children and Adolescents, No. 7).

302 Tokunaga, RS (2010). Following You Home from School: A Critical Review and Synthesis of Research on Cyberbullying Victimization. *Computers in Human Behavior,* 26(3): 277-287.

303 Levy N et al. (2012). Bullying in a Networked Era: A Literature Review. *Berkman Center Research Publication.* Available at: http://papers.ssrn.com/sol3/papers.cfm?abstract_id=2146877.

304 Kowalski, RM et al. (2014). Bullying in the Digital Age: a Critical Review and Meta-Analysis of Cyberbullying Research among Youth. *Psychological Bulletin,* 140(4): 1073-1137.

305 Kubiszewski, V et al. (2015). Does Cyberbullying Overlap with School Bullying when Taking Modality of Involvement into Account? *Computers in Human Behavior,* 43: 49-57.

306 Livingstone, S et al. (2011). *Risks and Safety on the Internet: The Perspective of European Children.* Full Findings. LSE, London: EU Kids Online. Available at: http://eprints.lse.ac.uk/33731/.

307 Waasdorp, TE, Bradshaw, CP (2015). The Overlap between Cyberbullying and Traditional Bullying. *Journal of Adolescent Health,* 56(5): 483-488.

308 Sticca, F et al. (2013). Longitudinal Risk Factors for Cyberbullying in Adolescence. *Journal of Community & Applied Social Psychology,* 23(1): 52-67.

309 Barlett, C, Coyne, SM (2014). A Meta-analysis of Sex Differences in Cyber-bullying Behavior: The Moderating Role of Age. *Aggressive Behavior,* 40(4): 474-488: p. 481.

310 Baek, J, Bullock, LM (2014). Op. cit.

311 Campbell, M et al. (2012). Victims' Perceptions of Traditional and Cyberbullying, and the Psychosocial Correlates of Their Victimisation. *Emotional and Behavioural Difficulties,* 17(3-4): 389-401.

312 Cassidy, W et al. (2013). Cyberbullying among Youth: A Comprehensive Review of Current International Research and its Implications and Application to Policy and Practice. *School Psychology International,* 34(6): 575-612.

313 Jose, PE et al. (2012). The Joint Development of Traditional Bullying and Victimization with Cyber Bullying and Victimization in Adolescence. *Journal of Research on Adolescence,* 22(2): 301-309.

314 ITU (2013). Measuring the Information Society 2013: *Measuring the World's Digital Natives.* Available at: http://www.itu.int/en/ITU-D/Statistics/Documents/publications/mis2013/MIS2013_without_Annex_4.pdf.

315 Aoyama, I, Talbert, TL (2010). Cyberbullying Internationally Increasing: New Challenges in the Technology Generation. *Adolescent Online Social Communication and Behavior: Relationship Formation on the Internet.* Hershey, NY: Information Science Reference, pp.183-201.

316 Cassidy, W et al. (2013). Op. cit.

317 Patchin, JW, Hinduja, S (2016). *Bullying Today: Bullet Points and Best Practices.* Thousand Oaks, CA: Sage.

318 Rivers I, Noret N (2010). 'I h8 u': Findings from a Five-year Study of Text and Email Bullying. *British Educational Research Journal,* 36: 643–671.

319 Valcke, M et al. (2011). Long-term Study of Safe Internet Use of Young Children. *Computers & Education,* 57(1): 1292-1305.

320 Hinduja, S, Patchin, JW (2012). Cyberbullying: Neither an Epidemic nor a Rarity. *European Journal of Developmental Psychology,* 9(5): 539-543: p. 541

321 Chester, KL et al. (2015). Cross-national Time Trends in Bullying Victimization in 33 Countries among Children Aged 11, 13 and 15 from 2002 to 2010. *The European Journal of Public Health,* 25(suppl 2): 61-64: p. 63.

322 Jones, LM et al. (2013). Online Harassment in Context: Trends from Three Youth Internet Safety Surveys (2000, 2005, 2010). *Psychology of Violence,* 3(1): 53.

323 Livingstone, S et al. (2014). *Children's Online Risks and Opportunities: Comparative Findings from EU Kids Online and Net Children Go Mobile.* LSE, London: EU Kids Online. Available at: http://eprints.lse.ac.uk/60513/.

324 Barbosa, A (2015). *ICT Kids Online Brazil.* Sao Paolo: Regional Centre for Studies on the Development of the Information Society, Cetic.br.

325 Haddon, L, Stald, G (2009). A Comparative Analysis of European Press Coverage of Children and the Internet. *Journal of Children and Media,* 3(4): 379–393.

326 Jang, H et al. (2014). Does the Offline Bully-Victimization Influence Cyberbullying Behavior among Youths? Application of General Strain Theory. *Computers in Human Behavior,* 31:85-93.

327 Baldry AC (2015). "Am I at Risk of Cyberbullying?" A Narrative Review and Conceptual Framework for Research on Risk of Cyberbullying and Cybervictimization: The Risk and Needs Assessment Approach. *Aggression and Violent Behavior,* 23: 36-51.

328 Livingstone, S et al. (2011). Op. cit.

329 Inchley, J et al. (2016) (Eds). Op. cit.

330 Modecki, KL et al. (2014). Bullying Prevalence Across Contexts: A Meta-analysis Measuring Cyber and Traditional Bullying. *Journal of Adolescent Health,* 55(5): 602-611.

331 Mitchell, KJ et al. (2015). The Role of Technology in Peer Harassment: Does It Amplify Harm for Youth? *Pscyhology of Violence,* 6(2): 193–204.

332 Erdur-Baker, O (2010). Cyberbullying and Its Correlation to Traditional Bullying, Gender and Frequent and Risky Usage of Internet-mediated Communication Tools. *New Media & Society,* 12(1): 109-125.

333 Kubiszewski, V et al. (2015). Does Cyberbullying Overlap with School Bullying when Taking Modality of Involvement into Account? *Computers in Human Behavior,* 43: 49-57.

334 Sittichai, R (2014). Information Technology Behavior Cyberbullying in Thailand: Incidence and Predictors of Victimization and Cyber-victimization. *Asian Social Science,* 10(11): 132.

335 Katz, I et al. (2014). *Research on Youth Exposure to, and Management of, Cyberbullying Incidents in Australia:* Synthesis Report. Social Policy Research Centre, UNSW Australia.

336 Wegge, D et al. (2016). Popularity through Online Harm the Longitudinal Associations between Cyberbullying and Sociometric Status in Early Adolescence. *The Journal of Early Adolescence,* 36(1): 86-107.

337 Ybarra, ML et al. (2014). Differentiating Youth Who Are Bullied from Other Victims of Peer-Aggression: The Importance of Differential Power and Repetition. *Journal of Adolescent Health,* 55(2): 293-300.

338 Görzig, A (2011). *Who Bullies and Who is Bullied Online? A Study of 9-16 Year-old Internet Users in 25 European Countries EU Kids Online.* London, UK. Available at: http://eprints.lse.ac.uk/39601.

339 Law, DM et al. (2012). The Changing Face of Bullying: An Empirical Comparison between Traditional and Internet Bullying and Victimization. *Computers in Human Behavior,* 28(1): 226-232.

340 Görzig A, Livingstone S (2012). Adolescents' Multiple Risk Behaviours on the Internet across 25 European Countries. *Neuropsychiatrie de l'Enfance et de l'Adolescence,* 60(5): S148.

341 Marwick, A, boyd, d (2014). 'It's Just Drama': Teen Perspectives on Conflict and Aggression in a Networked Era. *Journal of Youth Studies,* 6261(May 2015): 1-18.

342 Livingstone, S (2008). Taking risky opportunities in youthful content creation: teenagers' use of social networking sites for intimacy, privacy and self-expression. *New Media & Society,* 10(3): 393-411. Available at: http://eprints.lse.ac.uk/27072/

343 van Geel, M et al. (2014). Relationship Between Peer Victimization, Cyberbullying, and Suicide in Children and Adolescents: A Meta-analysis. *JAMA Pediatrics,* 168(5): 435.

344 Pabian S et al. (2016). Exposure to Cyberbullying as a Bystander: An Investigation of Desensitization Effects Among Early Adolescents. *Computers in Human Behavior,* 62: 480-487.

345 Sabella, RA et al. (2013). Op. cit.

346 Patchin, JW, Hinduja, S (2010b). Traditional and Nontraditional Bullying Among Youth: A Test of General Strain Theory. *Youth & Society.*

347 National Academies of Sciences, Engineering, and Medicine (2016). *Preventing Bullying Through Science, Policy, and Practice.* Washington, DC: The National Academies Press: p. S-3.

348 Del Rey, R et al. (2012). Bullying and Cyberbullying: Overlapping and Predictive Value of the Co-occurrence. *Psicothema,* 24(4): 608-613: p. 612

349 Casas, JA et al. (2013). Bullying and Cyberbullying: Convergent and Divergent Predictor Variables. *Computers in Human Behavior,* 29(3): 580-587.

350 Kwan, GCE, Skoric, MM (2013). Facebook Bullying: An Extension of Battles in School. *Computers in Human Behavior,* 29(1): 16-25.

351 Tanrikulu, I, Campbell, M (2015). Correlates of Traditional Bullying and Cyberbullying Perpetration among Australian Students. *Children and Youth Services Review,* 55: 138-146: pp. 143-4.

Maria learns computer skills at a teacher-training college, Angola
© UNICEF/UNI48650/Nesbitt

15. Bullying and Cyberbullying in Southern Africa

Patrick Burton

Introduction

Bullying is receiving increasing attention across a range of countries within Southern Africa. For example, in 2015, the Ministry for Arts, Education and Culture in Namibia, together with UNICEF, launched an anti-bullying campaign to raise awareness of the magnitude of the problem, and to attempt to harmonize efforts to address it. In South Africa, the Department of Basic Education has prioritized school bullying within its approach to the prevention of school violence more broadly. In Kenya, bullying has been criminalized through legislation. Despite this growing concern at a governmental level, there is little reliable, representative and recent data on the extent of bullying, or its relationship to other forms of violence, or related harms, and it is often seen as secondary to other forms of violence such as sexual violence or violent physical attacks. This lack of, or at best patchy, data, inhibits the evaluation of the impact of policies where they do exist, or the development of policies where none currently exist.

Where data does exist, estimates across studies and between countries vary considerably, explained in part by different focuses, definitions, sampling and representativeness. There are fewer cross-country comparative studies. One of the few are the TIMSS and PIRLS studies, which collect data using standardized definitions across South Africa, Ghana and Botswana.[352] These studies reveal relatively similar rates across the three countries, of between 40% of girls who report experiencing weekly bullying in schools in South Africa, to 54% of boys in Ghanaian schools. This data varies considerably from, for example, the 2013 National Schools Violence Study in South Africa, which shows that 13% of children had experienced some form of school bullying in the preceding year.[353]

Data collected in South Africa also highlights highly diverse incidence rates. A 2012 study examining bullying among secondary school learners in Gauteng Province found that 34.4% of children had been personally bullied, 38.1% of children knew peers who had been bullied and 23.3% of children admitted to perpetrating bullying themselves.[354] Older studies have found various rates, ranging from 61% of secondary school learners in South Africa's capital city, Tshwane,[355] to 41% of secondary school learners in a nationally representative sample[356] and 36.3% among grade 8 and grade 11 learners in the cities of Cape Town and Durban.[357]

Data from Zimbabwe reveals significantly higher levels of bullying: a 2014 study in the Chetegu district found that 64% of learners had observed bullying in their school, while 42% had themselves been bullied.[358] A 2010 situational analysis by the Namibian National Planning Commission found that 22.6% of learners interviewed reported being verbally teased, insulted and intimidated at school, with 18% saying they had been physically attacked at school.[359] In a 2008 study in Zambia, 60% of learners reported being bullied within a one month period, while in Kenya, a 2007 study of learners in Nairobi District reported that between 63% and 83% of learners experienced bullying.[360] The estimates are thus widely variable for bullying across studies, countries, and over the timeframes of the studies that do exist.

Defining bullying

Bullying is arguably one of the most common forms of violence that children experience during the course of the childhood, both within and outside of school. While there is some disagreement on what constitutes bullying, most research builds on the definition developed by Olweus, encompassing three core elements: bullying is characterised by the purposeful harming of victim in some way, occurs repeatedly over time and involves some form of power imbalance between the bully and the victim, whether it be physical power or social capital.[361]

Bullying is especially prevalent during adolescence. Some theorise that it is a developmental phenomenon that increases during childhood, peaks in early adolescence and starts to decline by late adolescence.³⁶² As a result, school going children are often most affected by bullying and schools are frequently the sites where this bullying plays out.

There has been much conjecture around why bullies may act out aggressively, with early research on the topic theorising that bullies may have poor social skills, low self-esteem or low intelligence.³⁶³ However, more recent research argues that bullies typically have good self-esteem, high intelligence and an understanding of the social and psychological impact of their actions, but engage in harmful behaviours nonetheless because it provides them with a social reward.³⁶⁴ Through their bullying behaviour and assertion of dominance, bullies accrue higher social status.

Critical to obtaining this status is the action of bystanders, who through their passive observation, or at times, active support of the bullying behaviour, provide the bully with the necessary social reward to motivate their behaviour.³⁶⁵ For the bystander, intervening to prevent bullying places the individual at significant social, as well as physical risk of becoming a victim of bullying themselves and succumbing to the bully's social dominance. That said, research has found that the more bystanders intervene in favour of the victim, the less bullying occurs, suggesting that this loss of social status acts as a deterrent to bullies.

Academics differentiate between three roles in bullying scenarios: the bully, the victim and the bully-victim. Bullies may tend to be aggressive and seek out social dominance while victims may tend to be more passive, anxious and have low self-esteem. In some cases, a single child may both bully others and be bullied themselves, possessing qualities of aggression and dominance but also low self-esteem.³⁶⁶ These children may attempt to bully others but perhaps not be perceived as sufficiently dominant and come to be viewed as irritating. As a result peers may bully this individual in return, and research suggests that this impacts greatly on the psychological wellbeing of the bully-victims, who often report greater negative psychological outcomes than other bullied children.

While there is some debate around this, gender is often thought to impact on the type and extent to which children experience bullying. Boys have been found to be both bully and be victimised (a bully-victim) more than girls, and to be exposed to more direct bullying.³⁶⁷ Girls meanwhile, have been found to be more likely to be the victims of bullying behaviours and be exposed to indirect bullying.³⁶⁸ Bullying may occur when a child is perceived from departing from conventional gender norms or stereotypes. In general, it has been found that bullying is more likely to take place within a gender, rather than between genders.

Harmful outcomes of bullying

Bullying has been found to have a number of potentially negative consequences for its victims, especially because bullying typically affects individuals when they are at their most psychologically vulnerable, during their teenage years. The effects of bullying can manifest behaviourally and psychologically, and impact on the life outcomes of individuals. Research has found associations between being bullied and anxiety, psychosomatic complaints, avoidance behaviour, depression, low self-esteem and general distress.³⁶⁹ For some victims this can escalate into self-harm, suicidal thoughts, attempted suicide and in the worst cases, suicide.³⁷⁰ It has also been found that in some cases victimisation is associated with behavioural problems, like substance abuse, engaging in violent behaviour and bringing weapons to school.³⁷¹

While bullying is clearly associated with a number of negative outcomes, it is often difficult to determine the direction of these relationships. A child may report experiences of being bullied and a number of negative psychological symptoms but whether a child experiences these negative outcomes as a result of the bullying they have experienced, or becomes susceptible to bullying as a result of these underlying vulnerabilities, is unclear.³⁷² This makes it difficult to determine the negative outcomes that come as a direct consequence of bullying.

Bullying has also been found to be linked to harmful outcomes for perpetrators. Some studies have found that bullying is associated with conviction for a crime in early adulthood, risk-taking behaviours like substance abuse and poor academic achievement.³⁷³ It has also been found that perpetrating bullying is associated with negative mental outcomes such as depression, conduct-disorder, psychosomatic complaints and suicide. Engaging in bullying may therefore be an indication of a broader range of problematic behaviours, as well as of poor emotional wellbeing.

Cyberbullying and its relation to bullying

Cyberbullying has emerged as a concern globally over the last decade. As with "offline"" or conventional bullying, the definition of cyberbullying is contested, and like bullying, variations in definitions between studies prevent accurate comparison between studies both within across countries.

Globally, researchers are defining and framing online violence in different ways, and there remains a need for a unified framework for defining and conceptualising cyberbullying. Terms like online harassment, digital violence, Internet harassment, electronic aggression and cyberbullying are often used interchangeably, while metrics for measuring these concepts also vary. As discussed below, the use of different terms, and different methods for 'measuring' definitions, has implications for empirical research, policy and children's rights.[374]

A recent systematic review of online violence literature shows that Olweus' definition of bullying is the most commonly used definition by online violence scholars.[375] This approach encompasses the same three core characteristics as bullying defined above, but incorporates the use of electronic contact: an aggressive, intentional act carried out by a group, or individuals, using electronic forms of contact, repeatedly and over time against a victim who cannot easily defend him or herself. The authors show that the inclusion of the concepts of 'intent to cause harm', 'imbalance of power', and 'repetition of the act', become critical when operationalizing the definition of cyberbullying in empirical research, and studies that incorporated 'imbalance of power' and 'repetition' into their survey design reported markedly lower rates of cyberbullying than those studies that relied on broader terms and definitions.

Perpetrators of internet harassment frequently target people they already know in an offline context, and both perpetrators and victims of online bullying often have similar psychological traits as their offline counterparts.[376] Indeed, the divide between online and offline is no longer binary, with more and more blurring between the two: "Drawing the line between offline and online is becoming close to impossible; almost any experience has an online dimension, whether through a direct engagement by the child or through provision of services designed to improve children's lives".[377] The blurring between online and offline forms of violence becomes an important factor in designing interventions.

However, some of the unique characteristics of cyberbullying, such as the permanency of the digital footprint, the capacity for aggressors to remain anonymous, the sheer scale of a viral offence, and the potential for online violence to permeate "all the spheres and spaces in which young people live their lives" may lead to distinct impacts and harms on children, schools, families, and community that require new research models to fully grasp.[378]

Cyberbullying in Southern Africa

There exists a dearth of literature and reliable studies within Southern Africa on cyberbullying, reflecting a wider imbalance between the Global North and the Global South in research on violence, and particularly on bullying.[379] It is only recently that cyberbullying has emerged as a concern in most Southern African countries. The difficulties in drawing conclusions on both the extent and the nature of cyberbullying reflect a wider lack of knowledge and data on children and Information and Communication Technologies (ICTs) in Southern Africa, and within urban and rural areas in general. Arguably, the issue of cyberbullying has also been perceived as relatively unimportant within the context of other forms of violence against children, and within a framework of more fundamental structural and institutional challenges in the region.

Much of the data that does exist on cyberbullying comes from South Africa. In a 2012 study of 5,939 secondary school learners in South Africa, one in five (20.9%) reported having experienced some form of cyberbullying over the last year.[380] The study located cyberbullying within a broader analytical framework of school violence. Like other forms of bullying, the most common perpetrators of cyberbullying were peers of the learner, either from within school or outside of school, and were generally known to the child. In the 2016 Optimus Foundation Study on Child Abuse, Violence and Neglect, just over one in ten (15.1%) of children between the ages of 15 and 17 reported being cyberbullied over a one year period.[381] Data from both studies suggest that girls tend to experience cyberbullying more than boys, or at least are more willing to disclose their experiences: 19% of females had experienced cyberbullying, compared to just over one in ten (12%) males. Like the 2012 study, the bully was usually known to the child, further reflecting international trends.[382]

Apart from South Africa, only Namibia has data on the extent of cyberbullying. Rates are similar to those in South Africa. A 2016 study on child online protection showed that 15% of children in five pilot sites reported being cyberbullied.[383] As in South Africa, girls were more likely to experience being cyberbullied than boys (17% as opposed to 14%). For both boys and girls, cyberbullying was ranked as the second most traumatic experience online, behind only requests for sexual images of oneself.

Shared vulnerabilities: bullying, cyberbullying and other experiences of violence

Research from the Global North points to the relationship between "offline" and "online" bullying and aggression, both in its form, and in the vulnerabilities to both perpetration and victimization. For example, victims of traditional bullying are more likely to experience cyberbullying,[384] and cyberbullying incidents are commonly linked to, or originate in, events or experiences that happen offline, particularly at school.[385]

Research shows similar findings for South Africa. A study by the Centre for Justice and Crime Prevention and the University of Cape Town found that 36% of children who report being bullied also experienced some form of cyberbullying, compared to 17% of those children who had not been bullied.[386] Similar findings are evident between cyberbullying and other forms of victimization, including sexual violence. The same study shows that children who experience cyberbullying are three times more likely than those who have not to experience some form of contact or non-contact sexual victimization, while 29% of those that had experienced cyberbullying reported they had "had an adult hit, kick or physically hurt (them)", compared to only 19% of those who did not report having been cyberbullied.[387] Similarly, of those who had experienced cyberbullying at some point in their life, 26% had also experienced psychological maltreatment, compared to just 14% of those who had not.[388]

Conclusion: towards a common bullying agenda for Southern Africa

Bullying, both traditional and cyber, is clearly related to other forms of violence, and to a multiple range of risk factors that cut across different forms of violence and vulnerabilities. Schools have been identified as a valuable intervention point to both build protective factors for bullying, and to prevent the development of bullying and other aggressive behaviour. Given the proven linkages between digital violence and traditional forms of peer violence experienced by children, taking systematic preventive measures to reduce one form of violence will yield results in reducing online violence. There is evidence to show that intervening through social and emotional learning initiatives focusing on bullying at schools can yield positive outcomes in the prevention of cyberbullying.[389] Yet within the Southern Africa region, there is as yet no evidence of effective bullying and cyberbullying interventions located within broader violence prevention and child safety policy initiatives.

South Africa's experience provides an example of how school violence, including bullying and cyberbullying, can be addressed at a national level, using a coordinated response that locates bullying within a broader violence prevention framework and simultaneously seeks to prevent all forms of violence. In response to calls for an integrated school safety framework that explicitly addresses all forms of violence at school within a whole school approach to violence prevention, the Department of Basic Education developed the National School Safety Framework.[390] This provides an integrated management tool to assist school managers, school governing bodies, district and provincial education officials, and all members of the larger school family, including learners, educators, parents, support staff and administrators, to deal more effectively with violence. The Framework also locates the school within the broader environment of local government and communities, mapping out the relationships between school and community, family and local government that are required to prevent bullying and all forms of violence. Rather than offering interventions, the Framework aims to equip schools with the tools to identify the risk of violence occurring, to identify gaps and weaknesses, and to direct schools to appropriate resources and interventions based on specific needs. Such a national policy response, and its recognition of the prerequisite of a whole school approach to preventing violence, is an important step in addressing all forms of violence, including bullying, and in its prevention, and the response to it when it occurs.

Yet, as noted earlier in this paper, there remains little reliable, nationally representative data on bullying to inform implementation, or around which evidenced-based policies and programming can be developed, or to measure its impact on other forms of violence. As such, the collection of nationally representative data should be a priority. Deepening the evidence base offers an opportunity to build on emerging national policies that seek to address all forms of violence, and to build a national and regional agenda that:

1. Defines and adopts common definitions of bullying that encompass its many forms, while also recognizing specific types, including bullying on the basis of sexual identify, race and culture, religion, or disability.

2. Locates bullying within a broader violence prevention paradigm that recognizes the profound psychological, emotional, physical, health and economic harmful outcomes of bullying, and positions bullying in relation to all other forms of violence experienced by children.

3. Emphasises the risk and protective factors that can provide the basis for evidence-based interventions.

4. Commits itself to the collection of data and the implementation of evidence-based programming, and the testing, scale-up and commitment of dedicated funding to support evidence-led interventions.

Through partnerships of researchers, governments and education systems throughout Southern Africa, such an agenda can be developed to combat the violence of bullying that so manifestly affects the lives of children throughout the region.

Endnotes

352. Mullis, IVS et al. (2012a). *TIMSS 2011 International Results in Mathematics*. TIMSS and PIRLS International Study Center, Boston College, Chestnut Hill, MA; Mullis, IVS et al.

353. One explanation here could be the different time frames within which experiences are located.; Burton P & Leoschut L (2013). *School violence in South Africa.* Monograph 12: The Centre for Justice and Crime Prevention. Available at: http://www.cjcp.org.za/uploads/2/7/8/4/27845461/monograph12-school-violence-in-south_africa.pdf

354. UNISA Bureau of Market Research (2012). *Nature, extent and impact of bullying among secondary school learners in Gauteng.* Available at: http://www.unisa.ac.za/contents/faculties/ems/docs/Gauteng_Technical%20Report_School%20violence_Bullying.pdf

355. Neser, JJ, Ovens, M, van der Merwe, E, Morodi, R & Ladikos, A (2003). *Peer victimisation in schools: The victims.* Available at: http://www.crisa.org.za/victimsp.pdf

356. Reddy, SP, Panday, S, Swart, D, Jinabhai, CC, Amosun, SL, James, S et al. (2003). *Umthenthe uhlaba usamila: The South African youth risk behaviour survey 2002.* Tygerberg: South African Medical Research Council.

357. Liang, H, Flisher, AJ, & Lombard, CJ (2007). Bullying, violence, and risk behavior in South African school students. *Child Abuse & Neglect,* 31(2): 161-171.

358. Gudyanga, E, Mudihlwa, C & Wadesango, N (2014). The Extent of Bullying in Some Schools in Zimbabwe: A Psychological Perspective, with the Notion of Designing an Intervention Model. Journal of Social Science 40(1): 65-74.

359. UNICEF Namibia and the Namibian National Planning Commission (2010). *Children and Adolescents in Namibia 2010: A situation analysis.* Available at: http://www.unicef.org/sitan/files/SitAn_Namibia_2010.pdf

360. Jones, N, Moore, K, Villar-Marquez, E & Broadbent, E (2008). *Painful Lessons: The Politics of Preventing Sexual Violence and Bullying at School-Working Paper 295.* London: Overseas Development Institute and Plan International. https://www.odi.org/sites/odi.org.uk/files/odi-assets/publications-opinion-files/3312.pdf, accessed 20 July 2016; Odhiambo, G, & Kokonya, DA (2007). Bullying in Public Secondary Schools in Nairobi, Kenya. *Journal of Child and Adolescent Mental Health* 19(1): 45-55.

361. Olweus, D (1993). *Bullying at school: What we know and what we can do.* Oxford, UK: Basil Blackwell.

362. Nocentini, A, et al (2013). Level and change of bullying behavior during high school: A multilevel growth curve analysis, *Journal of Adolescence,* http://dx.doi.org/10.1016/j.adolescence.2013.02.004

363. Protogerou, C, & Flisher, AJ (2012). Bullying in schools. In A van Niekerk, S Suffla & M Seedat (Eds), *Crime, violence and injury in South Africa: 21st century solutions for child safety* (pp 119-133).Tygerberg: MRC-University of South Africa Safety & Peace Promotion Research Unit.

364. Ibid.

365. Menesini, E, Nocentini, A, & Palladino, BE (2012). Empowering students against bullying and cyberbullying: Evaluation of an Italian peer-led model. *International Journal of Conflict and Violence (IJCV)* 6(2): 313-320.

366. Protogerou, C, & Flisher, AJ (2012). Op. cit.

367. Carbone-Lopez, K, Esbensen, FA & Brick, BT (2010). Correlates and consequences of peer victimization: Gender differences in direct and indirect forms of bullying. *Youth violence and juvenile justice* 8(4): 332-350.

368. Ibid.

369. Turner, MG, Exum, ML, Brame, R & Holt, T (2013). Bullying victimization and adolescent mental health: General and typological effects across sex. *Journal of Criminal Justice* 41(1): 53-59.

370. Ibid.

371. Ibid.

372. Turner, MG, Exum, ML, Brame, R & Holt, T (2013). Op. cit.

373. Protogerou, C, & Flisher, AJ (2012). Op. cit.

374. Jones, LM, Mitchell, KJ and Finkelhor D (2013) Online Harassment in Context: Trends From Three Youth Internet Safety Surveys (2000, 2005, 2010). *Psychology of Violence* 3(1): 53-69; Livingstone, S & Smith, PK (2014). Annual Research Review: Harms experienced by child users of online and mobile technologies: the nature, prevalence and management of sexual and aggressive risks in the digital age. *Journal of Child Psychology and Psychiatry* 55 (6): 635–654; Burton, P & Leoschut, L (2013). *Results of the 2012 National School Violence Study,* CJCP Monograph No 12. Cape Town: Centre for Justice and Crime Prevention.

375. Livingstone, S & Smith, PK (2014). Op. cit.

376. Ybarra, ML & Mitchell, KJ (2004). Online aggressor/targets, aggressors, and targets: a comparison of associated youth characteristics. *Journal of Child Psychology and Psychiatry* 45(7): 1308–1316.

377. Livingstone, S & Bulger, M (2013) *A Global Agenda for Children's Rights in the Digital Age.* UNICEF Office of Research: Florence.

378. Samuels, C, Brown, Q, Leoschut, L & Burton, P (2013). *Connected Dot Com: Young People's Navigation of Online Risks, Social Media, ICTs and Online Safety.* Cape Town, Centre for Justice and Crime Prevention and UNICEF South Africa.

379. Kleine, D, Hollow, D & Poveda, S (2013). *Children, ICT and Development: Capturing the potential, meeting the challenges.* Innocenti Insight. Florence, UNICEF Office of Research.

380. Burton, P & Leoschut, L (2013). *Results of the 2012 National School Violence Study,* CJCP Monograph No 12. Cape Town: Centre for Justice an Crime Prevention.

381. Data from Artz, L, Burton, P, Leoschut, L, Ward, C &Kassanjee, R (2016). *Optimus Study South Africa: Sexual Victimization of Children in South Africa.* Cape Town: Centre for Justice and Crime Prevention/University of Cape Town.

382. Mishna, F, Cook, C, Gadalla, T, Daciuk, J & Solomon, S (2010). Cyber bullying behaviours among middle and high school students. *The American Journal of Orthopsychiatry* 80(3): 362–374.

383. UNICEF Namibia (2016). *Child Online Protection in Namibia.* Research Report. Windhoek, UNICEF.

384 Raskauskas, J & Stoltz, AD (2007). Involvement in traditional and electronic bullying among adolescents. *Developmental Psychology* 43(3): 564–575.

385 Wolak, J, Mitchell, KJ & Finkelhor, D (2007). Does online harassment constitute bullying? An exploration of online harassment by known peers and online-only contacts. *Journal of Adolescent Health* 41: S51–S58; Raskauskas, J & Stoltz, AD (2007). Op. cit.; Mishna, F, Khoury-Kassabri, M, Gadalla, T & Daciuk, J (2011). Risk factors for involvement in cyber bullying: Victims, bullies and bully-victims. *Children and Youth Service Review* 34 (2012): 63-70.

386 Data from Artz, L, Burton, P, Leoschut, L, Ward, C &Kassanjee, R (2016). *Optimus Study South Africa: Sexual Victimization of Children in South Africa.* Cape Town: Centre for Justice and Crime Prevention/University of Cape Town.

387 Ibid.

388 Ibid.

389 Menesini, E & Salmivalli, C (2016). *Bullying:* Input Paper to the Know Violence in Childhood Global Learning Initiative. Full Report forthcoming.

390 South African Government Department of Basic Education (2015). National School Safety Framework, http://www.education.gov.za/Programmes/SafetyinSchools.aspx, accessed 25 July 2016

By studying in their mother tongue, children become more confident learners, Viet Nam
© UNICEF/UN09057/Lynch

16. Bullying and educational stress in schools in East Asia
Michael Dunne, Thu Ba Pham, Ha Hai Thi Le and Jiandong Sun[391]

Introduction

Bullying has been studied extensively in western countries for a long time. In the East Asia region there was relatively limited systematic research into bullying until recent years. The general nature of bullying in schools in this region appears similar to global trends. However, in Asia this occurs within a context of pervasive academic stress on children from demanding curricula, teachers and parents and inflexible school examination systems. Although some students thrive in this climate, many are constantly on edge, and some succumb to despair. The nexus between peer bullying and educational stress in Asian schools has not yet been researched in sufficient detail. In this paper we summarise trends in bullying across most countries in East Asia, and focus on recent studies of school bullying and study burden in China and Viet Nam. Much more work is needed to improve the quality of evidence to support systemic change and specialised programs to reduce educational stress and prevent interpersonal violence.

Bullying in East Asian schools

Given the wide cultural, religious and socioeconomic diversity of East Asian school systems, statements about typical characteristics that distinguish Asian education from other regions can easily ring hollow. Also, the rapid pace of change in East Asia defies solid generalisation about conditions in schools. Amid this complexity two intersecting themes recur in discussions of how school climate influences bullying: Collectivism and heavy educational pressure.[392] Of course, these two themes are common to many cultures, but it appears that both are more prominent in the daily lives of children in East Asia than in other parts of the world.

Generally, estimates of bullying prevalence in East Asia are similar to global patterns. A meta-analysis of 80 studies[393] mainly done outside of Asia found traditional bullying perpetration experience ranged from 9.7% to 89.6% of students (mean prevalence of 35%) and traditional bullying victimisation ranged from 9% to 97.9% (mean: 36%). The breadth in estimates of cyberbullying was more narrow, with online perpetration between 5.3% and 31.5% (mean: 16%) and victimisation ranging from 2.2% to 56.2% (mean: 15%). Craig and colleagues[394] reviewed prevalence statistics from 40 countries and also found wide diversity.

The range in prevalence estimates in western countries is also evident in mainland China, Taiwan, Hong Kong and Macau[395], although extremely high figures tend not to be found in Chinese surveys, with upper estimates rarely above 60%. In Southeast Asia, a systematic review of research in the ten ASEAN countries[396] found estimates of the prevalence of traditional bullying victimisation range between 6% and 85%, with the proportion of children admitting to traditional bullying perpetration ranging from 8% to 72%. Cyberbullying victimisation (from 4%

"I feel very stressed with my classmates. They are too diligent. Sometimes I want to relax for 30 minutes but I can't because my classmates keep studying all the time." Secondary school student, Viet Nam (Pham, 2015).

"My parents spend too much time and money for my study. They want me to be a lawyer. They always remind me to study. My duty is study and study and study. I feel bored." Secondary school student, Viet Nam (Pham, 2015).

"During my final year... there was no friendship among classmates....only fierce and cruel competition, betrayal of friends, endless verbal violence...we vented stress by hurting one another." Student in China (Zhao, Selman & Haste 2015, p2).

"I feel insecure if my son doesn't go to private tutors. Every parent sends their children to cram classes, so why not him?" Parent of a high school student, Viet Nam (Pham, 2015).

to 54%) and perpetration (from 5% to 35%) in ASEAN appear similar to non-Asian countries.

Comparative analysis of students' experience of specific acts of bullying victimisation in ten countries in the Asia-Pacific[397] also found considerable variation in prevalence of bullying. For example, being hurt on purpose was reported by 27% to 33% of girls in Indonesia and the Philippines, but only 2.7% of girls surveyed in the Republic of Korea. The differences in prevalence across the ten nations appeared to be greatest for girls; estimates of victimisation experiences of boys tended to be more similar across the region. As is often the case in self-report behavioural surveys, cross-cultural estimates differ for many reasons; arguably most variation between surveys is caused by study design, sampling, measurement and other methodological factors, although some of the diversity reflects actual differences in the underlying risk of bullying in different social, economic, family and school contexts.

The ranges in prevalence estimates in East Asia, like elsewhere in the world, are so wide that they beg the question: What do such prevalence data mean for policy and practice? If we try to understand the extent of the problem by making a graph of the many estimates, we can conclude that somewhere between very few and almost all children are physically bullied, and somewhere between one in twenty and one in two students experience cyberbullying! These estimates are so wide they evoke scepticism among policy makers. The picture is further complicated because measures of central tendency (such as the median prevalence) also vary across different global and regional reviews. Arguably, there is no 'true prevalence' estimate. The search for 'the' prevalence in a population is in some ways illusory. Even with high methodological rigour and validated measures, the beast we are trying to hold down and quantify changes its form and size depending on the culture, place and time in which a survey is done.

Despite this uncertainty, research produces useful insights by focusing on the causes of variability of bullying within a particular population. What individual, school, family and social factors explain why, within similar schools, some children report intense or frequent bullying, others less, and some none? How does children's experience of bullying change over time, and what factors might explain why bullying increases, decreases or remains stable? Of all probable determinants of change over time, which are deliberately modifiable through interventions in schools?

The specific acts of bullying reported by young people are fairly consistent across cultures, although Chan and Wong[398] suggested that collectivist culture in Chinese societies may lead to social exclusion being a more common form of peer victimisation. Consistent with research worldwide,[399] traditional bullying in East Asia is more prevalent than cyberbullying. Further, Asian region studies show the significant overlap in children's experience of traditional and cyberbullying, as the majority of students who report online bullying involvement also report bullying inside or nearby schools.[400] Asian boys are most likely to be victims and perpetrators of bullying[401] and younger students and those with low academic performance are more likely to be involved in bullying.[402] Similar to global patterns, use of multiple electronic devices, heavy internet usage and online gaming in East Asia is linked with higher risk of both traditional and cyberbullying.[403]

> *"Some students in grade 8 posted nasty comments on my Facebook…I didn't dare delete what they said, or did not dare to block them….if I did…they would hit me or threaten me. I had to keep their comments online."* Girl, grade 6, Viet Nam

The nexus between bullying and educational stress in East Asia

As Confucian tradition meets globalisation, a pressurised climate of "academic achievement at any cost" emerges. Demand for intensified and extended in-school and out-of-school training and exam preparation comes from all sides – from parents, employers, teachers and students themselves. According to Harvard education researchers Zhao, Selman and Haste[404] the much celebrated success of Asian students at home and abroad[405] has a significant downside for many young people. There are strong links between study burden and depression, anxiety, suicidal thoughts and actions and overall low wellbeing.[406] Zhao et al[407] emphasised that, for many children, the academic stress is debilitating.

> *"When riding my bike home, I often wish my mum would ask me "How are you feeling, are you happy?" But she never does. She just asks me about what I learned today and my homework. I feel very sad."* Year 8 girl in Viet Nam, 2015

Our research in East Asia has examined links between heavy use of private tutors and total study hours after formal school (private tutors, cram classes and/or self-study), subjective educational stress and bullying. We developed the Educational Stress Scale for Adolescents (ESSA) which has been validated in China and Viet Nam.[408] It is a brief 16-item scale with items such as "My parents care about my academic grades too much which brings me a lot of pressure". "I feel stressed when I do not live up to my own standards", and "I feel a lot of pressure in my daily studying" with children's responses ranging from strongly agree to strongly disagree on a 5-point scale. After-school study hours alone or with groups or private tutors were estimated, and we asked about the experience of various forms of bullying.

Nearly all of the 1,609 students surveyed in high schools in north, central and southern Viet Nam (94.5%) had private tutors, either one-to-one or in groups.[409] This is consistent with very high use of commercial tutors in most of East Asia.[410] Liu and colleagues[411] found that 72.4% of Taiwanese high school students had a personal tutor, which is similar to an estimated 71.8% of Hong Kong students.[412] Bray and Kwo[413] found that between 50% to 80% of high school students attend private tutoring across East and South Asian countries (including 70.6% in the Republic of Korea, 65.2% in Japan, 58% in India and 53.3% in China).

After-school study burden in Viet Nam appears especially heavy. Only 5.5% of students said they did not have tutors and on average, students dedicated 12 hours per week to this form of extra study, which is about double some estimates of the weekly hours for tutors and cram classes reported in Taiwan, Hong Kong, the Republic of Korea and Japan.[414]

How is students' mental health affected by heavy study burden?

The association between students' mental health and total extra study hours, use of tutors and self-study appears not to be simple or linear. In surveys in Shandong province China[415] and in three provinces of Viet Nam,[416] the link between subjective academic stress (ESSA scores) and study burden (as indicated by total homework hours) was U-shaped – the most academically stressed students were those who did the least homework alone or with tutors. Students who reported doing four or more hours of extra study per day were similarly distressed, while those who

> *"Extra study doesn't make me feel stressed, it makes me feel better. I study long hours to make me not anxious. If I don't study, I am worried."* Chinese undergraduate student, 2014.

studied between two to three hours per day reported good psychological well-being.

Interestingly, we did not find significant correlations between total study hours and most measures of poor mental health and behaviour (depression, anxiety, suicidal thinking, and health risk behaviours). However, when we looked at links between mental health and students' work with private, one-to-one tutors or attendance at cram classes, those who did both (compared to those with just one type or no type) were more depressed and anxious.[417] We also examined whether there were differences in mental health between those students who mainly relied on cram classes/tutors, those who had a fairly equal balance of hours in self-study and external classes/tutors, and those who relied on self-study as the primary method. There was a strong effect – the best mental health was found among those who mainly do self-study and supplement with a few hours of tutoring per week, while those who mostly or always did extra study with tutors or cram classes had considerably worse mental health on each measure.[418]

How is bullying associated with study burden and academic stress?

Zhao et al[419] argue that to understand the negative effects of intense study burden in China we need to look beyond the mental health of individuals. Evidence suggests that social relationships and interpersonal communications become dysfunctional under long periods of academic pressure. For example, in the educational cauldron of Shanghai, which is often praised for producing world-best grades in comparative rankings such as those of the Organisation for Economic Cooperation and Development's PISA assessment, many students experience substantial breakdown in formerly close relationships, with distrust, jealousy and animosity being common.[420]

In Viet Nam we asked students about multiple forms of bullying – physical, emotional, relational (mainly deliberate social exclusion) and cyberbullying. The bullying prevalence estimates were within the typical ranges for East Asian surveys.[421] We concurrently measured academic stress with the ESSA. Figure 1 shows a strong relationship between academic stress and the experience of nil, one, two, three or four forms of bullying. Clearly, students with the most extensive bullying victimisation were also under heavy academic stress.

These findings are consistent with insights from Shanghai.[424] Bullying and disharmony with peers are key features of the pervasive sense of burden and study-related anxiety throughout the school system and particularly during the key transition years where examinations are pivotal for

Figure 1.
Correlation between academic stress and exposure to multiple-forms of bullying in Viet Nam (1,609 high school students in 3 provinces)[422]

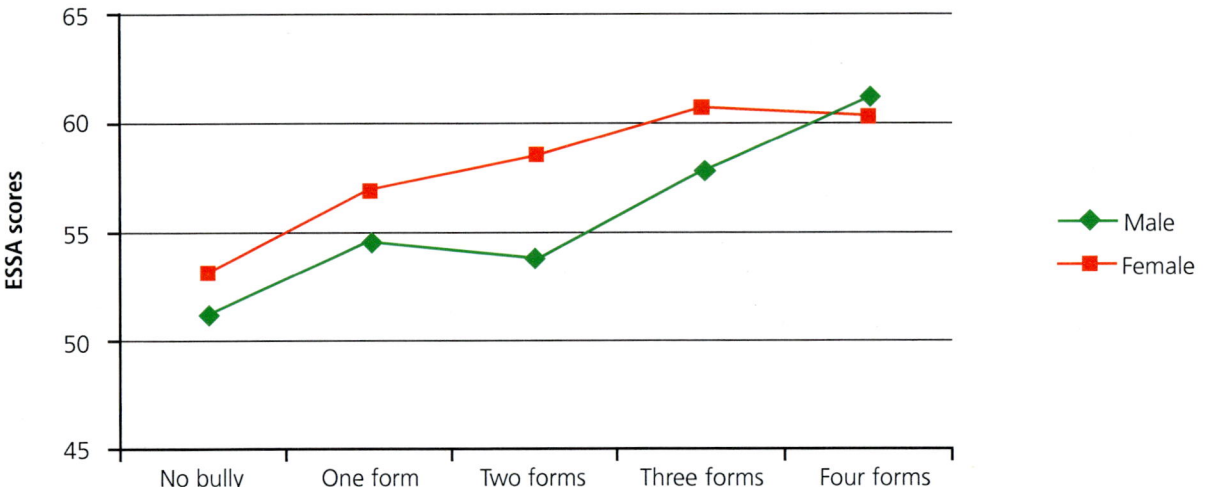

The data in Figure 1 are from a cross-sectional survey, so we do not know which factor may precede the other. It is possible that high academic stress makes students vulnerable to victimisation, or that victimised children consequently feel stressed by study.

Some light is cast on this by our research in Shandong province, China.[423] We asked high school students many questions about possible determinants of academic stress, including individual demographics, family factors (perceived parental care and protection, conflict with parents, parental punishment) and school factors (such as school connectedness, number of homework hours, extra classes, quarrels with teachers or peers, fighting, and experience of physical and emotional bullying victimisation). When all factors were considered together in a multivariate analysis, studying long hours was not significantly linked with educational stress. The three strongest correlates of academic stress were living in a rural location, having feelings of low school connectedness and reporting low grades. The next most influential cluster was peer-related, including emotional and physical bullying and frequent quarrels with classmates.

a young person's future and, to some extent, the social esteem and future wellbeing of their parents. The economic and family context is important. Although it may be expected that children in high pressure urban environments would have heaviest academic stress, in Shandong province we found that students in rural schools had significantly more academic stress. In part this may be due to the lower quality of many rural schools, making it more difficult to succeed in national exams, coupled with the heavy expectation on many rural students to use their education to move to the cities for a more affluent life for themselves and their families.

How stable or fluid is bullying involvement for children in East Asian schools?

Most international and Asian research to date has examined bullying using cross-sectional designs. There is limited evidence regarding ways in which individual, family and school factors affect change in bullying victimisation and perpetration over time.

Some research in western nations has captured the dynamic pattern of bullying involvement.[425] An important question is whether there are stable sub-types. Over time, do children usually stay within a sub-type of "bully", "victim" or "bully-victim"? What kinds of children remain uninvolved? Evidence on this issue should have important implications for prevention programs, because if stable sub-types of children are found, then support and prevention efforts might be targeted most effectively to individuals and small groups. On the other hand, if children's membership of sub-types is fluid over time, then prevention is best done at the whole group level.

Two studies in the USA suggest somewhat different patterns, but both recommend targeted prevention programs depending on the 'class' of bullying involvement. Bettencourt and colleagues[426] found that across two years of middle school, children tended to remain in stable sub-types of aggressor, victim, both aggressor and victim, or uninvolved. In a study by Ryoo et al[427] that tracked children over three years, most remained in stable sub-types (with those uninvolved being the largest group). However, they found considerable change in group membership among those with the most frequent, intense involvement as either victims or bullies.

To date there has been only one study on stability of traditional bullying over time in Asia.[428] Students in Seoul, Republic of Korea, were surveyed twice over nine months. Overall, bullying involvement was found to be quite stable, with 75% of students remaining either uninvolved (about half of the sample) or stable bullies, victims or both (25%).

In Viet Nam, our longitudinal study[429] was conducted in two northern provinces during the 2014-2015 academic years. Surveys were conducted at public middle schools (grades 6–8) and high schools (grades 10–11) in urban Hanoi city and semi-rural Hai Duong province, six months apart. We used an anonymous identity number matching technique employed in an earlier study of youth violence victimisation in Malaysia to reliably match individuals across surveys.[430]

Key findings are shown in Box 1. This first longitudinal study of bullying in South-east Asia estimated stability and change in bullying roles. Consistent with most international research,[431] traditional bullying victimisation and perpetration were more common than cyberbullying and cyber victimisation. This is unlikely to be due to limited online activity because over 90% of students reported using mobile phones and other devices that connect to the Internet for at least one hour daily online. A notable feature in the self-reports is the very substantial overlap between traditional and cyberbullying. About 90% of students who reported cyberbullying or perpetration also reported traditional bullying involvement. This is consistent with prior studies in the USA, Norway and elsewhere[432] and supports the view that cyberbullying is just another way by which adolescents are aggressive towards their peers.

Perhaps the most important insight from this study is that, over time, the majority of children who had bullying experience changed their bullying status. Among the 61% of students who reported any victimisation, perpetration or both, nearly three in every four had a different classifica-

---

Box 1: Change over one school year in Viet Nam 2014-2015: Traditional and cyberbullying victimisation & perpetration (N=1,424 students in middle and high schools

Bullying victimisation prevalence (any acts): 45% (Time 1) and 33% (Time 2)

- Traditional bullying victimisation: 43% and 32%; Cyberbullying victimisation:12% and 9%
- **The overlap: 90% and 92% of students experiencing cyber victimisation also had been bullied in at least one traditional way.**

Bullying perpetration prevalence (any acts): 29% (Time 1) and 20% (Time 2)

- Traditional bullying perpetration: 28% and 20% Cyberbullying perpetration: 6% and 5%

- **The overlap: 86% and 91% of students who perpetrated cyberbullying also bullied others in at least one traditional way.**

Stability and change in bullying over time

- 39% of respondents were not involved in bullying over an academic year. Six in ten students were involved in at least one form of bulling (61%). Among them, 26% remained stable as a victim, bully, or bully-victim.
- **74% changed their bullying role status over an academic year.**

tion across the two surveys. Change in the bullying role was the most stable characteristic. Of the 1,424 students in the sample, 635 changed their "type" over time; the second largest group was the 554 students who reported no involvement at either survey. The smallest groups were those children who were classified as bully-victims, victims or bullies at both times. These findings suggest greater fluidity in bullying involvement than has been found in the study in the Republic of Korea[433] and the USA.[434] Although much more research is needed to examine change in bullying experience in East Asia and globally, the findings in Viet Nam might reflect a sociocultural difference.

Conclusions

In general, the evidence from East Asia shows the universality of bullying experience. The growing number of local and regional surveys find that the types of aggressive acts in East Asia are much the same as elsewhere, although there are some indications that children in collectivist Asian countries may be more likely to use organised social exclusion to harm their peers. Unfortunately, the accumulating estimates of prevalence tend to vary too widely. Much more social science work is needed to standardise measures and survey methods to try to narrow the ranges; otherwise, it is difficult to advocate with education and health policy makers who may question the quality of evidence on the extent of bullying. Most importantly, this work should clearly demonstrate that the measures of bullying are valid and sensitive enough to detect real change in response to system-wide prevention efforts.

The dominance of traditional bullying victimisation and perpetration suggests that special programmes for cyberbullying among school students in East Asia should not be the primary focus for behaviour change. Also, the evidence so far is not clear about whether East Asian students should be classified into types of bullies or victims because the behaviours may be inherently fluid. If so, it would be best to focus on whole-of-school bullying prevention efforts that aim to enhance mutual respect and to improve interpersonal skills for conflict resolution for all students, with supplementary targeted psychological and behavioural interventions for the minority of children who are persistently and severely affected.

Bullying in East Asian schools is but one stressful element within a climate of heavy educational pressure and incessant competition. Systemic change is needed to find alternatives to fiercely difficult national examinations, including expanding parallel training pathways for aspirational students and their families.[435] Excessive reliance on the shadow education industry of cram classes and private tutors must be reduced to enable young people time to develop and enjoy their learning and social relationships. Such change is complex but essential for children to achieve their right to play.

Endnotes

[391] Michael P Dunne is at the School of Public Health and Social Work, Queensland University of Technology, Brisbane, Australia and is affiliated with the Institute for Community Health Research, Hue University of Medicine and Pharmacy, Hue, Viet Nam; Thu Ba Pham with the School of Public Health and Social Work, Queensland University of Technology, Brisbane, Australia and the Ministry of Education and Training, Hanoi, Viet Nam; Ha Hai Thi Le with School of Public Health and Social Work, Queensland University of Technology, Brisbane, Australia and Faculty of Social Science, Hanoi School of Public Health, Hanoi, Viet Nam; Jiandong Sun with School of Public Health and Social Work, Queensland University of Technology, Brisbane, Australia

[392] Chan, HC & Wong, DSW (2015). Traditional school bullying and cyberbullying in Chinese societies: Prevalence and a review of the whole school intervention approach. *Aggression and Violent Behavior* 23: 98-108; Sittichai, R & Smith, PK (2015). Bullying in South-East Asian countries: A review. *Aggression and Violent Behavior* 23: 22-35; Sun, J, Dunne, MP, Hou, XY & Xu, AQ (2011). Educational Stress Scale for Adolescents: Development, validity, and reliability with Chinese students. *Journal of Psychoeducational Assessment* 29: 534-546; Sun, J, Dunne, MP, Hou, XY & Xu, AQ (2013). Educational stress among Chinese adolescents: Individual, family, school and peer influences. *Educational Review* 65: 284-302; Zhao X, Selman RL & Haste H (2015). Op. cit.

[393] Modecki, KL, Minchin, J, Harbaugh, AG, Guerra, NG & Runions, KC (2014). Bullying prevalence across contexts: a meta-analysis measuring cyber and traditional bullying. *Journal of Adolescent Health* 55: 602-611.

[394] Craig, W, Harel-Fisch, Y, Vogel-Grinvald, H et al (2009). A cross-national profile of bullying and victimisation among adolescents in 40 countries. *International Journal of Public Health* 54: 216-224

[395] Chan, HC & Wong, DSW (2015). Op. cit.

[396] Sittichai, R & Smith, PK (2015). Op. cit.

[397] Lai, SL, Ye, R & Chang, KP (2012). Bullying in Middle Schools: An Asian-Pacific regional study. *Asia Pacific Education Review* 9: 503-515.

[398] Chan, HC & Wong, DSW (2015). Op. cit.

[399] Olweus, D (2013). School bullying: Development and some important challenges. *Annual Review of Clinical Psychology* 9:751-780

[400] Ibid.

[401] Chan, HC & Wong, DSW (2015). Op. cit.; Craig, W, Harel-Fisch, Y, Vogel-Grinvald, H et al (2009). Op. cit.

[402] Lai, SL, Ye, R & Chang, KP (2012). Op. cit.

[403] Chan, HC & Wong, DSW (2015). Op. cit.

[404] Zhao, X, Selman, RL & Haste, H (2015). Op. cit.

[405] Chua, A (2011). *Why Chinese mothers are superior.* Wall Street Journal, January 8, 2011.

[406] Sun, J, Dunne, MP, Hou, XY & Xu, AQ (2013). Op. cit.; Truc, TT, Loan, KX, Nguye,n ND, Dixon, J, Sun, J & Dunne, MP (2015). Validation of the educational stress scale for adolescents (ESSA) in Viet Nam. *Asia Pacific Journal of Public Health* 27: NP2112-NP2121.

[407] Zhao, X, Selman, RL & Haste, H (2015). Op. cit.

[408] Sun, J, Dunne, MP, Hou, XY & Xu, AQ (2011). Op. cit.; Truc, TT et al (2015). Op. cit.

[409] Pham, TTB (2015). Op. cit.

[410] Bray, M and Kwo, O (2014). *Regulating private tutoring for public good: Policy options for supplementary education in Asia.* Bangkok: Comparative Education Resource Centre.

[411] Liu, J (2012). Does cram schooling matter? Who goes to cram schools? Evidence from Taiwan. *International Journal of Educational Development* 32: 46-52.

[412] Bray, M (2013). Benefits and tensions of shadow education: Comparative perspectives on the roles and impact of private supplementary tutoring in the lives of Hong Kong students. *Journal of International and Comparative Education* 2: 18-30

[413] Bray, M and Kwo, O (2014). Op. cit.

[414] Liu, J (2012). Op. cit.: Bray, M (2013). Op. cit.; Hong, S & Park, YS (2012). An analysis of the relationship between self-study, private tutoring, and self-efficacy on self-regulated learning. *KEDI Journal of Educational Policy* 9: 113-144.

[415] Sun, J, Dunne, MP, Hou, XY & Xu, AQ (2011). Op. cit.; Sun, J, Dunne, MP, Hou, XY & Xu, AQ (2013). Op. cit.

[416] Pham, TTB (2015). Op. cit.

[417] Bray, M and Kwo, O (2014). Op. cit.

[418] Pham, TTB (2015). Op. cit.

[419] Zhao, X, Selman, RL & Haste, H (2015). Op. cit.

[420] Ibid.

[421] Lai, SL, Ye, R & Chang, KP (2012). Op. cit.; Pham, TTB (2015). Op. cit.

[422] Pham, TTB (2015). Op. cit.

[423] Sun, J, Dunne, MP, Hou, XY & Xu, AQ (2013). Op. cit.

[424] Zhao, X, Selman, RL & Haste, H (2015). Op. cit.

[425] Bettencourt, A, Farrell, A, Liu, W & Sullivan, T (2013). Stability and change in patterns of peer victimisation and aggression during adolescence. *Journal of Clinical Child & Adolescent Psychiatry* 42: 429-441; Ryoo, JH, Wang, C & Swearer, SM (2015). Examination of the change in latent statuses in bullying behaviors across time. *School Psychology Quarterly* 30: 105-122.

[426] Bettencourt, A, Farrell, A, Liu, W & Sullivan, T (2013). Op. cit.

[427] Ryoo, JH, Wang, C & Swearer, SM (2015). Op. cit.

[428] Kim, YS, Boyce, WT, Koh, YJ & Leventhal, BL (2009). Time trends, trajectories, and demographic predictors of bullying: A prospective study of Korean adolescents. *Journal of Adolescent Health* 45: 360-367.

[429] Le, HTH, Nguyen, HT, Campbell, WA, Gatton, ML, Tran, NT & Dunne, MP (2016). *Mental health consequences of bullying victimisation and perpetration among adolescents in Viet Nam.* (Under peer review)

[430] Choo, WY, Dunne, MP, Maret, MJ, Fleming, ML & Wong, YL (2011). Victimization experiences of adolescents in Malaysia. *Journal of Adolescent Health* 49: 627-634.

[431] Olweus, D (2013). Op. cit.

[432] Ibid.

[433] Kim, YS et al (2009). Op. cit.

[434] Bettencourt, A, Farrell, A, Liu, W & Sullivan, T (2013). Op. cit.; Ryoo, JH, Wang, C & Swearer, SM (2015). Op. cit.

[435] Bray, M and Kwo, O (2014). Op. cit.; Bray, M (2013). Op. cit.

Children attend class at a boarding school for nomadic Bedouin children, Syrian Arab Republic
© UNICEF/UNI44585/Noorani

17. Bullying in the Arab region: a journey from research to policy

Maha Almuneef

Introduction

The definition of bullying in the West can be phrased in many different ways. However, there is one unanimous term, bullying, that defines the repeated act of aggressive behaviour among school children. In the Middle East and North Africa region, however, there is no single word for bullying in the Arabic language. Each country in this region, despite having Arabic as the native language, has its own terminology for bullying. Searching for and collecting data on bullying, specifically among other forms of peer violence, is therefore challenging. Bullying can be translated to "tanamor," which literally means acting like a tiger. Another word used is "Al esti'sad" which means acting like a lion. "Al estqwa'a" means being strong and/or powerful. "Baltaja" is another word used by Egyptian researchers for bullying that originates from "Balta", a specific type of weapon in the old Egyptian dialect. So essentially "baltaja" translates as a person carrying a weapon.

There are 22 Member States in the Arab League, and while some countries do overlap in their dialect, others are quite different. This poses a huge difficulty for researchers collecting information on bullying in the Middle East as there is no single agreed term, and the word for bullying in a specific dialect in one country that is used to collect information may not correspond to that used in other countries.

The term bullying is relatively new to the Arab region, with published studies on this phenomenon dating back only to 2008. It is safe to say this topic is under-researched, but it has recently received greater attention. This could be due to the work done by researchers in the region that has demonstrated how widespread bullying is and how serious and long-lasting its physical and mental repercussions are for young people. More importantly, research has shown a link between bullying and criminal activity in adulthood against the community and violence towards the self (suicide). Longitudinal studies have examined the ways in which aggressive behaviour can continue from childhood to adolescence and then on to adulthood, creating a pattern of violent behaviour throughout a person's life.

Several studies from North America have shown that childhood aggression such as bullying can be a predictor of crimes and violence in adulthood.[436] A significant proportion of young people arrested for offences and violent behaviour were arrested also as adults for criminal offences. A study on childhood delinquency in Cambridge, England, found that one third of young males who had committed offences before the age of 18 were convicted again as adults (aged 21-40) compared only to 8% of those not convicted for violence during adolescent years.[437] With the increase in adult violence and armed conflict in the Arab region, more attention needs to be paid to child and adolescent aggression in order to prevent its development into adult aggression.

The Extent of Bullying

The problem of bullying among adolescents in the region cannot be viewed in isolation from other parts of the world. There is a wide variation in the prevalence rates of bullying between individual countries, but rates in the Arab region are among the highest.

Fleming and Jacobson's 2009 study confirms these findings.[438] The study was carried out in 19 countries with a sample size of 104,614 and the results showed a 20-40% incidence of bullying among students. Out of the 19 countries included, five were from the Middle East and North Africa region: Jordan, Lebanon, United Arab Emirates, Morocco and Oman. These countries had a rate of bullying of 29-44%, which is on the higher side of the overall rate of the 19 countries. To be specific, Jordan had a rate of 44%, followed by Oman at 38.8%, Lebanon 33.6%, Morocco 31.9% and United Arab Emirates 29.9%. According to the results from this study, Jordan has the highest rate of bullying amongst the five countries included in the study.

Further research into the prevalence of bullying in Jordan has yielded similar results. A study carried out by Abu Ghazal in 2009 with 1480 students in Jordan, found 14.9% prevalence of bullying among students in intermediate and high school (grades 7-10).[439] He later repeated the study in 2010 and found the rate of bullying to have tripled over one year. Another study in Jordan also measuring the prevalence of bullying is that by Al Bitar et al. in 2013 with 920 students in the grade 6. Their results showed an even higher prevalence rate at 47%.[440]

Shifting to Saudi Arabia, the first study was carried out by Al Bugami in 2009 on an all-girls school in Riyadh: the sample size was 369 and the prevalence of bullying was 56%.[441] Another major survey named "Jeeluna" was carried out by AlBuhairan et al. to assess the overall health of adolescents in Saudi Arabia. This was a cross sectional school-based national epidemiological observational study that was conducted nationwide in 2011- 2012 among adolescents from intermediate and secondary school. Over 12,500 pupils participated in this study and the results showed that 25% of the students were exposed to bullying during the 30 days preceding the study and that exposure to cyberbullying was 16.6%.[442]

Another source of valuable data on bullying in the Arab region has come from The International Society for Prevention of Child Abuse and Neglect's (ISPCAN) Child Abuse Screening Tool for Children, the home version (ICAST-CH), which was carried out in Saudi Arabia in 2013 with 15,264 high school students. The study was undertaken in five regions of the Kingdom: Riyadh, Tabouk, Jazan, Western Province, and Eastern Province. The rate of bullying was found to be 47.9% in the final year of the study. This result was the same as that from the pilot study, which took place in 2012 on a smaller sample in Al Kharj city close to Riyadh. In this study 2,835 intermediate and high school students were included and the prevalence of bullying was 41.7%.[443]

In the same year Almuneef et al. conducted the Adverse Childhood Experience (ACE) study using the International Questionnaire (ACE-IQ) of the World Health Organization (WHO) on all 13 regions of the Kingdom of Saudi Arabia.[444] The sample was 10,156 and bullying was one of the 13 ACE's examined under four main domains which included abuse, family dysfunction, community violence and collective violence. This study found that the rate of lifetime exposure to bullying in the first 18 years of life was 14% overall, a result which was very similar to those of the pilot study which was done in the city of Riyadh in 2012 with 920 participants: this had a rate of 11%.

In 2008, Al Gahtani conducted a study in Riyadh with 1877 students and found a prevalence of 31% of pupils exposed to violence in the previous month.[445]

Based on these studies from different countries in the region, there are clearly varying results on the prevalence rate of bullying. However, it is evident that bullying is a common problem among young people in the region and it is estimated that one in three children could be a victim of bullying. Further research should focus on bullying as a distinct and separate phenomenon to school violence or aggression in general in order to get a clearer picture of the extent of the problem. Understanding the problem and studying the conditions that lead to bullying during young people's formative years is an important factor in formulating sound policies for prevention and intervention.

Gender differences and types of bullying

In considering the gender differences in bullying Al Bitar of Jordan carried out some interesting research. He found that boys tended to be bullied more than girls, 55% against 40% respectively.[446] The ACE-IQ study conducted in Saudi Arabia likewise found that boys were bullied more than girls: 64% compared to 35%. However, IPSCAN's ICAST-CH study in Saudi Arabia found that girls tended to be victims more than boys. Girls reported more psychological and verbal bullying while boys tend to be engaged more in physical bullying. Similarly, another study carried out by AlQadah and Bashir in 2013 in Jordan showed that girls were bullied more than boys.[447] This was attributed to the difference between the genders in exploring their identities. According to their research, boys tend to use more logical belief systems and leadership models whereas girls tend to use conflict and abusing other peers as a way to establish their identity or sense of self-worth. Interestingly, AlQadah and Bashir also found that bullying tended to be more common in same sex schools than co-educational schools. The explanation for this was that the adolescents in co-educational schools were more focused on their appearance and behaviour in front of the opposite sex (attraction), whereas in same sex schools, students felt less obliged to care about their appearance. Cultural factors can also influence the extent and type of bullying in a society, for instance, when bullying is endorsed as a normal method of expressing strength and power this encourages boys to adopt the behaviour and take part in physical bullying. On the other hand, the increasing gender gap based on cultural values and norms appears to be linked with gender separation in many cultures: this appears to encourage bullying among girls especially bullying that is verbal or psychological.

From the available data it appears that the most common type of bullying in Arab countries is verbal, psychological, and name-calling. Al Bitar found the percentage of students in grade 6 subjected to name-calling was the highest at a rate of 40.9%.[448] The ICAST-CH study conducted in Saudi Arabia found that verbal bullying was also the most common form of bullying and practiced more by girls. The ACE –IQ study in Saudi Arabia in 2013 found that physical bullying rated highest at 21.9% followed by students being left out of activities or ignored at 17.5% and then verbal and name-calling at 15.3%. "Jeeluna" found that the prevalence of exposure to physical violence in school was also the highest at 20.8%.

A smaller study by Al Bugami in 2009 in an all-girls school found that the highest form of bullying was verbal at 73%.[449] This was followed by "Ijaab", a term in Arabic which translates to liking/admiring/having a crush, at 65%. This type of bullying occurs when one girl likes another and tries to befriend her but is met with rejection and then is bullied by the girl who she tried to befriend. Physical bullying was the next most prevalent in this study with 47.4%, raiding and stealing personal belongings occurred at a rate of 19% and sexual harassment was reported at 16.5%. This data suggests that society is influencing the type of bullying practiced. It is therefore important that society should be engaged in designing national programmes to prevent it. It is clearly important to address the problem not only from the individual, family and community aspect, but also at the societal level. Changing social and cultural norms is essential to combat bullying in the Arab region. Such an approach seeks to remove the economic and social barriers to young people's development, and to modify the cultural norms and values that stimulate violence in general and bullying in particular. Further studies are needed to study cyberbullying as an emerging form of bullying also particularly with the increase in use by young people of the internet and social media channels.

Overall, individual studies from the Arab region provide contradicting results on the prevalence of bullying and the influence of gender differences. This variability in research findings could be the result of methodological and other differences across individual studies. There is an urgent need for a synthesis of all available literature on this topic from the region in order to understand more clearly the phenomenon of bullying and cyberbullying among young people and children in the Arab region.

Characteristics of children who are bullied

The results from a number of studies in the Arab world have found that the majority of children and young people experienced bullying because of their dental or facial appearance (50%) followed by teasing about their weight and body appearance at 31%. Al Bitar's study found that teeth played the most significant role in being bullied, particularly if the teeth were protruding, spaced out or were missing.[450] The next most prevalent focus for bullying was body appearance and weight, followed by height and facial characteristics such as freckles, shape of eyes, chin, ears and lips. Al Bugami added to this list skin colour, where dark skin was a focus for bullying as were minority dialects, speech problems and perceived intellectual disabilities or skin problems.[451]

A number of studies in Western countries reviewed for this article have shown that gifted children tend to be targets for bullies. Peterson and Ray's study in 2006 showed that out of the 432 gifted children from 16 schools in the USA (48% boys and 52% girls) 67% were bullied.[452] The highest prevalence of bullying was in grade 6 after which it declined. For this specific group of students, the most common form of bullying was verbal and name-calling at 35% followed by teasing over appearance, level of intelligence, and finally physical bullying. Furthermore, Peterson and Ray's study showed that gifted students bullied in elementary school tended to become bullies in grade 9. None of the studies conducted in the Arab region have focused specifically on gifted children, as it is not a term recognized or used; it would be important therefore to add this category for future study. However, although not identified as a "gifted" category, Al Bitar's study found that 35% of the bullied children stated high grades as a reason for being bullied.[453]

Abu Ghazal's study focused on the "social status" of bullied children at school and found that most of these were signalled out for being a "teacher's pet" or being related to a teacher or faculty member.[454] Another common feature of bullied children was being rich or important. If the student did not have many friends, he/she also became a target for bullies, as was anyone perceived to be a tattletale or snitch.

Risk Factors for bullying

Individual factors

At an individual level, factors that affect the potential for practicing bullying include biological, psychological and behavioural factors. These factors can include influences from the individual's family and peers, or social and cultural factors. Al Adili's study with 180 students from grade 10 from four different schools found that the characteristics of the age group itself play a major role in bullying behaviour.[455] His study found that there tends to be competition amongst peers and teenagers: they can suffer from jealousy, a lack of sleep and a need to be the centre of attention; some of these characteristics manifest themselves in anger and stubbornness. Anger is sometimes felt to be the only way to express emotions in the struggle to establish identity in what is considered to be a confusing time in the transition from child to adult. At this age, anger stems from being scolded, belittled or humiliated and teased by family members or teachers.

While many of these studies offer interesting insights into some of the issues around bullying in the Arab region, studies on the personality traits of children involved in different bullying roles as bullies, victims, bully-victims and defenders, are still scarce in the region. These are needed to contribute to a deeper picture of the problem.

Family factors

International studies have shown that bullying has been linked to parental conflict and poor attachment and communication between children and parents.[456] Other factors that contribute to bullying include having a large number of children in the family, young mothers with low educational attainment, single parent households, and low socio-economic status. This finding is supported by a study carried out by AlNayrab in Ghaza in 2008 in an all-boys school with a sample size of 480.[457] This study found that one of the main factors that had a direct effect on bullying was the number of children in a family (families with more than 10 offspring). According to the research, this could be attributed to high levels of tension and conflict in these homes. The parent's level of education was another strong risk factor. His research found in particular that the mother's low education level had a negative effect on the children, leading them to practice bullying in schools. In comparison, he found that the father's level of education did not have an impact on bullying. This was attributed to the fact that the mother is considered the most influential in child rearing. Another factor contributing to bullying is the position of the child in the family. AlNayrab's research found that the fourth- to seventh-placed children tended to be bullies more than their other siblings. This was attributed to the fact that middle children do not have the attention and care of the first or last. The type of family also had a big impact on bullying depending on whether it was nuclear or extended. The research found that children from extended families have a higher chance of becoming bullies than children from nuclear families and this is attributed to the high number of arguments and conflicts between parents, grandparents and children and the great number of family members living under one roof.

Another risk factor that affects bullying is the parenting style. According to a study carried out by Al Sofi and Al Malki in 2012 in Iraq, factors such as neglect, leniency, inconsistency and being overly-strict increase the rates of bullying in children.[458] The results showed that neglect and domestic violence both led to children becoming bullies as such parenting appears to provoke a sense of anger or aggression or poor discipline in the children. In addition, the research indicated that bullying is also connected to inconsistent parenting where being strict and being lenient are used interchangeably or the parents do not agree on a parenting style.

School environment factors

AlQadah and Bashir found the school environment played a vital role in the prevalence of bullying. This included a lack of rules and regulations and little involvement of teachers or supervisors in punishing bullies or acknowledging the act as being in appropriate and undesirable.[459] The study found that schools that do not address the psychological and social needs of students sustain higher rates of bullying. Al Bugami adds to this that teachers who use corporal punishment in disciplining students increase a sense of anxiety and belittlement amongst students which in turn encourages them to take out their anger by bullying other students.

AlQadah and Bashir's study found that the geographic location of the school also played a role; schools located in poorer areas showed increased levels of bullying in comparison to schools located in high income areas.

Media factors

Young people's access to a wide range of media has increased dramatically in recent years. New forms of media such as videogames and smartphones and the proliferation of social media channels have multiplied the opportunities for young people to view violent behaviour and to be influenced by people in this virtual space. It also offers another channel for bullying. Despite its importance, there are very few studies in the Arab world that have considered or analyzed the impact of viewing violence in the media on rates of bullying. Al Nayrab's study did find that the media played an important role in teaching children about violence particularly through violent scenes in shows and movies.[460]

Consequences of Bullying

Fleming and Jacobson's study found that 25% of bullied students said they felt lonely and thought of suicide.[461] Smoking was found to be higher in bullied children than non-bullied children and the same results were seen for alcohol and drug use as well as early sexual relationships. Similarly, results from the ACE –IQ study among adults in Saudi Arabia, comparing the bullied with the non-bullied, showed a positive correlation between being bullied and risky health behaviours such as alcohol drinking (17% vs 7%), using drugs (18.7% vs 6.4%) and smoking (54.3% vs 35.5%). The results also showed a positive correlation between being bullied and long term physical chronic diseases in adulthood such as diabetes (OR-1.6) and hypertension (OR-1.8). Mental illness was also associated with bullying where the risk of anxiety and depression in adulthood increased twofold (OR-1.9 and 1.7 respectively).

Al Bitar's study found that being bullied had a negative effect on grades by 40%. In Ismail's study carried out in 2010 in Qina in Egypt on a sample size of 48 students from 9-12 years of age, she found that bullied children suffered from high levels of anxiety as a consequence of bullying in addition to preferring solitude over being with peers.[462] The study also found that bullied children tended to be challenged in forming social relationships and interacting with peers. AlBuhairan et al. also found that bullying negatively affected the academic performance and mental health of the bullied children and the effect was more prominent with verbal/psychological bullying compared to physical violence.[463]

Conclusion

Although bullying has started to be recognized only recently as a problem in the Middle East and North Africa region, we have seen progress in terms of research and policy making. As we have shown, research in developed countries shows little difference in terms of risk factors and consequences to our region, but it is worth noting that the Arab region ranks higher in terms of prevalence. As a result, research, policy development and legislation about bullying should be a political priority in all Arab countries. Many researchers from different fields are studying the phenomenon of bullying and comparing it to the available international studies in order to develop national policies based on local findings. All Arab countries have signed and ratified the Convention on the Rights of the Child and thus should be able to pass legislation and implement local policies effectively. Finally an emphasis on prevention should be a priority including a focus on increasing awareness of the issue, involving parents, and empowering teachers to take a stand against bullying.

Endnotes

436 Farrington, DP (2001) Predicting adult official and self-reported violence. In: Pinard GF, Pagantu L, eds. *Clinical assessment of dangerousness: empirical contributions.* New York, NY, US: Cambridge University Press (pp 68-88); Loeber R, Wung P, Keenan K, et al (1993) Developmental pathway in disruptive child behavior. *Development and psychopathology* 5(1-2):103-133. Peterson JS, Ray KE (2006) Bullying and the gifted: Victims, perpetrators, prevalence, and effects. *Gifted child quarterly* 50(2):148-168.

437 Farrington, DP (2001). Op. cit.

438 Fleming, L & Jacobsen, K (2009). Bullying among middle-school students in low and middle income countries. *Health promotion international* 25(1):73-84.

439 Ghazal, A (2010). Causes of Bullying from the perspective of bullied children. *Al Sharjah University for Human and Social Sciences* 7(2):306-275.

440 Al-Bitar, Z, Al- Omari, I, Sonbol, H, et al (2013). Bullying among Jordanian schoolchildren, its effects on school performance, and the contribution of general physical and dentofacial features. *American Journal of Orthodontics and Dentofacial Orthopedics* 144(6):872-878.

441 Al-Bugami, F (2009) *The Phenomenon of Bulling between students in high school in Riyadh.* (Master Thesis, King Saud University, Riyadh, Saudi Arabia). Unpublished Master Thesis.

442 AlBuhairan, F, AlDubayee, M, Tamimi, H, et al (2015). Time for adolescent health surveillance system in Saudi Arabia: Findings from "Jeeluna". *Journal of Adolescent Health* (57):263-269.

443 IPSCAN, The International Society for Prevention of Child Abuse and Neglect, *Child Abuse Screening tool for children, the home version, (ICAST-CH),* conducted in Saudi Arabia, 2013.; Eissa, M, AlBuhairan, FS, Qayad, M et al (2013). Determining Incidence of Child Maltreatment in Saudi Arabia Using ICAST-CH Tool: A Pilot Study. *Child abuse and neglect journal* (42):147-182.

444 Almuneef, MA, Hollinshead, D, Saleheen, H, et al (2016). Adverse Childhood Experiences and association with health, mental health, and risky behavior in the Kingdom of Saudi Arabia. *Child abuse and neglect journal.* Under peer review.; World Health Organization (WHO) *World report on violence and health: Summary (2002):* pp. 25-55. Retrieved from: http://www.who.int/violence_injury_prevention/violence/world_report/en/summary_en.pdf

445 Al-Gahtani, N (2008). *Bullying among middle school pupil in Riyadh city: A survey and recommendation for intervention programs against bullying in school environment.* (Master Thesis, King Saud University, Riyadh, Saudi Arabia). Unpublished Master Thesis.

446 Al Bitar, Z, Al- Omari, I, Sonbol, H, et al (2013), op. cit.

447 AlQadah, M, Bashir, A (2013). Predictive ability of the educational environment in the emergence of bullying in primary school students in private schools in Amman. *University of Al Najah for Research Journal Human studies* (4):27.

448 Al Bitar, Z, Al- Omari, I, Sonbo,l H, et al (2013). Op. cit.

449 Al-Bugami, F (2009). Op. cit.

450 Al Bitar, Z, Al- Omari, I, Sonbol, H, *et al* (2013). Op. cit.

451 Al-Bugami, F (2009). Op. cit.

452 Peterson, JS, Ray, KE (2006). Bullying and the gifted: Victims, perpetrators, prevalence, and effects. *Gifted child quarterly* 50(2):148-168.

453 Al Bitar, Z, Al- Omari, I, Sonbol, H, *et al* (2013). Op. cit.

454 Ghazal, A (2010). Op. cit.

455 Al Adili, R. *Abnormal sibling competition and relationship with anger, bullying, in middle school pupils in Iraq.* University of Bagdad, Master thesis (unpublished).

456 Eron, LD, Huesmann, LR, Zelli, A (1991). The role of parental variables in the learning of aggression. In: Pepler DJ. Rubin KJ, (eds). *The development and treatment of childhood aggression.* Hillsdale, NJ Lawrence Erlbaum: 169-188.

457 AlNayrab, A (2008). *Psychological and social factors contributing to violence in schools in middle school as reported by teachers and students in Ghaza.* Islamic University of Ghaza. Unpublished master thesis.

458 Alsufi, O, AlMalki, F (2012). Bullying amongst children and its relationships to Parental treatment. *Psychology and Education Journal* 35:146-188.

459 AlQadah, M, Bashir, A (2013). Op. cit.

460 AlNayrab, A (2008). Op. cit.

461 Fleming, L & Jacobsen, K (2009). Op. cit.

462 Ismail, H (2010). Psychological changes bullying victims go through in elementary school. *Qina, South Valley University, Egypt* 16(2).

463 AlBuhairan, F, AlDubayee, M, Tamimi, H, et al (2015). Op. cit.

Three girls in the photograph were participants in a photography workshop, Netherlands
© UNICEF/UNI201382/Mona

18. Lithuanian anti-bullying campaign and child helplines
Robertas Povilaitis and Child Helpline International

Introduction

This article uses the examples of case studies to highlight effective interventions against bullying and cyberbullying. It consists of two parts: the first, by Robertas Povilaitis, shares the details, and reviews the efforts, of the Lithuanian NGO "Child Line" in its work to combat bullying against children since 1997. The second part, by Child Helpline International, considers the nature and value of the services provided by child helplines in many countries around the world and the efforts of Child Helpline International to coordinate and share the invaluable data collected from such organisations.

Lithuanian NGO "Child Line"

The Lithuanian NGO "Child Line" established in 1997 provides free and anonymous help for children and teenagers. The "Child Line" mission is to provide help to children and teenagers by phone and on-line by accepting them the way they are, and helping them to look for the answers to the questions that worry them. It also aims to encourage children and teenagers to help themselves and their peers and to raise awareness among adults about their problems and the ways in which adults might help. Bullying is one of the main themes that comes up in the conversations.

"Child Line" is a member of the Lithuanian Association for Emotional Support Services, Child Helpline International[464] and a founding member of the European Anti-bullying Network[465] that unites 20 organizations from 15 European countries. "Child Line" is also a member of the Safer Internet consortium in Lithuania[466] and is associated with INSAFE network.[467]

Prevalence of bullying in Lithuania

According to the Health Behaviour in School-aged Children Study (HBSC) the prevalence of bullying in Lithuania is one of the highest among all countries taking part in the study.

The survey[468] reveals that 31.6% of boys and 26.3% of girls were bullied while 16% of girls and 30% of boys were bullying others (see Tables 1 and 2).

"Child Line" Campaign: "WITHOUT BULLYING"

"Child Line" initiated an anti-bullying campaign in 2004 in an attempt to address some of the challenges facing Lithuania. The campaign aims to create a safer environment in schools and kindergartens; it also aims to ensure the active participation of all members of society who are dealing with this issue. The campaign has focused on raising societal awareness of bullying and it has also contributed to the introduction of methods for prevention. Campaign activities have been implemented at various levels (societal, school, individual) in order to effectively reach the audience and to encourage changes in society.

In 2004, "Child Line" produced a public letter that was signed by NGOs and other organisations involved in children's issues. This was sent to the Lithuanian President and the Government of Lithuania with the aim of drawing attention to the problem of bullying among children. This and other activities initiated by "Child Line" have increased awareness of the problem of bullying in the media and among policy makers and the wider society.

The year 2007 finally marked a turning point in the prevention of bullying in Lithuania. The issue was addressed in the special international meeting in the Parliament of Lithuania in January, and by the President's Office in April. The Prime Minister of Lithuania formed a task force to prepare an action plan for the prevention of school vio-

Table 1.
Prevalence of children being bullied. Health Behaviour in School-aged Children Study, 2013/2014[469]

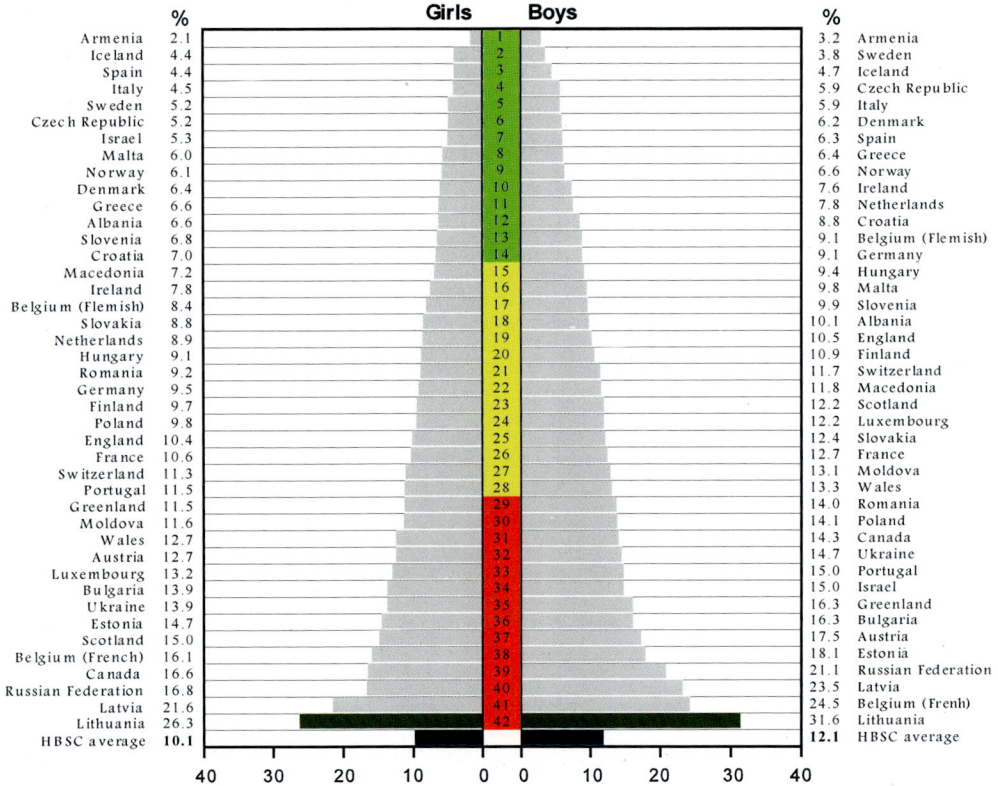

Table 2.
Prevalence of children bullying others. Health Behaviour in School-aged Children Study, 2013/2014[470]

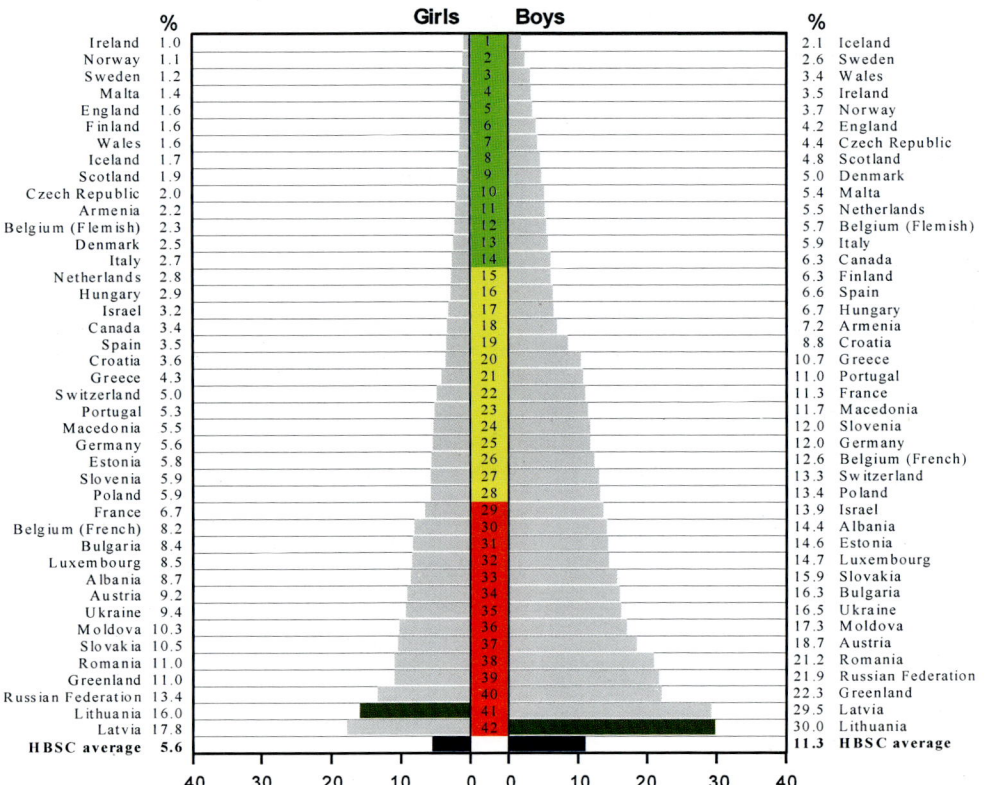

lence in May. Results show that there was a peak in the increased awareness of the issue of bullying at the time of the international conference "Modern Approaches in Prevention of Violence and Bullying in Schools" that took place in Vilnius in 2007.[471]

The Prime Minister's task force drew up the National Programme for the Prevention of Violence against Children and Provision of Assistance to Children to cover the years 2008-2010. It was an extensive plan that included various measures against bullying, including a proposal to implement bullying prevention programmes in schools.

In March 2010, the Memorandum on Childhood Without Bullying[472] was initiated by the President of Lithuania, Dalia Grybauskaitė. This Memorandum was signed by ministers, leaders of various state institutions and representatives of NGOs. It was signed on the first day of the "Action week Without Bullying" in 2010 initiated by "Child Line".

More recent actions to combat bullying have also been undertaken. The President of Lithuania in 2016 initiated the campaign "For a Safe Lithuania".[473] This campaign aims to stop bullying and violence, to diminish substance abuse and other addictions, and to tackle issues such as social exclusion. "Child Line" contributed to this campaign also by providing recommendations for working with children involved in bullying.[474]

In March 2016, the Parliament of the Republic of Lithuania took action also and passed a resolution assuring students' rights to a safe environment in all educational institutions.[475] This resolution requires all schools in Lithuania to implement violence and bullying prevention programmes.

"Child Line" has also been involved in providing advice to the President's Office on the draft law it presented to the Parliament. "Child Line" took part in the consultation process for the amendment of the Education Law, which was initiated by the President. The amendment of the law was registered in May 2016.[476] This amendment states that a unified system of fighting bullying should be established in all Lithuanian schools for both general and vocational education.

Raising societal awareness on bullying

The internet is one of the most efficient methods of publishing the latest information on bullying and sharing research data. In order to take advantage of the opportunities presented by the internet, "Child Line" has created a web site for its campaign "Without bullying".[477] The information shared on the site is targeted to different groups: children, parents and caregivers, school educators and staff, and all others who are seeking to obtain more information on the bullying phenomenon. All information on the web site is publicly available, including to download and share. On this site, "Child Line" has also involved celebrities who share their own experiences of bullying, and who go on to encourage children to seek help if they too are being bullied.[478] A Facebook profile "Without Bullying"[479] has also been created to promote anti-bullying activities on social networks. This is also seen as a useful platform to widely share information about bullying and ways to manage it.

Another campaign launched on the internet by "Child Line" is the "Museum of Bullying".[480] This virtual "Museum of Bullying" is a website, where visitors are welcome to inspect the exhibits used in one way or another in bullying situations faced every day by Lithuanian children and teenagers. Visitors can see the broken doll, the school bag full of rubbish, the torn child's painting, a mobile phone with hurtful messages, and a video with bullying scenes shown on a computer screen. All of these presentations look real and the visitors to the site are then encouraged to contribute to suggesting ways to prevent such bullying. Recommendations on how to provide support to a child who is being bullied, or how to respond to bullying, are described on the website as well.

"Child Line" is also involved in measuring and monitoring societal attitudes towards bullying. A public opinion survey conducted in 2016 revealed that 76% of respondents now thought that bullying in schools is an important issue. Since the beginning of the anti-bullying campaign, "Child Line" has sent a clear message that bullying is not a natural stage of child's development and should be actively addressed, and this message is apparently being understood more widely in society.

As part of its ongoing work, "Child Line" has organised several international and national conferences that have brought together policy makers, researchers, professionals, pupils, and representatives of schools, NGOs and state institutions in order to share experiences on preventive activities against bullying.

"Child Line" also continuously provides information about the campaign to the mass media by providing press releases on bullying prevention activities, details of the latest national and international studies, and on policy developments. The media have drawn on the expertise of specialists associated with "Child Line" for interviews and comments on the issue of bullying.

Action Week Without Bullying campaign

Since 2010, "Child Line" has organised the "Action Week WITHOUT BULLYING" campaign[481] with the aim of changing the attitudes in society towards bullying. More than a thousand educational institutions (schools, kindergartens, NGOs) usually take part in this anti-bullying week every year by organizing various activities for their communities.

Support to schools

"Child Line" has produced a number of books and other information material on the prevention of bullying and cyberbullying. The publications are developed for schools, parents and children. Also, a questionnaire for the measurement of the prevalence of bullying in the school is available for their use. The organisation has also produced various short films that can be viewed on the Internet and used as educational tools. These include a short film about cyberbullying and an educational video "Be safe on the internet".[482]

Support to parents and guardians

"Child Line" has developed various recommendations to parents and guardians that are available in the form of books,[483] brochures and information on the website. Parents have an important role in the prevention of bullying and in intervening in bullying situations. It is therefore imperative that they should be involved in the process and offered advice and information.

Such information is also available through several social advertisements on bullying produced by "Child Line". The advertisement "Beware of the smart phone in your child's hands"[484] urges parents to be more attentive to their children's behaviour online using smart phones. Lithuanian National Television has widely broadcast this advertisement.

Support to children

"Child Line" offers individual support to children and teenagers by phone and on-line in a tremendously important part of its campaign. By providing help to children on the European helpline number 116111, "Child Line" cooperates with the professionals of the National Children's Rights Protection and Adoption Institution, which provides access to emotional support and to social and legal counselling services. "Child Line" answered nearly 140,000 calls from children in 2015. Emotional support for children is provided by almost 200 counsellors. The most frequently mentioned issues by the children are problems and worries about relationships with parents and peers and experiences of bullying and abuse. The bullying is the most frequently mentioned issue in children and adolescents' talks with "Child Line's" counsellors.

Child Helpline International – Work and Data

by Child Helpline International

Child Helpline International is the global network of child helplines, working to protect children's rights throughout 142 countries. It has 183 members worldwide. Child hel-

The map of Lithuania with schools registered for "Action Week Without Bullying 2016"

plines are safe, confidential and accessible for children. The counsellors are often children's first point of contact with child protection services and children themselves are able to approach them voluntarily.

Child Helpline International annually collects data on the contacts with children established by its network of child helplines. It uses this data to advocate for better child protection services and to highlight gaps in existing child protection services. In 2014, Child Helpline International collected data on bullying and cyberbullying from 96 child helplines as part of a report on Violence Against Children. This data illustrates the incidence of violence, gives information about the experiences of children themselves and provides invaluable information through its insights and testimonies for policy makers and practitioners working with children.

Child helplines play an important role in protecting children from abuse and violence. For many children, child helplines are the first point of contact with any kind of protection, and they serve as critical gateways to further help and support. All child helplines provide active listening, counselling and referral services to children who suffer abuse. In countries with low and medium Human Development Index (HDI) levels, where resources are often scarce and as a consequence child-protection systems are more porous, many child helplines also have to provide additional services, such as direct intervention, shelter, education, and legal services.

In 2014, 732,768 violence-related contacts were made by children to these helplines: 26% of these contacts concerned bullying, and 4% cyberbullying.

Child Helpline International's contacts on bullying and cyberbullying

Peer violence (bullying and cyberbullying) and physical abuse form the largest concerns for children and young people. Most of the violence-related contacts made to child helplines were about these two topics. Bullying is a common behaviour in schools and among peers across the world. It is also one of the greatest worries for children attending school. Child helplines worldwide receive a large number of contacts regarding bullying. In 2014 alone, counsellors at child helpline call centres worldwide received 190,521 cases about bullying. Most contacts about bullying concern emotional bullying, followed by physical bullying (see figure 3).

More girls than boys contact child helplines regarding bullying (see figure 4). In the experience of child helpline counsellors, the type of bullying for which girls and boys

Figure 1
Types of violence against children (2014 CHI data N = 732,768)

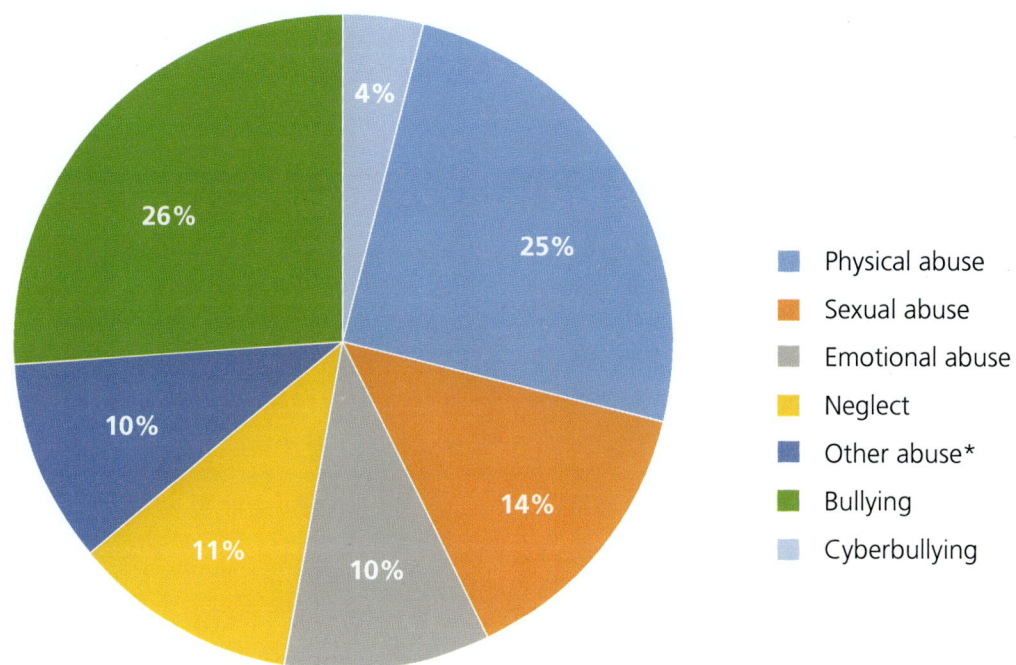

Figure 2.
Children affected by bullying (2014 CHI data N=190,521)

Figure 3.
Shares of contact by types of bullying (N=29,084 excluding "unspecified and other")

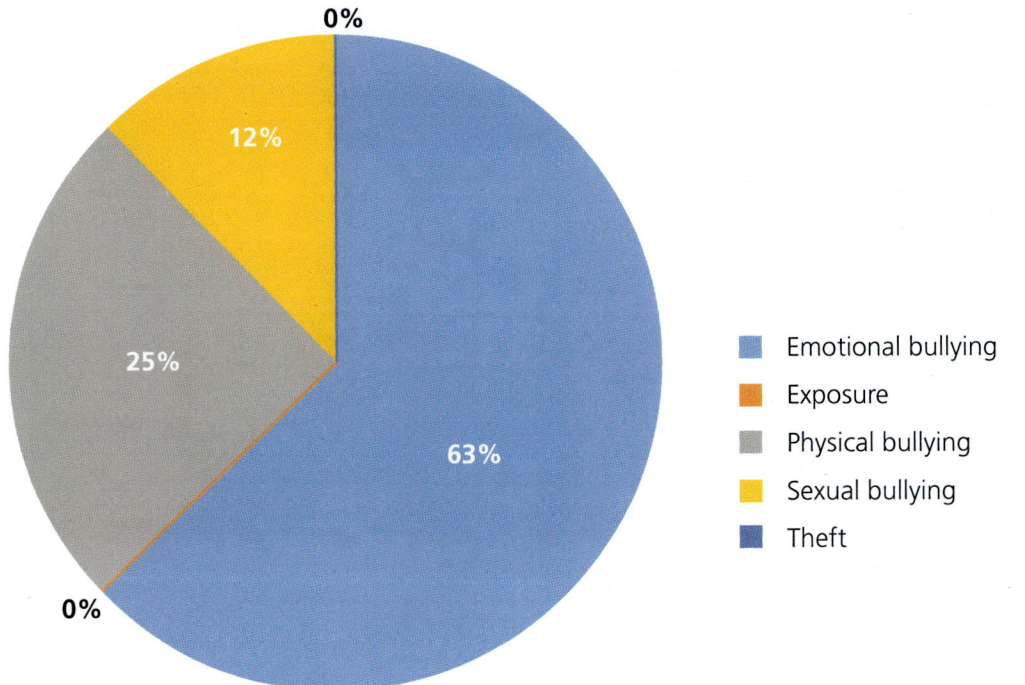

Figure 4.
Bullying and cyberbullying victims by sex

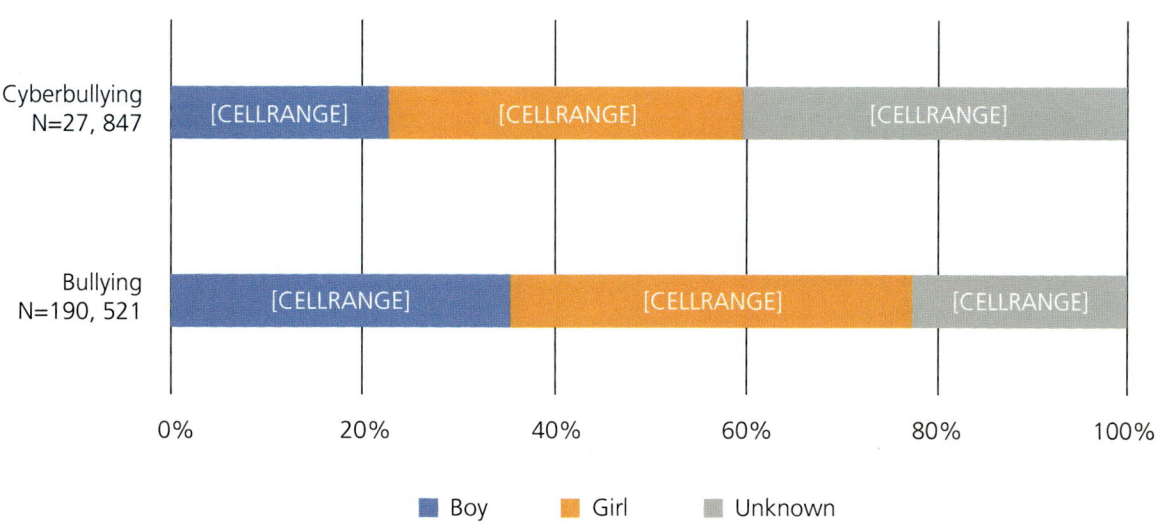

contact child helplines also differs. Girls seem to be more affected by embarrassing stories spread by peers — often amplified by the use of social media while boys more often report being subjected to physical bullying and extortion.

Globally, Child Helpline International 2014's data show 27,847 cases of cyberbullying. Cyberbullying is a form of abuse that occurs through the Internet and social media. Cyberbullying can occur in isolation, but it also often occurs as an extension of face-to-face bullying. Cyberbullying can cause even more harm to young people because of its near-indelible nature: it is difficult to remove content from the Internet; and the insults, comments or images can be preserved by others and used to inflict further harm with each posting, reading or viewing. Furthermore, the audience on social media is larger, and many social media platforms allow the possibility of co-ordinated 'campaigns' against the victim. Lastly, the speed at which messages reach an audience is near-instantaneous and the spread of information uncontrollable.

Child Helpline International will continue to collect data on bullying and cyberbullying to share and advocate for more awareness and improved protection measures.

Examples of individual case studies

The following examples of individual case studies from Child Helpline International serve to illustrate the range of difficulties and the levels of distress caused by bullying. They also demonstrate the effectiveness of the child helpline support. Names have been changed to protect the identity of the children.

Grooming: Brazil A sexual molester gained Laura's trust online when she was surfing the Internet. At the age of 15, she ended up recording herself in a video with explicit sexual content. When this video became viral, Laura and her father contacted the child helpline to help them remove it from both national and international websites. While doing this, counsellors also offered psychological support to help her cope with the consequences of this type of abuse. A few days after contacting the helpline for the first time, Laura's father sent an email saying: "We feel much better now. The school and the prosecutor offered us all necessary support to solve this. Thank you very much."

Bullying: Romania 15-year-old Alicia used to be bullied "because" she was adopted when she was four. During her fourth suicide attempt, she called the child helpline and said "Please, please, help. I am doing it again." The counsellor offered psychological support and helped her to identify who would able to help her further. They identified both Alina's parents and her school counsellor. By the end of that conversation, the counsellor also helped her to come up with a plan on what to do to help reduce the effects of bullying on her life.

Bullying and Extortion: Kazakhstan Several senior students from the school attended by a 17-year-old male caller would consistently and aggressively ask him for money. Failure to deliver resulted in severe physical and verbal abuse and each time the amount demanded would double. Needless to say, the boy was terrified and reluctant to give information about his abusers or details of what was going on in school. Compounding the issue, teachers were not available to talk to about this type of bullying. This type of bullying/extortion is widespread and generally continues uninterrupted at the victim's expense. After a number of counselling sessions through the child helpline, the boy began to feel more confident and disclosed the requested information. The offenders were taken into custody and the 17-year-old called the helpline back to thank the counsellors.

Bullying and Cyberbullying: Belgium A girl was being bullied by another girl at school. The other girl and her friends were physically harassing the caller and sending hate messages through SMS and Facebook. The caller had tried ignoring the girl, reasoning with her and blocking her on Facebook, but nothing seemed to help. She was feeling quite desperate about it and was even thinking of moving to a different school. Then she contacted the helpline. The counsellor congratulated her on the steps that she had already taken and encouraged her to talk to an adult at school (a teacher or school counsellor) about the situation. As the victim was worried this might make things worse if the other girls found out, the counsellor suggested that she express this worry to the chosen adult confidant. She also checked that the caller had kept some evidence of the cyberbullying, which she had, and encouraged her to show this proof to a teacher or school counsellor. The caller said that she subsequently felt more confident in handling the situation.

Bullying, Cyberbullying and Sexting: Brazil A 16-year-old girl begins her call by saying: "I'm not pretty, and people "throw it in my face". They laugh at me and talk about the way I dress; what should I do?" During almost two hours of conversation, the girl shared that "friends" had taken a picture of her drunk and without clothes on at a party, and everybody at school received the photo through SMS. After that they started to cyberbully her, with boys telling everyone that she was "easy". She contemplated suicide twice and had started cutting herself, "to punish me for being who I am". Due to her thoughts about suicide and actual self-harm, the counsellor referred the girl to a psychologist for face-to-face counselling and assured her that she could always call again.

Abuse and Technology: Mauritius A young girl's Facebook account was being hacked and posted with inappropriate content. She did not know why her account was hacked, but was very weary of the content now posted. She was also afraid that her friends might receive threats and strange e-mails. She wanted advice on how to handle this situation and called the child helpline. The counsellor supported the girl and talked to her about who might possibly have hacked her account. The counsellor also discussed with the girl the possibility that somebody might want to threaten her and blackmail her with the threat of posting even more damaging content. The girl and the counsellor discussed that it is never good to give in to blackmail, but that reporting the issue would help. Then the counsellor took all the information the girl had and asked for the girl's consent to report the hacking to the appropriate authorities and to Facebook. The coordinator of the child helpline then provided the information to the appropriate Facebook agency and within minutes the account was closed. This case was also highlighted in the media in Mauritius, giving credit to the work being conducted by the local child helpline.

Conclusion

The evidence presented here demonstrates clearly the value of child helplines in many parts of the world. The individual case studies can give invaluable insights into the issues facing real children in their daily lives and the aggregated data is an essential tool in the development of effective policies, laws and practical activites to support the fight against the threats of bullying and cyberbullying.

Endnotes

464 Child Helpline International. Web site: http://www.childhelplineinternational.org/about/
465 European Anti-bullying Network (EAN). Web site: http://www.antibullying.eu
466 Lithuanian Safer Internet Centre. Web site: www.draugiskasinternetas.lt
467 Better Internet for Kids. Web site: http://www.saferinternet.org
468 Zaborskis, A (2016). National Conference "Prognosis for bullying in Lithuania 2020-2030", March 16.
469 Ibid
470 Ibid
471 Conference "Modern Approaches in Prevention of Violence and Bullying in School`s" (2007) Vilnius. http://bepatyciu.lt/kampanija-be-patyciu/renginiai/
472 Press Centre of the President of the Republic of Lithuania (2010). *Lithuania without bullying - an obligation for everyone, March 22*. Web site: https://www.lrp.lt/lt/lietuva-be-patyciu-ipareigojimas-kiekvienam/pranesimai-spaudai/8363
473 The campaign "For a Safe Lithuania" http://uzsaugialietuva.lt/english
474 Guidelines for children "Do you experience violence and bullying?" Web site: https://www.lrp.lt/data/public/uploads/2016/04/patiri-smurta-ar-patycias.pdf
475 The Parliament of the Republic of Lithuania (2016). *The Resolution on pupils' rights to a safe environment in educational institutions.* 2016.03.17 (Nr. XII-2260), Vilnius. Web site: http://www3.lrs.lt/pls/inter3/dokpaieska.showdoc_l?p_id=1128513
476 The amendment of the Law of Education, http://www3.lrs.lt/pls/inter3/dokpaieska.showdoc_l?p_id=1147264&p_tr2=2
477 Web site of the campaign "Without Bullying": http://bepatyciu.lt/
478 Celebrities about bullying. Web sites: https://www.youtube.com/watch?v=mLlkrdE7E8A , https://www.youtube.com/watch?v=I5Ssa9yNTxU, https://www.youtube.com/watch?v=W2jLqyWLEWs, https://www.youtube.com/watch?v=6fHLy_5GOgs, https://www.youtube.com/watch?v=5ol6z2Gb8Co, https://www.youtube.com/watch?time_continue=5&v=4_pd5UAsno0
479 Facebook profile of the campaign "Without Bullying" https://www.facebook.com/bepatyciu/
480 "Child Line" awareness campaign "Museum of Bullying". http://www.museumofbullying.com
481 "Child Line" initiative "Action Week Without Bullying" website: http://bepatyciu.lt/veiksmo-savaite-be-patyciu/
482 Educational video about cyber bullying: https://www.youtube.com/watch?v=NCuudFQxMIk; Educational video "Be safe in internet": https://www.youtube.com/watch?v=Hf_4YNxoZmY
483 Jasiulionė, JS, Mažionienė, M, Suchodolska, I, Povilaitis, R (2011). How I can help my child? *Answers to parent's questions about bullying among children* (In Lithuanian).
484 Social advertisement "Beware of smart phone in your child's hands": https://www.youtube.com/watch?v=9CccXEutlfc

Notes on the Contributors

Maha Almuneef, M.D., is a pioneer in the field of child maltreatment in Saudi Arabia. A paediatrician, she is passionate about advocating for child's rights and well-being. She established National Family Safety Program to combat violence through awareness, advocacy, training professionals in the field and conducting research.

Katharina Anton-Erxleben, PhD, is a Monitoring and Evaluation Fellow in the Education, Youth, and Childhood Development Office at USAID/Uganda. She holds university degrees in Psychology and Neuroscience and has more than 10 years of experience in research. Prior to joining USAID/Uganda, she has worked on the USAID Bureau for Africa's efforts to generate data and improve measurement around School-Related Gender-Based Violence.

Patrick Burton, M.Sc., is the Executive Director of the Centre for Justice and Crime Prevention (CJCP), a Cape Town-based NGO engaged in the field of social justice and crime prevention, with a particular focus on children and youth. While at CJCP, Patrick has worked on the first national youth victimisation study to be conducted in South Africa, youth resilience to violence study, a national school violence baseline study and a cyber-violence pilot study. Other more recent projects undertaken include explorations into the causes and nature of youth violence, and extensive work into the extent and nature of school violence in South Africa and the region. He has undertaken work in South Africa, South Sudan, Ethiopia, Malawi, Tanzania, Mozambique, Namibia, the Democratic Republic of Congo, India and Bangladesh.

Christophe Cornu, is a Senior Program Specialist at UNESCO, Health and Education Section. He has coordinated UNESCO's international initiative on education sector responses to homophobic and transphobic violence since 2011 and has also worked and consulted in more than 45 countries for a range of organizations including UN agencies, and international NGOs.

Eric Debarbieux, Professor of Education at University of Bordeaux, and University of Paris-Est Créteil. Since 1998 he has been the President of the European Observatory on Violence in Schools. Between 2003-2011 he was the President of the International Observatory of Violence in Schools. From 2012-2015 he was a ministerial delegate in charge of prevention and fight against school bullying. Currently he is responsible of an important action against school bullying in 32 deprived areas in France.

Michael Dunne, PhD, is a psychologist who teaches and does research in the fields of population mental health, particularly regarding East Asian communities. His primary interest is in social epidemiology, including studies of the prevalence, causes and consequences of violence and childhood adversities in China, Vietnam, Malaysia and Indonesia. His co-authors: **Thu Ba Pham** is with the School of Public Health and Social Work, Queensland University of Technology (QUT) and the Ministry of Education and Training, Hanoi, Viet Nam; **Ha Hai Thi Le** is with the School of Public Health and Social Work, QUT, and the Faculty of Social Science, Hanoi School of Public Health, Viet Nam; and **Jiandong Sun** is with the School of Public Health and Social Work, QUT.

Patricia Espinoza is a Quantitative Research Officer at Young Lives. Her research focusses on inequality, poverty, and on the relationship of social stratification, mobility, and ethnicity. She has a DPhil in International Development from the University of Oxford.

Bernard Gerbaka, M.D., is a Professor of Paediatrics in St. Joseph University in Beirut, and a member of the Faculty of Medicine Council. He works in the fields of child health, child abuse, violence against children, injuries prevention and safety promotion. He is President of the Lebanese Institute for Child Rights (President of ChildOfLebanon.org), former President of the Lebanese Union for Child Protection and Vice-President of the University Child and Youth Observatory in Lebanon. He is published on child health, child injuries, child safety, child abuse, violence against children and child protection. Dr. Gerbaka co-founded the Arab professional society for the prevention of violence against children (www.APSPVAC.org). He is currently President Elect of ISPCAN. His co-authors are **Fares BouMitri, M.D. and Carla Haber, M.D.**

Sanna Herkama, PhD, is a communication scholar currently working as a senior research fellow in the Division of Psychology, University of Turku, Finland. Her research focuses on the development and implementation of intervention programs as well as to school bullying and the communication and cognitive processes connected to it.

Susan Limber, PhD., MLS, is the Dan Olweus Professor at the Institute on Family and Neighborhood Life within the Department of Youth, Family & Community Studies at Clemson University. She is a developmental psychologist who also holds a Masters of Legal Studies. Dr. Limber's research and writing have focused on youth participation, children's rights, and legal and psychological issues related to bullying among children and youth.

Anne Lindboe, M.D., is the Norwegian Children's Ombudsman. She obtained her medical degree (MD) at the University of Oslo in 2000. Prior to being the Ombudsman, Dr. Lindboe was a medical expert for the police in cases of violence and abuse as well as a researcher at the Norwegian Institute of Public Health. Her co-author is child rights' expert, **Anders Cameron.**

Yongfeng Liu, is a Programme Specialist at UNESCO in the Section of Health and Education. He has supported UNESCO's international initiative on education sector responses to homophobic and transphobic violence since 2013 . Before joining UNESCO in 2003, he worked for 20 years in development and implementation of national education programmes and projects for family planning, reproductive health and HIV prevention, in China.

Sonia Livingstone, OBE, is a professor in the Department of Media and Communications at London School of Economics and Political Science. She researches opportunities and risks for children and young people afforded by digital and online technologies, focusing on media literacy, social mediations, and children's rights in the digital age. A fellow of the British Psychological Society, she leads the projects Global Kids Online, Preparing for a Digital Future and EU Kids Online. Her co-authors, **Mariya Stoilova** and **Anthony Kelly,** are both in the Department of Media and Communications at the London School of Economics and Political Science.

Ersilia Menesini, PhD, is a Professor of Developmental Psychology at the University of Florence. Her research is related to violence and aggressive behaviour in adolescence and childhood, school bullying, peer rejection, dating aggression, cyberbullying and risk behaviours in virtual contexts. Dr. Gerbaka is President elect of the Association of Developmental Psychology Council for the period 2017-2019.

George Moschos, Deputy Ombudsman for Children's Rights. He studied Law and Criminology. In 2003 he was appointed as the first Deputy Ombudsman for Children's Rights at the Independent Authority "The Greek Ombudsman" and was re-appointed twice in this position. He has served as Chairman and member of Bureau of the European Network of Ombudspersons for Children (ENOC) and has participated in numerous national and international committees, consultation meetings and conferences. He is committed in carefully listening to children and in defending their rights.

Annalaura Nocentini, PhD, is a researcher on Developmental Psychology at the University of Florence. Her research is related to aggressive behaviour from childhood to young adults, school bullying and cyberbullying, dating aggression, and conduct disorders.

María José Ogando Portela is an ODI Fellow in the National Institute of Statistics of Rwanda (NISR). From 2011 to 2015 she worked with Young Lives as a research assistant and survey coordinator of the fourth round of the quantitative surveys in Ethiopia, and in the development of the fifth round. Ms. Ogando Portela continues to work with Young Lives on research related to psychosocial well-being and violence affecting children.

Dan Olweus, PhD, has been affiliated with the Department of Psychology at the University of Bergen in Norway since 1970. He has been involved in research and intervention work in the area of school bullying for more than forty-five years. His anti-bullying program, the Olweus Bullying Prevention Program (OBPP), has been implemented in a large number of schools in several countries, including Norway, the U.S.A., Sweden, Iceland, and Lithuania. Dr. Olweus is generally recognized as a pioneer of research and intervention on bully/victim problems and as a world-leading expert in this area. He has received a number of awards and recognitions for his research and intervention work.

Brian O'Neill, PhD, is Director of Research, Enterprise and Innovation Services at Dublin Institute of Technology. Brian has 25+ years researching and working in areas of media policy and digital technologies; media and information literacy, e-safety and information society policy for children. He is a member of the Management Group for EU Kids Online network responsible for its policy work package. He sits on Ireland's Internet Safety Advisory Committee.

Kirrily Pells, PhD, is a Lecturer in Childhood at UCL Institute of Education. Her research focuses on childhoods globally and children's rights, especially in relation to poverty, development and conflict. Ms. Pells is also a research associate with Young Lives, a longitudinal study of childhood poverty where her research focuses on children's experiences of violence in Ethiopia, India, Peru and Vietnam and includes collaborating with UNICEF on a multi-country study of violence affecting children.

Robertas Povilaitis, PhD, is the Director of the NGO "Child Line" (www.vaikulinija.lt) and a lecturer at Vilnius University. A clinical psychologist, he is the Secretary General of the European Federation of Psychologists' Associations and a Board Member of the European Anti-Bullying Network (www.antibullying.eu.)

Dominic Richardson joined UNICEF Office of Research Innocenti in 2015, working on issues of equity in education and the relationships between schooling, school outcomes and child well-being. He has worked extensively with OECD Social Policy Division in evaluating child and family policies and in designing frameworks through which indicators of child well-being outcomes can be compared. Dominic has been a contributor to UNICEF Innocenti Report Cards on child well-being in rich countries, and authored a joint EC OECD project evaluating large international surveys of school children in developed countries. His co-author, **Chii Fen Hiu,** is at Oxford University, UK.

Christina Salmivalli, PhD, is a psychology professor at the University of Turku. Her specialty field is children's peer relationships, especially bullying and its evidence-based prevention. She has led the development of the KiVa antibullying program. The Finish Psychological Association, in 2009, awarded Ms. Salmivalli for her work in investigating bullying and conceptual development in the field of prevention.

Maria Luisa Sotomayor works in UNICEF's Global Innovation Center, on the U-Report Global Coordination team. Before joining UNICEF, she worked at Ciudadano Inteligente, an NGO dedicated to empowering people's rights and responsibilities as citizens through the use of new information and communication technologies in Chile and Latin America. She was also an active board member of Todo Mejora, a Chilean NGO working to prevent adolescent suicide resulting from homophobic bullying. She has a master's degree in Latin American Literature This article was written in collaboration with UNICEF Child Protection division.

Julie Hanson Swanson, EdM, is the Deputy Education Chief, Bureau for Africa, USAID. Prior to this position, she spent eight years in USAID's Office of Gender Equality and Women's Empowerment. Ms. Swanson has over 25 years of experience developing, managing, and implementing programs in formal and non-formal education, adolescent reproductive health, girls' education, gender, and school-related gender-based violence."